*f*P

THE QUESTION

OF GOD

C. S. Lewis and Sigmund Freud

Debate God, Love, Sex, and the

Meaning of Life

DR. ARMAND M. NICHOLI, JR.

THE FREE PRESS
New York   London   Toronto   Sydney   Singapore

THE FREE PRESS
A Division of Simon & Schuster, Inc.
1230 Avenue of the Americas
New York, NY 10020

The Free Press and colophon are trademarks
of Simon & Schuster, Inc.

For information regarding special discounts for bulk purchases,
please contact Simon & Schuster Special Sales at
1-800-456-6798 or business@simonandschuster.com

Designed by Leslie Phillips
Manufactured in the United States of America

5   7   9   10   8   6

LIBRARY OF CONGRESS CATALOGING-IN-PUBLICATION DATA IS AVAILABLE.

ISBN 0-7432-0237-6

To my wife, Ingrid, and to my children,
Kimberly and Armand III, with love

Contents

Prologue

On the morning of September 26, 1939, at Golders Green in north-west London, a group of friends and family gathered to mourn the death of Sigmund Freud. After his body was cremated, Ernest Jones, in his funeral oration, noted that "he was being buried . . . [as] he would have wished . . . in sheer simplicity, without a note of pomp or ceremony." Stefan Zweig, the author, closed his remarks by predicting that "wherever we seek to advance into the labyrinth of the human heart, henceforth his intellectual light will shine upon our path."

The front page of the Sunday *New York Times* declared in a headline: "Dr. Sigmund Freud Dies in Exile at 83." And in the subheadlines: "Founder of Psychoanalysis . . . Succumbs at His Home Near London." The article described his recent escape from the Nazis, who burned his books, dismissed his theories as pornographic, and demanded a ransom for his freedom. It also mentioned Freud's "worldwide fame and greatness," referring to him as "one of the most widely discussed scientists," mentioning that "he set the entire world talking about psychoanalysis" and noting that his ideas had already permeated our culture and language.

As a young teenager, Freud demonstrated academic brilliance, ranking at the top of his class for seven years and graduating *summa cum laude* from the "Gymnasium." He entered the University of Vienna when seventeen years old, read widely in several languages, conducted research, and studied subjects ranging from physics to philosophy.

Today historians rank Freud's scientific contributions with those of Planck and Einstein. He appears on most lists of the greatest physicians in history. He was recently on the cover of *Time* (with Albert Einstein) for an issue dedicated to the greatest scientific minds of the century and ranked sixth in a book on the hundred most influential scientists. Yet if Freud's fame and influence have continued to grow since his death more than sixty years ago, so have the criticism and the controversy surrounding him. He persists in spite of it all. Freud's photo graces Austrian currency. His ideas remain permanently embedded in our culture and our language.

We use terms such as *ego, repression, complex, projection, inhibition, neurosis, psychosis, resistance, sibling rivalry,* and *Freudian slip* without even realizing their source. Freud's model of the mind is still perhaps the most developed of all. Of the more than one hundred forms of psychotherapy, many continue to use one or another of Freud's concepts. Perhaps most important of all, his theories influence how we interpret human behavior, not only in biography, literary criticism, sociology, medicine, history, education, and ethics— but also in the law. We now take for granted the basic psychoanalytic concept that our early life experiences strongly influence how we think, feel, and behave as adults. Because of the unmistakable impact of his thought, some scholars refer to the twentieth century as the "century of Freud."

As part of his intellectual legacy, Freud strongly advocated an atheistic philosophy of life. He referred to this view as the "scientific *Weltanschauung.*" Freud also waged a fierce, ongoing battle against the spiritual worldview that he referred to as "the religious *Weltanschauung.*" Freud's philosophical writings, more widely read than his expository or scientific works, have played a significant role in the secularization of our culture. In the seventeenth century people turned to the discoveries of astronomy to demonstrate what they considered the irreconcilable conflict between science and faith; in the eighteenth century, to Newtonian physics; in the nineteenth century, to Darwin; in the twentieth century and still today, Freud is the atheist's touchstone.

*　*　*

Twenty-four years after Freud's death, on the morning of November 26, 1963, at Oxford, England, northwest of London, a group of friends and family gathered at the Holy Trinity Church at Headington Quarry to mourn the death of C. S. Lewis. The service began with the quote "I am the resurrection and the life, saith the Lord." After the service, the group walked slowly into the cold, clear day, and watched silently as the coffin was carried from the church to the churchyard for burial.

The *New York Times* of November 25, 1963, amid numerous articles on the assassination of John F. Kennedy, announced in a headline: "C. S. Lewis Dead: Author, Critic 64." Under a photo, and an article of several columns, the *Times* surveyed Lewis's prolific life, mentioned his reputation as a brilliant scholar, reviewed some of his scholarly and popular works that had already sold millions of copies, and noted that his success as a writer occurred after his change of worldviews, from atheist to believer.

Lewis, the celebrated Oxford don, literary critic, and perhaps the twentieth century's most popular proponent of faith based on reason, won international recognition long before his death in 1963. During World War II, his broadcast talks made his voice second only to Churchill's as the most recognized on the BBC. A few years after the war, a cover article in *Time* magazine described him as the most influential spokesman for the spiritual worldview. His books continue to sell prodigiously and his influence continues to grow. During 1998, the centennial year of his birth, conferences focusing on his work were held throughout the United States and Europe.

His extraordinarily popular *Chronicles of Narnia* ignites the imagination of children around the world. The sheer quantity of personal, biographical, and literary books and articles on Lewis, the vast number of C. S. Lewis societies in colleges and universities, and *Shadowlands,* the award-winning London and Broadway plays and the movie based on his life—all attest to the ever-growing interest in the man and his work.

Lewis began his brilliant academic career as an undergraduate student at Oxford, where he won a triple first, the highest honors in three areas of study—a feat seldom achieved. After finishing his studies, he stayed on at Oxford as a member of the faculty. For the next thirty years, he taught philosophy and then English language and literature. In 1955, he left Oxford to accept a chair in medieval and Renaissance English literature at Magdalene College, Cambridge University. At both Oxford and Cambridge, his immensely popular lectures often filled lecture halls to standing room only.

Lewis embraced an atheistic worldview for the first half of his life and used Freud's reasoning to defend his atheism. Lewis then rejected his atheism and became a believer. In subsequent writings, he provides cogent responses to Freud's arguments against the spiritual worldview. Wherever Freud raises an argument, Lewis attempts to answer it. Their writings possess a striking parallelism. If Freud still serves as a primary spokesman for materialism, Lewis serves as a primary spokesman for the spiritual view that Freud attacked.

Sadly the two men never debated directly. When Lewis began teaching at Oxford, he was in his twenties, and Freud was already in his mid-seventies. Lewis was well aware of Freud's theories; the new psychology was widely discussed. Even earlier, by the time Lewis enrolled as an undergraduate at Oxford, Freud had already become father of the new literary criticism that Lewis studied. Later, Freud may very well have read some of Lewis's early writings—such as *The Allegory of Love,* published to critical acclaim several years before

Freud died. He may have read Lewis's *Pilgrim's Regress*, in which Lewis satirizes Freudian psychology. Lewis named one of the characters Sigismund, Freud's real name until, at the age of twenty-two, he changed it to Sigmund.

Unfortunately, because Lewis trailed Freud by a generation, his responses to Freud's arguments were the last written word. Freud never had the chance to rebut. Yet if their arguments are placed side by side, a debate emerges as if they were standing at podiums in a shared room. Both thought carefully about the flaws and alternatives to their positions; each considered the other's views.

Thirty years ago, Harvard invited me to teach a course on Freud. I have been teaching it ever since to the undergraduates, and also for the last ten years to the Harvard Medical School students. At first, the course focused solely on Freud's philosophical views. Roughly half of my students agreed with him, the other half strongly disagreed. When the course evolved into a comparison of Freud and Lewis, it became much more engaging, and the discussions ignited. I have been teaching it that way ever since. I found, however, that a third voice needs to be added to that of their writings, in the form of their biographies. Their arguments can never prove or disprove the existence of God. Their lives, however, offer sharp commentary on the truth, believability, and utility of their views. (In analyzing their biographies, however, we do well to keep in mind that human beings do not always live what they profess, nor profess what they live.)

○ ○ ○

The purpose of this book is to look at human life from two diametrically opposed points of view: those of the believer and the unbeliever. (Freud divided all people into these two catagories.) We will examine several of the basic issues of life in terms of these two conflicting views. We will look at both views as objectively and dispassionately as possible and let the arguments speak for themselves. (I am aware that no one—including the author—is neutral on such emotionally charged issues. None of us can tolerate the notion that our worldview may be based on a false premise and, thus, our whole life headed in the wrong direction.) Because of the far-reaching implications for our lives, we tend to dismiss and contradict arguments for the worldview we reject. I hope each reader will critically assess the arguments of both Freud and Lewis and follow Sir Francis Bacon's advice to "Read not to contradict . . . but to weigh and consider."

Socrates said "the unexamined life is not worth living." Within the university, students and professors scrutinize every possible aspect of our universe—from the billions of galaxies to subatomic particles, electrons, quarks—but they assiduously avoid examining their own lives. In the wider world, we keep hectically busy and fill every free moment of our day with some form of diversion—work, computers, television, movies, radio, magazines, newspapers, sports, alcohol, drugs, parties. Perhaps we distract ourselves because looking at our lives confronts us with our lack of meaning, our unhappiness, and our loneliness—and with the difficulty, the fragility, and the unbelievable brevity of life. Pascal may have been right when he observed that "if our condition were truly happy we should not need to divert ourselves from thinking about it . . . the sole cause of our unhappiness is that we do not know how to sit quietly in our room." One of my Harvard students stated during a class discussion that "living a human life is a scary business." Perhaps the reason we find it difficult to sit quietly and examine our lives is because doing so makes us anxious. But until we examine our lives, we can do little to make them less unhappy and more fulfilling. It is my hope that Freud and Lewis can jointly guide us through just such an examination.

✿   ✿   ✿

Whether we realize it or not, all of us possess a worldview. A few years after birth, we all gradually formulate our philosophy of life. Most of us make one of two basic assumptions: we view the universe as a result of random events and life on this planet a matter of chance; or we assume an Intelligence beyond the universe who gives the universe order, and life meaning. Our worldview informs our personal, social, and political lives. It influences how we perceive ourselves, how we relate to others, how we adjust to adversity, and what we understand to be our purpose. Our worldview helps determine our values, our ethics, and our capacity for happiness. It helps us understand where we come from, our heritage; who we are, our identity; why we exist on this planet, our purpose; what drives us, our motivation; and where we are going, our destiny. Some historians of science such as Thomas Kuhn point out that even a scientist's worldview influences not only what he investigates but also how he interprets what he investigates. Our worldview tells more about us perhaps than any other aspect of our personal history.

Both Freud's and Lewis's views have existed since the beginning of recorded history—the spiritual worldview, rooted primarily in ancient Israel, with its emphasis on moral truth and right conduct and its motto of Thus saith the Lord; and the materialist or "scientific" worldview, rooted in ancient Greece, with its emphasis on reason and acquisition of knowledge and its motto What Says Nature? All of us embrace some form of Freud's or Lewis's worldview. If we accept Freud's materialism, we may call ourselves atheists, agnostics, or skeptics. There are likewise many different expressions of Lewis's worldview. We will consider the specific form of the spiritual worldview embraced by Lewis and, according to a recent Gallup poll, by more than 80 percent of Americans.

Why Freud and Lewis? For several reasons. First, both write extensively about a specific, representative worldview with great depth, clarity, and conciseness. Freud won the coveted Goethe Prize for literature, and Lewis became a professor of literature, a noted literary critic, and a widely read, prolific author. Furthermore, both wrote autobiographies and thousands of letters that provide a reasonably good perspective on how they lived their lives. Freud and Lewis provide a particularly clear lens through which we can examine these two views.

Are these worldviews merely philosophical speculations with no right or wrong answer? No. One of them begins with the basic premise that God does not exist, the other with the premise that He does. They are, therefore, mutually exclusive—if one is right, the other must be wrong. Does it really make any difference to know which one is which? Both Freud and Lewis thought so. They spent a good portion of their lives exploring these issues, repeatedly asking the question "Is it true?"

Freud was preoccupied with the question of whether or not God exists. In a collection of letters he wrote as a college student at the University of Vienna, the question of God's existence arises constantly. It continues throughout his philosophical writings until his last major work, *Moses and Monotheism*. In "The Question of a *Weltanschauung*," Freud argues against the existence of God. He points to the problem of suffering and he develops the psychological argument that the whole concept is nothing but a projection of a childish wish for parental protection from the vicissitudes and sufferings of human existence. He also argues against the objection of those holding the spiritual worldview that faith "is of divine origin and was given us as a revelation by a Spirit which the human spirit cannot comprehend." Freud says this "is a clear case of begging the question" and adds this comment: "The actual question raised is whether there is a divine spirit and a revelation by it, and the matter is certainly not decided by saying this question cannot be asked."

Lewis agrees with Freud that this is indeed the most important question. He writes: "Here is a door behind which, according to some people, the secret of the universe is waiting for you. Either that's true or it isn't. If it isn't, then what the door really conceals is simply the greatest fraud . . . on record." Because so many people embrace Lewis's answer—a recent Gallup poll reports that the vast majority of adult Americans believe in God—Lewis is right: if not true, then the spiritual worldview is not only a fraud but also the cruelest hoax ever perpetrated on the human race. And the only alternative is to follow Freud's advice to grow up and face the harsh reality that we are alone in the universe. He says we may find less consolation, but the truth, harsh as it is, will ultimately set us free from false hopes and unrealistic expectations. But if the spiritual worldview is true, then all other truth fades in significance. Nothing has more profound and more far-reaching implications for our lives.

If both Freud and Lewis thought the question of God's existence to be life's most important question, let's see how they arrived at their conflicting answers. And let's see if their biographies—how they actually lived their lives—strengthen or weaken their arguments and tell us more than their words convey.

PART ONE

WHAT SHOULD
WE BELIEVE?

$-\infty 1 \infty-$

THE PROTAGONISTS

*The Lives of Sigmund Freud
and C. S. Lewis*

Although C. S. Lewis, a full generation younger than Sigmund Freud, embraced Freud's atheism during the first half of his life, he eventually rejected that view. When Lewis began teaching at Oxford, Freud's writings had already influenced many intellectual disciplines, including Lewis's field, literature. Lewis knew well all of Freud's arguments—perhaps because he used them to bolster his position when he himself was an atheist. In his autobiography he writes: "The new Psychology was at that time sweeping through us all. We did not swallow it whole . . . but we were all influenced. What we were most concerned about was 'Fantasy' or 'wishful thinking.' For (of course) we were all poets and critics and set a very great value on 'Imagination' in some high Coleridgean sense, so that it became important to distinguish Imagination .. . from Fantasy as the psychologists understand that term."

Rare indeed is the person whose views never change throughout his life. Before we compare the views of Lewis and Freud, therefore, we need to know something about how they reached them.

Freud's Background

On May 6, 1856, in the town of Freiberg, Moravia, Amalia Freud gave birth to a son. Little did she realize her child would someday be listed among the most influential scientists in history. Her husband, Jacob, named him Sigismund Schlomo and inscribed these names in the family Bible. The young boy eventually dropped both of these names. He never used "Schlomo," his paternal grandfather's name, and, while a student at the University of Vienna, changed "Sigismund" to "Sigmund."

A nursemaid took care of the young Freud for the first two and a half years of his life. A devout Roman Catholic, she took the young boy to church with her. Freud's mother, many years later, told Freud that on returning from church he would "preach and tell us what God Almighty does." The nursemaid spent considerable time with Freud, especially when his mother became pregnant and delivered a younger sibling. Freud considered her a surrogate mother and became very attached to her. When less than two years old, he lost his younger brother, Julius, whose sickness and death must have absorbed all of his mother's time and left him almost totally in the care of his nanny. He wrote that although "her words could be harsh," he nevertheless "loved the old woman." In a letter to Wilhelm Fliess, an ear, nose, and throat specialist with whom Freud developed a close friendship for several years, he stated "in my case the 'prime originator' was an ugly, elderly, but clever woman, who told me a great deal about God Almighty and hell and who instilled in me a high opinion of my own capacities." During this time the nanny, after being accused of stealing, left the household suddenly. As an adult, Freud would dream about her.

Scholars have speculated that Freud's antagonism to the spiritual worldview and specifically to the Catholic Church stemmed in part from his anger and disappointment at being left by the Catholic nanny at a critical time in his life. Freud acknowledged that "if the woman disappeared so suddenly . . . some impression of the event must have been left inside me. Where is it now?" He then also recalled a scene that had been "for the last twenty-nine years turning up in my conscious memory . . . I was crying my heart out . . . I could not find my mother . . . I feared she must have vanished, like my nurse not long before." Still, it is itself a Freudian stretch to assume that his feelings toward the church were formed by one person's departure from his life.

What is true is that the nanny exposed Freud to Catholic practices. When the nanny took the little boy to mass, Freud apparently observed worshippers kneeling, praying, and making the sign of the cross. These early childhood impressions may be what he had in mind when, as an adult, he wrote papers comparing religious practices with obsessive symptoms and referring to religion as the "universal obsessional neurosis." They may also have been Freud's first exposure to music, Rome, and the holidays of Easter and Pentecost (also known as Whitsunday—the celebration of the descent of the Holy Spirit upon the disciples). Although Freud disliked music, he appeared to possess a strange attraction to Rome and an unusual awareness of these two holidays. He mentioned them often in his letters. He writes of his "longing for Rome," of his wish to spend "next Easter in Rome," and how he "so much wanted to see Rome again."

Sigmund Freud grew up in an unusual, complicated family. Freud's father Jacob married Amalia Nathansohn when she was still a teenager and he was forty years old and already a grandfather. Amalia was Jacob's third wife. Jacob had two sons from his first marriage, one older than Amalia, and one a year younger.

Freud's father had been educated as an Orthodox Jew. He gradually gave up all religious practice, celebrating only Purim and Passover as family festivals. Nevertheless, he read the Bible regularly at home in Hebrew, and he apparently spoke Hebrew fluently. In his autobiography, written when almost seventy years old, Freud recalled, "My early familiarity with the Bible story (at a time almost before I had learnt the art of reading) had, as I recognized much later, an enduring effect upon the direction of my interest." During several visits to the Freud home in London, I spent time alone in Freud's study perusing his bookshelves. I noticed a large copy of a Martin Luther Bible. Many of Freud's numerous biblical quotations suggest that he read this translation. The Bible that he read as a boy, however, appears to be the Philippson Bible, consisting of the Old Testament and named after a scholar of the Reform Movement that led to Reform Judaism. On Freud's thirty-fifth birthday Jacob Freud sent his son a copy of the Philippson Bible with the following inscription in Hebrew:

> My dear Son:
>
> It was in the seventh year of your age that the spirit of God began to move you to learning. I would say the spirit of God speaketh to you: "Read in my Book; there will be opened to thee sources of knowledge and of the intellect." It is the Book of Books; it is the well that wise men have digged and from which lawgivers have drawn the waters of their knowledge.
>
> Thou hast seen in this Book the vision of the Almighty, thou hast heard willingly, thou hast done and hast tried to fly high upon the wings of the Holy Spirit. Since then I have preserved the same Bible. Now, on your thirty-fifth birthday I have brought it out from its retirement and I send it to you as a token of love from your old father.

Freud naturally associated the spiritual worldview with his father. His feelings toward his father were at best ambivalent. Unlike him,

Freud never learned to speak Hebrew and knew only a few words of his mother's Yiddish.

Jacob Freud struggled to make a living as a wool merchant, and the entire family occupied a single rented room in a small house. The Freuds lived above the owner, a blacksmith, who occupied the first floor. During the time of Freud's birth the population of Freiberg—later known as Příbor in modern Czechoslovakia—ranged from about 4,000 to 5,000. The Catholic population of Freiberg far outnumbered the Protestant and Jewish populations of about 2 to 3 percent each.

When he was about three years old, in 1859, Freud and his family moved to Leipzig, and then a year later to Vienna. He lived and worked the rest of his life in Vienna—until in 1938, when eighty-two years old, after the Nazi invasion, he escaped to London with the help of colleagues, the American secretary of state, and President Franklin Roosevelt.

During his adolescent years in Vienna, Freud studied Judaism under Samuel Hammerschlag, who emphasized the ethical and historical experience of the Jewish people more than their religious life. Hammerschlag remained a friend and benefactor to Freud for many years. When he was fifteen, Freud also began corresponding with a friend named Eduard Silberstein. These letters, extending over a full decade, give us some insight into the theological and philosophical thoughts and feelings of the young Freud, especially on the question of whether or not an Intelligence exists beyond the universe. Silberstein was a believer who became a lawyer and married a young woman whom he sent to Freud for treatment of her depression. After arriving at Freud's office, she told her maid to wait downstairs. Instead of going to Freud's waiting room, she went up to the fourth floor and jumped to her death.

When Freud entered the University of Vienna in 1873 and studied under the distinguished philosopher Franz Brentano, a former Catholic priest who left the priesthood because he did not accept the infallibility of the pope, he wrote about it to Silberstein. Brentano made a profound impression on the young Freud. Eighteen years old, Freud exclaimed in a letter to his friend: "I, the godless medical man and empiricist, am attending two courses in philosophy . . . One of the courses—listen and marvel!—deals with the existence of God, and Prof. Brentano, who gives the lectures, is a splendid man, a scholar and philosopher, even though he deems it necessary to support his airy existence of God with his own expositions. I shall let you know just as soon as one of his arguments gets to the point (we have not yet progressed beyond the preliminary problems), lest your path to salvation in the faith be cut off."

A few months later Freud comments further on his impressions of Brentano: "When you and I meet, I shall tell you more about this remarkable man (a believer, a teleologist . . . and a damned clever fellow, a genius in fact) who is in many respects, an ideal human being." Under Brentano's influence Freud wavered and considered becoming a believer. Freud confided to Silberstein the strong influence Brentano had on him: ". . . I have not escaped from his influence—I am not capable of refuting a simple theistic argument that constitutes the crown of his deliberations . . . He demonstrates the existence of God with as little bias and as much precision as another might argue the advantage of the wave over the emission theory." Freud also encouraged Silberstein to attend Brentano's lecture: "The philosopher Brentano, whom you know from my letters, will lecture on ethics or practical philosophy from eight to nine in the morning, and it would do you good to attend, as he is a man of integrity and imagination, although people say he is a Jesuit, which I cannot believe . . ."

Then Freud made a startling quasi-admission: "Needless to say, I am only a theist by necessity, and am honest enough to confess my helplessness in the face of his argument; however, I have no intention of surrendering so quickly or completely." In the same paragraph, he made a contradictory statement: "For the time being, I have ceased to be a materialist and am not yet a theist." This confusion and ambivalence would stay with him, despite his many ringing pronouncements in favor of atheism.

In another letter a few weeks later, Freud continued to share his struggle: "The bad part of it, especially for me, lies in the fact that science of all things seems to demand the existence of God . . ."

Freud may have repressed the experience of becoming a "theist by necessity." When he was seventy years old, in an address to the B'nai B'rith (Sons of the Covenant), he stated: "What bound me to Jewry was (I am ashamed to admit) neither faith nor national pride, for I have always been an unbeliever . . ." If Freud found the arguments by Brentano for the existence of God so compelling, what made him so reluctant to accept them, to "surrender" to reasoning he was unable "to refute"? Some answers to these questions may lie among the other influences on the young Freud during his long years of medical education.

First, in his letters to Silberstein, Freud mentioned reading another philosopher, Ludwig Feuerbach. "Feuerbach is one whom I revere and admire above all other philosophers," Freud wrote his friend in 1875. Ludwig Feuerbach, born in 1804, studied theology at the University of Heidelberg. A student of Hegel, he wrote books critical of theology, stating that one's relationship to others—the "I-and-thou" relationship—was more compelling than one's relationship to God. Although he claimed to be a believer, his writings reinforced the atheism of both Marx and Freud. His main thesis in *The Essence of Christianity* is that religion is simply the projection of human need, a fulfillment of deep-seated wishes.

The purpose of his book, Feuerbach wrote, was "the destruction of an illusion." He summarized the work in his conclusion: "We have shown that the substance and object of religion is altogether human; we have shown that divine wisdom is human wisdom; that the secret of theology is anthropology; that the absolute mind is the so-called finite subjective mind." Freud spent many years of his adult life working out the implications of Feuerbach's assertions.

Other influences that may have played an important role in Freud's rejection of the spiritual worldview include the cultural environment of Europe during the late nineteenth and early twentieth centuries and the specific environment of the medical school where Freud trained. During the late nineteenth century many publications discussed the assumed conflict between science and religion. Two well-known books—John William Draper's *History of the Conflict Between Religion and Science* and Andrew Dickson White's *History of the Warfare of Science with Theology in Christendom*— illustrate the prevailing perception. Historian Peter Gay refers to "sizable pockets of anticlericalism and of secularist contempt for all religion" that pervaded European culture during Freud's years in medical school. Many of these "pockets" involved the medical community, whose acceptance Freud strongly desired—for his professional advancement early in his career, and later, for the acceptance of his theories.

Freud worked in the laboratory of Ernst Brücke, one of a group of physiologists who had attempted to found a science of biology on thoroughly materialistic grounds. In his autobiography, Freud described Brücke as the person "who carried more weight with me than anyone else in my whole life." Brücke, along with many other of the medical faculty that Freud admired, took a strong stand against the spiritual worldview, insisting that irreconcilable differences exist between science and religion and that no truth existed except that attained through the scientific method. As Freud would write late in his life, "there are no sources of knowledge of the universe other than . . . what we call research."

Freud coveted a prestigious professorship at the University of Vienna. For many years his appointment was turned down. Other colleagues who spent the same number of years teaching received professorships, and yet Freud year after year watched a parade of promotions pass him by. Refusing to wait passively any longer, he used a friend and former patient of his to exert political influence, and finally obtained the post. The usual wait for a member of the faculty with Freud's experience was four years; Freud had waited seventeen. Freud had been warned by an old physiology professor of his that there was prejudice against him in official circles. In addition, the two professors who proposed his promotion reminded him of the anti-Semitism prevalent in Austria at that time and hinted that he might meet resistance.

During the years of Freud's medical training the intense anti-Semitism of the political world of Austria, and of the general population, also infected the medical profession. For the Jews living in Vienna at the close of the nineteenth century, this atmosphere produced a kind of psychological holocaust—a precursor to what took place under the Nazis a generation later. The medical literature at that time reflected intense racism and anti-Semitism. As historian Sándor Gilman points out, the European medical journals reflected the eighteenth-century view that "Jews were profoundly flawed . . . and predisposed to a host of illnesses." Freud's official biographer, Ernest Jones, notes that Freud had the "common Jewish sensitiveness to the slightest hint of Anti-Semitism—and had suffered much from school days onward, and especially at the University, from the anti-Semitism that pervaded Vienna."

Freud's early experiences with anti-Semitism critically influenced his attitude toward the spiritual worldview. In Austria over 90 percent of the population registered as Catholic. Freud said that in this environment "I was expected to feel myself inferior and an alien because I was a Jew." One can understand Freud's motivation to dis-

credit and destroy what he called the "religious *Weltanschauung*"
and why he referred to religion as "the enemy." Without this "enemy" he would not be in a tiny minority and expected to feel himself "inferior and an alien."

Freud recalled all of his life a story his father told him when he was
about ten years old. His father had been approached by an anti-
Semitic bully who knocked his father's cap off into the mud and
shouted, "Jew! Get off the pavement!" Freud asked about his father's
reaction. His father replied, "I went into the roadway and picked up
my cap." Freud said that struck him "as unheroic conduct on the part
of the big, strong man . . ." Freud confronted anti-Semitism not like
his father, with a passive acceptance, but with a strong desire to fight
it tooth and nail.

In April of 1882, Freud met Martha Bernays, and two months
later they became engaged. Her grandfather had been the chief
rabbi of Hamburg, and her father maintained the Orthodox Jewish
faith of her grandfather.

When he was twenty-seven years old, Freud wrote his fiancée
of an experience he had on a train: "You know how I am always
longing for fresh air and always anxious to open windows, above
all in trains. So I opened a window now and stuck my head out to
get a breath of air. Whereupon there were shouts to shut it . . . I
declared my willingness to close the window provided another,
opposite, were opened, it was the only open window in the whole
long carriage. While the discussion ensued and the man said he
was prepared to open the ventilation slit instead of the window,
there came a shout from the background: 'He's a dirty Jew!'—
And with this the whole situation took on a different color."
Freud describes how one of the men involved in the argument
threatened to settle the fight physically. Freud said he was "not in
the least frightened of the mob, asked the one to keep to himself
his empty phrases which inspired no respect in me, and the other

to step up and take what was coming to him. I was quite prepared to kill him . . ."

On Easter Sunday 1886, when he was thirty years old, Freud opened a private practice in neuropathology. From that time on, Easter would remind him of this event. A half century later, he wrote in a letter: "Easter Sunday signifies to me the fiftieth anniversary of taking up my medical practice." Many scholars note that Easter had a special significance for him, dating back to his Catholic nanny taking him to church. Some write that opening his practice on Easter Sunday reflected the special respect Freud gave the day, others that it reflected defiance or disrespect.

The opening of his private practice provided Freud with sufficient income to marry and support a family. On September 13, 1886, he and Martha married. He did not want a Jewish wedding because he found the religious aspects uncomfortable. For a brief time he even considered becoming a Protestant to avoid the Jewish religious ceremony, but his friend and mentor Josef Breuer advised against it. So the couple married in Germany, first in a civil ceremony in the Town Hall and, the next day, in a brief Jewish ceremony in the home of the bride, with only a few members of the family present.

A decade later, in October 1896, Freud's father died. Freud wrote in a letter to Fliess that this death "has affected me profoundly . . . has reawakened all my early feelings . . . I feel quite uprooted." He noted that the death of one's father is "the most important event, the most poignant loss, in a man's life." Jacob had struggled financially, had not been able to support his son through his long medical training, and had had the humiliating experience of having to accept assistance from his wife's family. Freud considered his father a failure. Yet the death struck him hard. Indeed, in my own clinical practice I have observed that one has more difficulty resolving the loss of a parent when negative feelings toward that parent remain unresolved. The death of Freud's father stimulated his self-analysis, the writing of what he considered his most significant work, *The Interpretation of Dreams,* and the beginning of the formulation of his theory of the Oedipus complex. This object of so much controversy both outside of and within psychoanalytic circles may help explain Freud's personal feelings toward the concept of an Ultimate Authority and his sustained attack on the spiritual worldview.

The Oedipus theory, so easily and so often caricatured, bears restatement. Freud observed clinically that children experience a phase in their psychosexual development during which they experience positive feelings toward the parent of the opposite sex and feelings of rivalry toward the parent of the same sex. "While he is still a small child, a son will already begin to develop a special affection for his mother, whom he regards as belonging to him; he begins to feel his father as a rival who disputes his sole possession," Freud explains in a lecture delivered in 1915. "And in the same way a little girl looks on her mother as a person who interferes with her affectionate relation to her father and who occupies a position which she herself could very well fill. Observation shows in us to what early years these attitudes go back. We refer to them as the 'Oedipus complex,' because the legend of Oedipus realizes, with only a slight softening, the two extreme wishes that arise from the son's situation—to kill his father and take his mother to wife."

Freud observed this complex of feelings in his own analysis. In a letter to Fliess he admitted that "I have found, in my own case too, [the phenomenon of] being in love with my mother and jealous of my father, and I now consider it a universal event in early childhood. If this is so, we can understand the gripping power of Oedipus Rex, in spite of all the objections that reason raises against the presupposition of fate." (If Freud based his Oedipus complex theory only on his self-analysis, one could certainly question whether or not it is a "universal event." Freud's family, with an elderly father, an attractive teenager for a mother, and half brothers who were about the age of his mother, was hardly typical.)

Freud acknowledged that people who first hear about this theory think it absurd: "the discovery has provoked the most violent opposition among adults . . ." He suggested, however, that if the theory contains truth—regardless of how distasteful—we must accept it. "It is my unaltered conviction that there is nothing in this to be disavowed or glossed over. We must reconcile our-selves to the fact which was recognized by the Greek legend itself as an inevitable fate."

Why did Freud think this concept so important? Because he thought the failure to resolve these universal childhood feelings contributed to the development of many emotional disorders later in life. "It became ever clearer," Freud wrote in 1924 in *A Short Account of Psychoanalysis,* "[that] the complicated emotional relation of children to their parents—what is known as the Oedipus complex . . . was the nucleus of every case of neurosis." These early feelings of children toward parents also formed the basis for Freud's main argument against the existence of an Intelligence beyond the universe. Freud asserts that one's ambivalence toward parental authority—especially the positive feelings of that ambivalence—forms the basis of one's deep-seated wish for God.

Today, in psychoanalytic circles, the Oedipus complex is still debated. But even among those who question the universality of this theory, it is widely agreed that early relationships with parents strongly influence later psychological health. And perhaps these early family relationships predispose us toward or away from belief in God.

Lewis's Background

On November 29, 1898, on the outskirts of Belfast, Ireland, Florence Hamilton Lewis gave birth to a son. She and her husband, Albert James Lewis, named their newborn infant Clive Staples. Little did they realize the child would someday become a brilliant scholar, a celebrated author whose works would be read by millions, and whose many honors would include being offered the Commander of the Order of the British Empire (an honor which Lewis declined).

C. S. Lewis, in his autobiography *Surprised by Joy,* describes his family succinctly. Though born in Ireland, his father was Welsh and his mother Scottish. The families of his parents "were as different in temperament as in origin." His father's family "were true Welshmen, sentimental, passionate, and rhetorical, easily moved both to anger and to tenderness; men who laughed and cried a great deal and had not much the talent for happiness." His mother's family, on the other hand, "were a cooler race. Their minds were critical and ironic and they had the talent for happiness in a high degree . . ." Lewis believed that his "mother's cheerful and tranquil affection" and "the ups and downs" of his father's emotional life bred in him "a certain dislike or distrust of emotion as something uncomfortable and embarrassing and even dangerous."

Before marrying Lewis's father, Albert, Florence Hamilton attended Queen's College in Belfast and won honors in logic and mathematics. Albert Lewis attended boarding school in England and studied under W. T. Kirkpatrick, a very strict but excellent headmaster, who would later instruct the young Lewis. When Albert finished boarding school, he was apprenticed to a solicitor, a lawyer in the British system who can try cases only in the lower courts. Albert eventually finished his apprenticeship and set up his own practice in Belfast, where he worked for the remainder of his life. He married Florence on August 29, 1894.

Lewis's grandfather served as vicar of the local church attended by the Lewis family. The grandfather preached highly emotional sermons and often wept in the pulpit. Lewis remembered that, as a very young boy, he and his brother Warren would find these church services uncomfortable and embarrassing—so embarrassing they would struggle to keep from giggling out loud. These early experiences with formal religion played no small role in Lewis's later repudiation of his nominal childhood faith, his seeing the spiritual worldview as "silly" and his embrace of a materialist alternative.

When he was about four years old, Lewis announced to his parents that his name was "Jacksie," eventually shortened to "Jack," the name always used by those who knew him well.

When writing his autobiography, Lewis recalled certain early experiences that he realized were spiritually meaningful. One of these events occurred before he was six years old. In *Surprised by Joy* he explains: "Once in those early days my brother brought into the nursery the lid of a biscuit tin which he had covered with moss and garnished with twigs and flowers so as to make it a garden or a toy forest. This was the first beauty I ever knew . . . As long as I live my imagination of Paradise will retain something of my brother's toy garden." Lewis suggested that this memory, along with the view of the "Green Hills" which "we saw from the nursery window," taught him "longing." After he rejected atheism, he looked back and realized that these experiences occurred periodically. He described them as "Joy" and said they must be "sharply distinguished both from Happiness and from Pleasure." He later concluded that this longing was not for a "place," as he first thought, but for a "Person."

When Lewis was seven years old, his family moved to a new house called Little Lea, a larger country home. Lewis noted in his autobiography that "the New House is almost a major character in my story." Here he spent many of his most formative years reading books, amid "long corridors, empty sunlit rooms, upstairs indoor silences, attics explored in solitude, distant noises of gurgling cisterns and pipes, and the noise of wind under the tiles." Because of the frequent wet weather in the Belfast area of Ireland, Lewis and his brother spent many hours in the new house drawing and writing stories: ". . . we always had pencils, paper, chalk and paint boxes, and this recurring imprisonment gave us occasion and stimulus to develop the habit of creative imagination . . . together we devised the imaginary country of 'Boxen' which proliferated hugely and became our solace and joy for many years to come." Lewis was beginning to develop both the imagination and writing skills that characterized his adult life. Then his brother Warren "was packed off to an English boarding school," and Lewis spent a considerable amount of time alone. He recalled that "at the age of six, seven, and eight—I was living almost entirely in my imagination."

When Lewis was nine years old, his cozy, comfortable world came to a cataclysmic end. First, his paternal grandfather died. Then his mother became seriously ill. After consultations with many medical specialists the doctors diagnosed cancer and recommended surgery. The operation took place in the home, a not unusual occurrence among middle-class families in Ireland. Lewis recalled the sounds and the smells as people hurried into and out of his mother's room during the surgery. Almost a half century later, he remembered vividly how his father tried to "convey to my terrified mind things it had never conceived before." His mother's illness, her frightening operation, and then her death overwhelmed the little boy. He recalled being taken into her bedroom to observe her corpse and that his "grief was overwhelmed in terror."

The impact of this loss—the change in his father's demeanor and subsequently the change in his relationship to his two boys, Lewis's depression and pessimism of many years, and the "first religious experience" of praying in vain for his mother's recovery—all were crucial.

Albert Lewis, grief-stricken over the death of his wife, decided he could not care adequately for his sons and sent them both to boarding school in England. Boarding schools (called public shools) were then and are still private, independent schools. Perhaps because of his very young age (nine years old) and because he associated leaving home with the loss of his beloved mother, Lewis reacted to England "with immediate hatred." He hated "the strange English accents . . . the flatness . . . the miles and miles of featureless land, shutting one in from the sea, imprisoning, suffocating. Everything was wrong; wooden fences instead of stone walls and hedges, red brick farmhouses instead of white cottages, the fields too big . . . at that moment I conceived a hatred for England which took many years to heal." The painful feelings of grief and loneliness within the young Lewis might have caused him to hate any place away from the comfort and security of his home and those who cared for him.

The first school Albert Lewis chose for his sons turned out to be an unhappy one. Lewis experienced it as a kind of hell. It contained only about twenty students. The headmaster—nicknamed "Oldie"— whipped his students with a cane and had a reputation for cruelty. The teaching staff consisted mainly of the headmaster and his son and daughter. Lewis described the cruelty as "irrational and unpredictable." His brother Warren wrote of this headmaster: "I have seen him lift a boy of twelve or so from the floor by the back of his collar, and holding him at arm's length, as one might a dog . . . apply his cane to his calves." The father of one boy brought a High Court action against the headmaster for extreme brutality. Eventually the school closed down because of lack of pupils. The headmaster, after being diagnosed as psychotic, died two years later. Oldie, a clergyman of the Church of England, made a lasting impression on Lewis. A half century later Lewis had difficulty forgiving him. Some may have wondered if the headmaster had obtained sexual pleasure from his violent behavior, but Lewis doubted it: "Everyone talks of sadism nowadays but I question whether his cruelty had any erotic element in it." That the headmaster was a clergyman did not escape the perceptive mind of the young Lewis.

But not all of his experiences proved negative. As he looked back, he realized that some helped prepare him for the faith he would eventually embrace. He recalled in his autobiography: "Life in a vile boarding school . . . teaches one to live by hope. Even in a sense, by faith; for at the beginning of each term, home and the holidays are so far off that it is as hard to realize them as to realize heaven." Lewis recalled going to church during these years and beginning "to pray and to read my Bible and to attempt to obey my conscience." What prompted him to do this? "I feared for my soul; especially on certain blazing moonlit nights in that curtainless dormitory."

After the first boarding school closed down, Albert Lewis sent his son to another, Cherbourg, in the town of Malvern. Here he came under the influence of a Miss Cowie, the school matron, who became his first surrogate mother. She apparently noticed that Lewis was unusually sensitive and felt isolated and lonely. Lewis responded to her attention. Once the headmaster found her holding Lewis in her arms, and although she apparently had held other boys with what they considered motherly affection, he promptly fired her. Lewis missed her and wrote of her some fifty years later: "No school ever had a better Matron, more skilled and comforting to boys in sickness, or more cheery and companionable to boys in health. She was one of the most selfless people I have ever known. We all loved her."

Miss Cowie had another, more profound effect on Lewis. She "was still in her spiritual immaturity" and "floundering" in many different cults, which she discussed with him. This caused considerable confusion in the thirteen-year-old boy, and his nominal faith began to falter and finally disappear. "Little by little, unconsciously, unintentionally, she loosened the whole framework, blunted all the sharp edges of my belief. The vagueness, the merely speculative character, of all this Occultism began to spread . . ."

The framework continued to collapse when he began to read the classics. Lewis remembered: "Here, especially in Virgil, one was presented with a mass of religious ideas; and all teachers and editors took it for granted from the outset that these religious ideas were sheer illusion . . . the impression I got was that religion in general, though utterly false, was a natural growth, a kind of endemic nonsense into which humanity tended to blunder."

Lewis described his years at boarding school as times of loneliness and unhappiness. As he looked back, Lewis became acutely aware of the negative impact it all had. "If the parents in each generation . . . knew what really goes on at their son's schools, the history of education would be very different." He recalled one instructor instilling within his students "the desire for glitter, swagger, distinction, the desire to be in the know" and influencing Lewis "to labor very hard to make myself into a fop, a cad, and a snob."

Lewis did not like what he saw himself becoming nor did he like what he observed happening to the young men around him. "I have never seen a community so competitive, so full of snobbery and flunkeyism, a ruling class so selfish and so self-conscious, or a proletariat so fawning, so lacking in all solidarity and sense of corporate honor." The environment fostered pride and arrogance and the tendency to look down on others. He wrote many years later: "For the last thirty years or so England has been filled with a bitter, truculent, skeptical, debunking, and cynical *intelligentsia*. A great many of them were at public [private] schools, and I believe very few of them liked it." Lewis added that those who defend these schools will say these are the cases which the "system failed to cure; they were not kicked, mocked . . . flogged, and humiliated enough."

Lewis's father finally decided his son would fare better studying with a private tutor than he would in boarding school. As he explained in a letter to Lewis's brother, "In a word, the whole thing is a failure and must be ended. His letters make me unhappy . . . I think . . . the best thing I can do is to send him to 'Kirk' after next term."

William T. Kirkpatrick, a retired headmaster who once taught Lewis's father, now taught private pupils to prepare them for the university. Lewis spent the next two and a half years studying under "the Great Knock," as he called him, years that proved to be the most formative and happy of his life. He spent many hours of each day delving into books of his own choice. Every afternoon he was free "to read, write or moon about in the golden-tinted woods and valleys of this country."

During these leisure hours Lewis discovered George MacDonald, an author who made a profound impact on him and on his writing. "I have never concealed the fact that I regard him as my master; indeed, I fancy I have never written a book in which I did not quote from him," Lewis wrote some thirty years later. The book that introduced Lewis to MacDonald, *Phantastes,* "had about it a sort of cool morning innocence . . . What it actually did to me was to convert, even to baptize . . . my imagination." Lewis did not at that time realize that MacDonald was writing about the spiritual worldview that he, Lewis, would embrace some fifteen years later.

Kirkpatrick, a militant atheist and logician, taught Lewis to think critically and within the strict rules of logic. Under the "Great Knock" Lewis developed work habits that he kept for the rest of his life. He insisted, however, that Kirkpatrick did not impose atheism on his students: "The reader will remember that my own Atheism and Pessimism were fully formed before I went to Bookham. What I got there was merely fresh ammunition for the defense of a position already chosen. Even that I got indirectly from the tone of his mind or independently from reading his books." Lewis considered Kirkpatrick one of his greatest teachers and always spoke fondly of him: "My debt to him is very great, my reverence to this day undiminished."

Both Lewis and the Great Knock based their atheism on anthropological studies such as Frazer's *Golden Bough.* Lewis considered that "all religions, that is all mythologies, to give them their proper name, are man's own invention." Lewis believed the New Testament to be like other pagan myths about a god coming to earth, dying and rising again. He spelled out his views in a letter written during this time to his friend Arthur Greeves: ". . . great men were regarded as gods after their death—such as Heracles or Odin: thus after the death of a Hebrew philosopher Yeshua (whose name we have corrupted into Jesus) he became regarded as a god, a cult sprang up . . . and so Christianity came into being—one mythology among many . . . Superstition of course in every age had held the common people, but in every age the educated and thinking ones have stood outside it . . ."

Lewis went to Oxford on December 4, 1916, to take a scholarship exam in classics. He received approval from University College. He had to pass another set of exams called Responsions before he could be admitted, however, and he failed the math part of that exam. Fortunately he was allowed to enter Oxford to pass into the Army by way of the Officers Training Corps. (Although he never passed the math exam, he was allowed to return to Oxford after his war service because ex-servicemen were then exempt from it.) During his officer training course, his roommate was a young man named Edward "Paddy" Moore. Lewis and Paddy formed a close friendship, and each promised that if one should be killed in the war, the other would look after his parent.

Lewis arrived in the trenches on his nineteenth birthday. The terror of seeing friends slaughtered and of being wounded with shrapnel and hospitalized caused Lewis to relive these scenes for years in repetitive dreams. Nevertheless, Lewis wrote little about his war experiences. Perhaps they evoked too much anxiety. He sometimes tended to make light of some of them: "How 'I took' about sixty prisoners—that is, discovered to my great relief that the crowd of field-gray figures who suddenly appeared from nowhere, all had their hands up—is not worth telling, save as a joke."

Paddy, however, was killed in action. Lewis remembered his promise and took it seriously. He moved in with Mrs. Moore and her daughter. He helped run the household, doing an endless number of menial tasks as well as helping to pay the rent. Mrs. Moore, some thirty years older than Lewis, became a surrogate mother. Some biographers have speculated that Lewis and Mrs. Moore were lovers, but the evidence weighs against this notion. In his letters, Lewis makes unmistakably clear his mother-son relationship: "She is the old lady I call my mother and live with"; "She is really the mother of a friend"; "My ailing mother"; "My aged mother."

After Mrs. Moore's death, Lewis continued to refer to her this way: "There has been a great change in my life owing to the death of the old lady I called my mother. She died without apparent pain after many months of semi-conscious existence, and it would be hypocritical to pretend that it was a grief to us." George Sayer, a student and later a close friend and biographer, described the relationship with Paddy's mother as he observed it: "Jack's relationship with Mrs. Moore . . . was compounded of gratitude for her motherly kindness and generous hospitality, of pity for her as the mother of his closest wartime friend, and of the undertaking he may have been given to look after her if Paddy was killed."

In 1919, Lewis returned to Oxford, where he would spend the next thirty-five years. During his freshman year he published his first book, *Spirits in Bondage,* a collection of poems that sold poorly. Once he finished his undergraduate work, he taught philosophy for one year and then, in 1925, was elected to a fellowship in English literature at Magdalen College. The rest is history.

✿   ✿   ✿

The early life experiences of Freud and Lewis show a striking parallelism. Both Freud and Lewis, as young boys, possessed intellectual gifts that foreshadowed the profound impact they would make as adults. Both suffered significant losses early in life. Both had difficult, conflict-ridden relationships with their fathers. Both received early instruction in the faith of their family and acknowledged a nominal acceptance of that faith. Both jettisoned their early belief system and became atheists when in their teens. Both read authors that persuaded them to reject their nominal childhood beliefs: Freud was strongly influenced by Feuerbach and the many scientists he studied under as a medical student and Lewis by his teachers who gave him the impression that "religious ideas were sheer illusion . . . a kind of endemic nonsense."

Lewis, however, eventually rejected atheism and embraced the very view he once thought to be nonsense. How did he explain this dramatic change? What caused Freud to continue to reject the rich spiritual heritage of his family and to remain an atheist?

2

THE CREATOR

Is There an Intelligence Beyond the Universe?

As an atheist, Lewis agreed with Freud that the universe is all that exists—simply an accident that just happened. But eventually Lewis wondered whether its incredible vastness, its precision and order, and its enormous complexity reflected some kind of Intelligence. Is there Someone beyond the universe who created it?

Freud answers this "most important question" with a resounding "No!" The very idea of "an idealized Superman" in the sky—to use Freud's phrase—is "so patently infantile and so foreign to reality, that . . . it is painful to think that the great majority of mortals will never rise above this view of life." He predicted, however, that as the masses of people become more educated, they would "turn away" from "the fairy tales of religion." He reminds us that "the world is no nursery" and strongly advises us to face the harsh reality that we are alone in the universe. In short, he shouts, "Grow up!"

Lewis, after his changed worldview, answers with a resounding "Yes!" He asserts that the universe is filled with "signposts" like the "starry heavens above and the moral law within"—Immanuel Kant's phrase—all pointing with unmistakable clarity to that Intelligence. Lewis advises us to open our eyes, to look around, and understand what we see. In short, Lewis shouts, "Wake up!" Both Freud and Lewis give bold, clear, unequivocal, and mutually exclusive answers.

❖   ❖   ❖

In his scholarly works, his autobiography, and his letters written throughout his life, Freud refers to himself as "a materialist," "an atheist," "a godless medical man," "an infidel," and "an unbeliever." When eighty-two, a year before his death, he wrote a letter to Charles Singer, the historian, stating, "Neither in my private life or in my writing have I ever made a secret of being an out-and-out un-believer." Freud appears to have forgotten that he did waver once, in that letter to Silberstein, but that was just a brief student episode that quickly passed

In his philosophical writings Freud divides all people not into psychiatric categories, but into "believers" and "unbelievers." Un-der unbelievers he includes all those who call themselves material-ists, seekers, skeptics, agnostics, and atheists; under believers he includes a spectrum from all those who merely give intellectual as-sent to some kind of Supernatural Being to those, like Lewis, who describe a transforming spiritual experience that revolutionizes their lives and literally makes them into "new creatures."

Freud calls his worldview "scientific," because of its premise that knowledge comes only from research. Of course, this basic premise cannot itself be based on scientific research. Rather, it is a philo-sophical assumption that cannot be proven. One can only *assume* that all knowledge comes from "research" and that "no knowledge" comes "from revelation."

Freud appears to realize that logically one cannot prove a nega-tive—one cannot *prove* that God does not exist. The only real de-fense of his worldview is to discredit its alternative. Thus, Freud undertook a systematic and sustained attack on the spiritual world-view. He attacked it with sledgehammer blows. He wrote that the "tales of miracles . . . contradicted everything that had been taught by sober observation and betrayed too clearly the influence of the activity of the human imagination." He asserted that the Scrip-tures "are full of contradictions, revisions and falsifications"; he said no intelligent person can accept the "absurdities" or "fairy tales" of believers.

Freud wrote that the doctrines of religion "bear the imprint of the times in which they arose, the ignorant times of the childhood of humanity," that the specific doctrine that "the universe was cre-ated by a being resembling a man, but magnified in every respect . . . an idealized superman . . . reflects the gross ignorance of primitive peoples."

He described the spiritual worldview as "distorting the picture of the real world in a delusional manner . . . and . . . forcibly fixing [peo-ple] in a state of psychical infantilism." He wrote that "the religions of mankind must be classed among the mass delusions," and he re-ferred to religion as "the universal obsessional neurosis of human-ity." He wondered if "Jesus Christ . . . is not a part of mythology" or merely "an ordinary deluded creature." In a letter to Oskar Pfister, a friend and clergyman, Freud referred to the teachings of Jesus as "psychologically impossible and useless for our lives" and con-cluded, "I attach no value to the 'imitation of Christ.'" Freud refers here to the famous, influential book *The Imitation of Christ,* be-lieved to have been written by Thomas à Kempis between 1390 and 1440, encouraging readers to follow the example of Jesus Christ in self-denial and in love for others.

o   o   o

For the first thirty years of his life, Lewis shared Freud's atheism. His materialism took definitive form soon after he entered his teens. Before that time he participated in traditional religious practices—complying with his family and with the rules of the boarding schools he attended. Mandatory chapel was an "opportunity to daydream." In his autobiography, he recalled that "religious experiences did not occur at all . . . I was taught the usual things and made to say my prayers and in due time taken to church." But Lewis found himself bored and disinterested. He pursued this form of religiosity mechanically, "without feeling much interest in it."

His experiences in boarding school gradually erased all vestiges of his childhood religiosity. "I believe in no God," Lewis wrote in a letter to his friend Arthur Greeves when both were in their late teens. Even at that early age Lewis expressed himself with simplicity and clarity.

A decade later, as a faculty member at Oxford, Lewis experienced a radical change—a change from atheism to belief based on the Old and New Testaments. Through a series of discussions with faculty members whose intelligence he greatly respected, and through the reading of certain authors over a period of many years, Lewis came to a firm belief, not only in a Creator of the universe, but also a belief that that Creator stepped into human history.

In the preface to his most widely read book, Lewis described his worldview in eleven words: "There is one God and . . . Jesus Christ is His only Son." Later in the book, Lewis gave more detail. He wrote that all of humanity can be divided into "the majority who believe in some kind of God or gods, and the minority who do not."

Lewis added that among those who believe, another division exists: one group, the Hindus, believe "God is beyond good and evil"; the other group, the Jews, Mohammedans, and Christians believe "God is definitely 'good' or 'righteous,' a God who takes sides, who loves love and hates hatred." The biblical worldview states "that

God made the world . . . space and time, heat and cold, and all the colours and tastes, and all the animals and vegetables . . ." but also "that a great many things have gone wrong with the world that God made and that God insists, and insists very loudly, on our putting them right again."

But God was not the only supernatural being. There was also "a Dark Power in the universe . . . the Power behind death and disease, and sin . . . [who] was created by God, and [who] was good when he was created, and went wrong." Lewis asserted that this Dark Power is "the Prince of this world" and we now live in "enemy-occupied territory."

Why would a good, omnipotent Creator make a world that could go and has gone so wrong? "God created things which had free will—and free will, though it makes evil possible, is also the only thing that makes possible any love or joy worth having." The abuse of this freedom, however, has made the human race a horror to God and to itself. The result is human history, with its slavery, war, prostitution, and poverty, "the long, terrible story of man trying to find something other than God which will make him happy."

Lewis describes how God has intervened repeatedly in our lives. "First, He left us conscience, the sense of right and wrong: and all through history there have been people trying . . . to obey it. None of them ever quite succeeded." Second, God gave the human race stories "scattered throughout the heathen religions about a god who dies and comes to life again and, by his death, has somehow given new life to men." Third, God selected a particular people—the Jews—to instruct them in the kind of God he was, "that there was only one of Him and that He cared about right conduct." The Hebrew Scriptures record this period of instruction.

Then something shocking happened. "Among these Jews there suddenly turns up a man who goes about talking as if He was God." Lewis wrote that if this man turned up among Hindus or other Pantheists, where people often say they are one with God or a part of God, we could understand his claim. But this man was a Jew, to whom God "meant the Being outside the world Who had made it." Lewis argued that in this context this man's claim to be God "was the most shocking thing that has ever been uttered by human lips."

o　o　o

Freud was less shocked. He proffers two main arguments against the existence of an Intelligence beyond the universe: one, the psychological argument concerning wish fulfillment, and two, the argument concerning human suffering. Both arguments prevail in our culture today. To the psychological argument, used long before Freud, he gave an innovative twist. Human suffering was also hardly a new argument; indeed, for centuries it had been the most serious obstacle to faith for both believers and unbelievers. It too was well employed by Freud.

Freud's psychological argument against the spiritual worldview rests on the notion that all religious ideas are rooted in deep-seated wishes and are therefore illusions—false beliefs. He writes in his widely read *Future of an Illusion,* "We shall tell ourselves that it would be very nice if there were a God who created the world and was a benevolent providence and if there were a moral order in the universe and an afterlife, but it is a very striking fact that all this is exactly as we are bound to wish it to be." Freud therefore concludes that belief in God is merely a projection of powerful wishes and inner needs. He writes: ". . . religious ideas, which are given out as teachings . . . are illusions, fulfillments of the oldest, strongest and most urgent wishes of mankind. The secret of their strength lies in the strength of these wishes."

Freud admits that many before him recognized and wrote about this argument—especially the German philosopher Ludwig Feuerbach. "I said nothing which other and better men have not said be-

fore me in a much more complete, forcible manner," Freud acknowledges modestly. He then confesses "their names are well
known, and I shall not cite them, for I should not like to give the impression that I am seeking to rank myself as one of them."

Many scholars have recognized that Freud's argument reflects
the thinking of several writers of the Enlightenment—mainly
Voltaire, Diderot, and Darwin, in addition to Feuerbach. In a letter
to Freud, the Swiss clergyman Oskar Pfister argued that materialism was simply another religion and that "your substitute religion is
basically the idea of the eighteenth-century Enlightenment in
proud modern guise."

In his Future of an Illusion, Freud asserts somewhat less modestly yet more accurately that "all I have done—and this is the only
one thing that is new in my exposition—is to add some great psychological foundation to the criticism of my great predecessors."
Many writers before Freud wrote about God being a projection of
human needs and wishes. What Freud accomplished was to identify
those wishes quite specifically.

Freud asserts that the deep-seated wishes we project onto our
concept of God stem from early childhood. First among them is a
feeling of helplessness that carries over into adulthood. Freud
writes: "Biologically speaking, religiousness is to be traced to the
small human child's long-drawn-out helplessness and need of help."
He argued we all share a less conscious but very strong wish for the
protection of our parents, especially that of our fathers. When we
become adults, we still find ourselves helpless when confronted
with the great forces of life, and so we conjure up a figure like the
one who protected us as a child. "Psychoanalysis," Freud writes in
his 1910 paper on Leonardo da Vinci, "has shown us that a personal
God is, psychologically, nothing other than an exalted father . . . and
it brings us evidence every day of how young people lose their religious beliefs as soon as their father's authority breaks down."

Three years later, Freud wrote in *Totem and Taboo* that "psycho-analysis of individual human beings . . . teaches us with quite special insistence that the god of each of them is formed in the likeness of his father, that his personal relation to God depends on the relation to his father in the flesh and oscillates and changes along with that relation, and that at bottom God is nothing other than an exalted father." And twenty years later, in *Civilization and Its Discontents*, he writes: "The derivation of religious needs from the infant's helplessness and the longing for the father aroused by it, seems to me incontrovertible . . . The common man cannot imagine this Providence otherwise than in the figure of an enormously exalted father." Freud observed that "this god-creator is undisguisedly called 'father'" and asserted that "psycho-analysis infers that he really is the father, with all the magnificence in which he once appeared to the small child."

Freud insisted that one's personal relationship with God depends entirely on one's relationship with one's father. As he explained: "For the same person to whom the child owed his existence, the father (or more correctly, no doubt, the parental agency compounded of the father and the mother), also protected and watched over him in his feeble and helpless state, exposed as he was to all the dangers lying in wait in the external world; under his father's protection he felt safe."

Freud explained that when the child grows up "he knows, to be sure, that he is in possession of greater strength, but his insight into the perils of life has also grown greater, and he rightly concludes that fundamentally he still remains just as helpless and unprotected as he was in his childhood, that faced by the world he is still a child." As an adult plagued with feelings of helplessness, he "cannot do without the protection which he enjoyed as a child." He is imprinted with the "image of the father whom in his childhood he so greatly overvalued. He exalts the image into a deity and makes it into something contemporary and real." Freud concluded that "the effective strength of this . . . image and the persistence of his need for protection jointly sustain his belief in God."

In *The Future of an Illusion,* Freud pointed out that the mother becomes the child's "first protection against all of the undefined dangers which threaten it in an external world—its first protection against anxiety, we may say." But then a change takes place: "In this function (of protection) the mother is soon replaced by a stronger father, who retains that position for the rest of childhood. But the child's attitude to its father is colored by a particular *ambivalence.* The father himself constitutes a danger for the child, perhaps because of its earlier relation to its mother. Thus it fears him no less than it longs for him and admires him." Freud then asserted that "the indications of this ambivalence in the attitude to the father are deeply imprinted in every religion . . . When the growing individual finds that he is destined to remain a child for ever, that he can never do without protection against strange superior powers, he lends those powers the features belonging to the figure of his father." Thus, God is often depicted as someone to be feared as well as loved.

Freud wrote that the individual creates for himself the God "whom he dreads, whom he seeks to propitiate, and with whom he nevertheless entrusts with his own protection." In summary, "the defense against childish helplessness is what lends its characteristic features to the adult's reaction to the helplessness which he has to acknowledge—a reaction which is precisely the formation of religion."

So Freud asserts we possess intense, deep-seated wishes that form the basis for our concept of and belief in God. God does not create us in His image; we create God in our parents' image—or, more accurately, into the childhood image of our father. God exists only in our minds. Freud cannot help but advise us to grow up and give up the "fairy tales of religion."

o   o   o

C. S. Lewis countered Freud's wish-fulfillment argument with the assertion that the biblical worldview involves a great deal of despair and pain and is certainly not anything one would *wish* for. He argued that understanding this view begins with the realization one is in deep trouble, that one has transgressed the moral law and needs forgiveness and reconciliation. He wrote that this worldview begins to make sense only "after you have realized that there is a real Moral Law, and a Power behind the law, and that you have broken that law and put yourself wrong with that Power." Only after we realize that our position is "nearly desperate" will we begin to understand the Scriptures. Although this biblical faith is "a thing of unspeakable comfort," Lewis wrote, "it does not begin in comfort; it begins in dismay." And "it is no use at all trying to go on to that comfort without first going through that dismay."

Until one experiences the dismay of realizing how far short one falls of meeting the Creator's standards and how much one needs alteration, one can never experience the comfort of belief. Lewis wrote that in faith "as in war and everything else, comfort is the one thing you cannot get by looking for it. If you look for truth, you may find comfort in the end: If you look for comfort you will not get either comfort or truth—only soft soap and wishful thinking to begin with and, in the end, despair."

Lewis adds that any attempt to live this particular worldview also involves pain, and is certainly not something one would wish for. In *The Problem of Pain* he notes that the process of "rendering back one's will which we have so long claimed for our own, is, in itself, extraordinarily painful. To surrender a self-will inflamed and swollen with years of usurpation is a kind of death."

In addition, Lewis astutely notes that Freud's argument stems from his clinical observations that a young child's feelings toward the father are always characterized by a "particular ambivalence"—i.e., strong positive *and* strong negative feelings. But if Freud's observations hold true, these ambivalent wishes can work both ways. Would not the negative part of the ambivalence indicate the wish that God *not* exist would be as strong as the wish *for* his existence?

Lewis found this to be true in his own life. He notes in his autobiography that as an atheist his strongest wish was that God *not* exist. Lewis wanted no one to interfere with his life. "No word in my vocabulary expressed deeper hatred than the word *Interference*," he wrote in *Surprised by Joy*. And he found himself acutely aware that the Old and New Testaments "placed at the center what seemed to me a transcendental Interferer." Atheism appealed to Lewis because it satisfied his deep-seated wish to be left alone. Lewis says that Freud's clinical observations tell us something about our thoughts and feelings—but that those feelings may involve either a wish for or a wish against God's existence. Freud failed to follow through with his own observations.

Lewis takes his argument a step further. Not only does wishing for something not rule out the existence of the object wished for—it may itself be evidence *for* its existence. In his own life, Lewis experienced periodically a deep-seated desire that he called "joy" and that he eventually concluded was a desire for a relationship with his Creator. Lewis notes we usually possess desires for things which exist. He asserts that "Creatures are not born with desires unless satisfaction for those desires exists. A baby feels hunger: well, there is such a thing as food. A duckling wants to swim: well, there is such a thing as water. Men feel sexual desire: well, there is such a thing as sex." He then implies we all have a deep-seated desire, or wish for, a relationship with the Creator and for an existence beyond this life, though we often mistake it for something else. Recent research by neuroscientists adds a twist here. Evidence exists that the human brain is "hardwired" (genetically programmed) for belief. Whether, if true, this wiring reflects an Intelligence beyond the universe depends on one's worldview. As Lewis states, what we learn from evidence "depends on the kind of philosophy we bring" to the evidence.

Lewis writes: "If I find in myself a desire which no experience in this world can satisfy, the most probable explanation is that I was made for another world." Lewis continues: "If none of my earthly pleasures satisfy it, that does not prove that the universe is a fraud. Probably earthly pleasures were never meant to satisfy it, but only to arouse it, to suggest the real thing. If that is so, I must take care, on the one hand, never to despise, or be unthankful for, these earthly blessings, and on the other, never to mistake them for the something else of which they are only a kind of copy, or echo, or mirage."

Lewis relates this desire to one's purpose in life: "I must keep alive in myself the desire for my true country, which I shall not find till after death; I must never let it get snowed under or turned aside; I must make it the main object of life to press on to that other country and to help others to do the same."

In short: "All your life an unattainable ecstasy has hovered just beyond the grasp of your consciousness. The day is coming when you will wake to find, beyond all hope, that you have attained it, or else, that it was within your reach and you have lost it forever."

Freud recognized a similar desire in himself. He used the German word *Sehnsucht*, the same word Lewis uses to describe the desire. In a paper published in 1899, Freud described a "longing" that haunted him all of his life. This longing he associated with a desire to walk in the woods with his father, as he did as a child. He writes: "I believe now that I was never free from a longing for the beautiful woods near our home, in which . . . I used to run off from my father, almost before I had learnt to walk."

❖   ❖   ❖

Clinically, I have observed that all of us have some conflict with our parents and therefore some ambivalence toward authority. The differences are in degree and not in kind. Remember that Freud said of the child's attitude toward his father: "It fears him no less than it longs for him and admires him." Freud may be correct that these early feelings toward parental authority influence one's concept of and attitude toward God. They may determine as adults whether we remain open to or defiant and closed to even the possibility of an Ultimate Authority. Freud's atheism and the atheism Lewis embraced for the first half of his life may be explained in part on the basis of early negative feelings toward their fathers. A considerable amount of evidence supports this notion. Both Freud and Lewis describe strong negative feelings toward their fathers when they were children—feelings that they wrote about often as adults—and, in addition, both associated their fathers with the spiritual worldview they rejected as young men.

Freud's father was already a grandfather when he married Freud's mother, his third wife. Freud always felt considerably closer to his young mother than to his much older father. In his self-analysis Freud discovered feelings of intense jealousy and rivalry toward his father. His father's financial reverses did not help. The son turned out to be a great success, but he considered his father a failure. When almost sixty years old, Freud wrote an article reflecting on his schoolboy experiences and describing a boy's relationship with his father in a manner that clearly reflects his own experience. "In the second half of childhood a change sets in in the boy's relation to his father—a change whose importance cannot be exaggerated . . . He finds that his father is no longer the mightiest, wisest and richest of beings; he grows dissatisfied with him, he learns to criticize him and to estimate his place in society; and then as a rule, he makes him pay heavily for the disappointment that has been caused by him . . . he becomes a model not only to imitate but also to get rid of, in order to take his place. Thenceforward affectionate and hostile impulses towards him persist side by side, often to the end of one's life . . ."

Freud remembered all his life the disgust and bitter disappointment he felt as a boy of ten years when hearing that his father refused to defend himself against the anti-Semitic bullies who pushed him off the sidewalk. He also associated religious faith with his Orthodox father, who read the Bible and who spoke Hebrew fluently.

C. S. Lewis also had a conflict-ridden relationship with his father. After he lost his mother when he was nine years old, Lewis described how his father had difficulty controlling his temper and "spoke wildly and acted unjustly." He could never forgive his father for sending him away during a time of desperate emotional need. Over the next few years, Lewis became progressively more alienated from him. In his autobiography, Lewis describes their strained relationship, how his father irritated him, how almost any attempt to discuss an issue with him resulted in an argument, how his father failed to visit him when Lewis, recovering from war wounds, pleaded for him to come.

Lewis described his father as both "pathetic and comic." Long after his father's death, Lewis realized his conflict with his father was more his doing than his father's. In his autobiography Lewis admits: "With the cruelty of youth I allowed myself to be irritated by traits in my father which, in other elderly men, I have since regarded as lovable foibles."

As with Freud, Lewis associated the spiritual worldview with his father. His father encouraged him to attend church and to become a believer. Once Lewis became an atheist in his early teens, he not only avoided informing his father; on at least one occasion he pretended to be a believer. In his autobiography he confesses that "my relations to my father help to explain one of the worst acts of my life." Though an atheist, he prepared for confirmation and took his first Communion "in total disbelief." In his autobiography he states, "Cowardice drove me into hypocrisy and hypocrisy into blasphemy . . . I was acting a lie . . . it seemed impossible to tell my father my real views."

Lewis appears to be aware of some relationship between his atheism and his negative feelings toward his father. He not only associated the spiritual worldview with his father, but knew that his embracing atheism would be in defiance of and disturbing to his father. When his father died, Lewis expressed remorse for feeling so alienated, so angry, and so impatient with him.

Both Freud and Lewis, as adults, experienced great difficulty with authority, not only with the Ultimate Authority, but with all authority. In Freud's autobiography he notes how he struggled to get rid of the last shred of "the innocent faith in authority of which I was not yet free." He mentions how he works well with people under him but has difficulty with "those above me or who are in some other respect my superiors." Lewis also writes of the "deep-seated hatred of authority" he felt as an atheist. So perhaps these intense negative childhood feelings in Freud and Lewis toward the first authority in their lives caused resistance to the very notion of an Ultimate Authority.

Freud's argument, however, cannot explain changes of view very easily. How did Lewis overcome his resistance to belief? He did, and Freud did not. Freud cannot tell us why.

As with much of Freud's teachings, the great psychiatrist offers a partial truth that supports his philosophy but omits crucial aspects that question his conclusions. Freud's arguments were militantly hostile to God's existence. Yet his logic predicted ambivalence. Reflecting this ambivalence, he himself remained preoccupied throughout his life with the question of God's existence. He was indeed preoccupied with the "infantile" "fairy tale" of God's existence. This may come as a surprise to some readers of Freud, but it is true. The evidence lies in his letters.

Freud's daughter Anna, the only child to carry on his work, once said to me: "If you want to know my father, don't read his biographers, read his letters." A careful reading of his letters reveals some rather surprising—if not perplexing—material. First, Freud frequently quoted from the Bible, both the Old and New Testaments. In his autobiography Freud writes: "My early familiarity with the

Bible story . . . had, as I recognized much later, an enduring effect upon the direction of my interest." Second, letters written throughout his life are replete with words and phrases such as "I passed my examinations with God's help"; "if God so wills"; "the good Lord"; "taking the Lord to task"; "into the keeping of the Lord"; "until after the Resurrection"; "science seems to demand the existence of God"; "God's judgment"; "God's will"; "God's grace"; "God above"; "if someday we meet above"; "in the next world"; "my secret prayer." In a letter to Oskar Pfister, Freud writes that Pfister was "a true servant of God" and was "in the fortunate position to lead (others) to God." What does this mean? Can we not dismiss all this as merely figures of speech—common in English as well as in German? Yes, if it were anyone but Freud. But Freud insisted even a slip of the tongue had meaning.

This preoccupation continues until his last book, *Moses and Monotheism,* written over a half century later, when he was in his eighties. Why? Why couldn't he put the question to rest? If he had all the answers, why did the question of God's existence continue to preoccupy him? Perhaps Lewis would say we can never explain away God. Nor can we find rest until that deep-seated desire (experienced by both Freud and Lewis) is satisfied.

Some of my students dogmatically deny the existence of God— but at the same time acknowledge that whenever their plane hits turbulence, they find themselves praying. Many facets of Freud's life likewise appear to be in contradiction to his atheism. Lewis said that when he was an atheist, his life also was full of contradictions. He writes: "I was at this time living, like so many Atheists . . . in a whirl of contradictions. I maintained that God did not exist. I was also very angry with God for not existing. I was also equally angry with Him for creating a world . . . why should creatures have the burden of existence forced on them without their consent?" Even as an atheist, Lewis realized his ambivalence toward God—a part of him wanting desperately that God not exist, another part strongly desiring His existence.

*   *   *

Lewis's early life resembled Freud's in some important ways. Both Freud and Lewis received religious instruction as children. Nevertheless, both of them, as adolescents, became avowed atheists. Something happened in the minds of Freud and Lewis as highly intelligent adolescents that caused them to repudiate their religious upbringing and to embrace an atheistic worldview. Did they carefully examine the evidence for their faith and find it intellectually unsound? They each faced specific conscious influences in their academic environments, and less conscious ambivalence toward their fathers and toward authority generally.

To understand what happened, we may find helpful the classification of religious faith according to a scheme developed by Gordon W. Allport. He used two categories: *extrinsically* and *intrinsically* religious. Extrinsically religious people are those whose expressions of faith are motivated by a need to attain status or be accepted by others. Usually a child's faith, motivated by a need to please parents, falls into this category. Intrinsically religious people are those who internalize their beliefs so that they become the primary motivating influence in their lives. Many of this group speak of a specific time when they came to faith; some speak of the experience as a rebirth. Modern medical research has shown that extrinsic religiosity can have a negative effect on physical and emotional health, whereas intrinsic faith often has a scientifically demonstrable positive effect (see Notes at the back of the book).

With both Freud and Lewis, their childhood religiosity, motivated by a desire to please their parents, would be considered extrinsic, and easily eroded by outside influences. As we have seen, their rejection of this nominal or extrinsic childhood faith was also motivated by external factors: they were each rebelling against their father. Both rejected their nominal faith after they left home, Lewis for boarding school and Freud for college. They were no longer under the authority of their fathers. In the analysis of his patients (and perhaps in his own analysis), Freud noted that young people lose their religious beliefs "as soon as their father's authority breaks down."

Freud's philosophical works are not characterized by the objective, dispassionate tone of the clinician or scientist. Instead, they exhibit an intense, emotional, argumentative and, at times, desperate and pleading tone. Freud obviously feels intensely about these issues. He appears to be determined to destroy every possible reason for accepting the spiritual worldview.

At times Freud's attack becomes overdetermined and contradictory. For example, he makes the sweeping statement that believers are simply not very intelligent, suffering from a "weak intellect." Freud asserts that "when a man has once brought himself to accept uncritically all the absurdities that religious doctrines put before him and, even so, overlook the contradictions before them, we need not be greatly surprised at the weakness of his intellect." To be sure, Freud had a low opinion of people generally and considered them lazy, influenced not by reason but by their passions. He writes, "For the masses are lazy and unintelligent . . . men are not spontaneously fond of work and . . . arguments are of no avail against their passions." When almost eighty years old, he wrote that "there has been little occasion for me to change my opinion of human nature." Yet Freud realized that many of the great minds that he admired had been men of faith. He considered Sir Isaac Newton a genius and quoted him often. He wrote that St. Paul "stands alone in all history." Oskar Pfister, a Swiss pastor and psychoanalyst from whom Freud "accepted the most varied suggestions for the technique of child analysis," remained one of Freud's closest friends throughout his adult life.

These men were exceptions; in general, Freud scoffed at believers.

Lewis argues just the opposite. He makes the observation that the biblical worldview has certain characteristics that simulate our physical universe—it is extremely complex and different from what we would expect it to be. He points out, for example, that a table is not simply a table—it comprises atoms, electrons, etc. Moreover, the universe is not simply the sum of its physical parts. Lewis believes that anyone trying to understand and live this worldview "will find his intelligence sharpened . . . That is why an uneducated believer like Bunyan was able to write a book that has astonished the world."

Freud characterized people who embrace the spiritual worldview not only as lacking in intelligence, but also as suffering from the "universal obsessional neurosis." As a little boy taken to church, Freud saw people kneeling frequently and making the sign of the cross. He may also have observed the rocking movements of Orthodox Jews when they prayed. Later, in his clinical practice, when he treated patients suffering from obsessive-compulsive disorder (OCD) he noticed symptoms that reminded him of these earlier observations. A person with OCD may experience the need to repeat certain behaviors—such as praying, counting, or hand washing—to reduce the anxiety caused by obsessive thoughts—persistent, repeated impulses or images that are intrusive and cause marked anxiety.

In Freud's first paper on the religious worldview, "Obsessive Actions and Religious Practices," he noted "the resemblance between what are called obsessive actions in sufferers from nervous afflictions and the observances by means of which believers give expression to their piety." Freud believed that the human race experienced stages of development that paralleled the stages experienced by the individual. The universal obsessional neurosis, he thought, paralleled the childhood neurosis that he believed every individual experienced in the process of growing up. Freud thought that the human race would someday outgrow the need for belief—especially as the masses became more educated. In fact, according to a recent Gallup poll, though more Americans are more educated today than ever before, more also believe God plays a direct role in their lives than ever before.

Psychiatrists use clinical terms, many of which stem from Freud. Freud thought that people who embraced the spiritual worldview suffered from a neurotic illness that sometimes bordered on a psychosis. Freud makes clear he thinks that religious beliefs "are so improbable, so incompatible with everything we have laboriously discovered about the reality of the world, that we may compare them . . . to delusions." Psychiatry defines delusions as false, fixed beliefs. We all possess false beliefs. Lewis points out that when we know little about a subject, we possess few correct concepts, but many false concepts. But these false concepts or beliefs change— they are not fixed—as our knowledge increases and shows us where the belief does not correspond with reality. A delusional person, on the other hand, does not change his views in response to contrary evidence. He is psychotic.

When an American physician wrote Freud about his conversion experience, Freud dismissed the experience as a "hallucinatory psychosis." Freud asserts in *Civilization and Its Discontents:* "The religions of mankind must be classed among the mass-delusions. No one, needless to say, who shares a delusion ever recognizes it as such."

Did Freud really believe that everyone who embraced the spiritual worldview was emotionally ill? Findings from a Gallup poll published recently indicate that 96 percent of Americans report they believe in God and 80 percent believe they have a personal relationship with God. Are so many Americans really emotionally ill?

To criticize Freud's rhetoric on spirituality is not to diminish Freud's scientific contributions. Lewis reminds us that "the medical theories and technique of the psychoanalysts" do not conflict with the spiritual worldview. The conflict occurs only with the "general philosophical view of the world which Freud and some others have gone on to add to this." Lewis adds that "when Freud is talking about how to cure neurotics he is speaking as a specialist on his own subject, but when he goes on to talk general philosophy he is speaking as an amateur . . . I have found that when he is talking off his own subject and on a subject I do know something about . . . he is very ignorant."

In sum, Freud's and Lewis's arguments can be subjected to tests of evidence and plausibility. We need to understand their arguments and to assess how much they are based on evidence and how much on emotion that caused them to distort reality. Freud associated the vehement anti-Semitism he experienced growing up with the spiritual worldview and this undoubtedly contributed to his intense desire to discredit and destroy it. In addition, Freud apparently treated many patients whose faith was based on neurotic need or whose psychotic symptoms contained religious content—i.e., patients whose faith reflected pathology. Oskar Pfister reminded Freud that he had seen only pathological forms of religious faith. Pfister wrote Freud: "Our difference derives chiefly from the fact that you grew up in proximity to pathological forms of religion and regard these as 'religion.'" As we continue to focus on the arguments that Freud and Lewis proffer, we need to ask which corresponds best to reality as we have experienced it. And we need to continue to observe how their lives strengthen or weaken their arguments.

—ఌ3ౚ—

CONSCIENCE

Is There a Universal
Moral Law?

One basic premise most believers hold is that every individual "just knows" right from wrong, because of an absolute moral law that has always existed in all cultures. If I think stealing a person's money or making love to his wife is alright—if he has a lot of money and if his wife consents—is that wrong? If you disagree with me, who is right? If we have no moral point of reference, what you think is no more right or wrong than what I think. This moral relativism, prevalent in our culture today, prompts an important question addressed by both Freud and Lewis. Is there a universal moral law?

We conduct our lives according to our sense of right and wrong. We somehow possess an awareness of what we "ought" to do. When we fail to do what we "ought," a part of our mind we call "conscience" evokes an unpleasant feeling we call "guilt." Is that feeling—present in almost all individuals—an indication of a God-given

moral law? Or does it simply reflect what we have been taught by
our parents?

Our conscience influences the decisions we make throughout the
day. If we find a wallet with hundreds of dollars in it, we decide to
return the wallet, or we keep it, depending on our moral code.
Where does this code come from? It influences not only our behavior, but also how we feel about our behavior. Do we simply make it
up? Freud thinks we do, as we make up our traffic laws, and that
moral codes can change from culture to culture. Lewis says we discover this code, as we discover the laws of mathematics, and that
this universal moral law transcends time and culture.

An important difference between the views of Freud and those
of Lewis concerns epistemology, the source of knowledge. Freud
wrote, ". . . there are no sources of knowledge of the universe other
than carefully scrutinized observations—in other words what we
call research—and along side it no knowledge derived from revelation." The Ten Commandments of the Old Testament and the two
great commandments (to love God, and to love one's neighbor as
oneself), according to Freud, come from human experience, not
from revelation. The scientific method, he writes, is our only source
of knowledge.

Lewis strongly disagrees. The scientific method simply cannot
answer all questions, cannot possibly be the source of all knowledge.
He says the job of science—a very important and necessary job—is
to experiment and observe and report how things behave or react.
He writes, "But why anything comes to be there at all, and whether
there is anything behind the things science observes . . . this is not a
scientific question."

Lewis argues that the question of whether or not an Intelligence
exists beyond the universe can never be answered by the scientific
method. When anyone attempts to answer that question, he makes
a philosophical or metaphysical assumption, not a scientific state-

ment. Similarly, we cannot expect science to answer questions concerning the existence of a moral law.

Lewis continues: "We want to know whether the universe simply happens to be what it is for no reason or whether there is a power behind it that makes it what it is . . ." He thinks that one way we could expect this power to show itself would be "inside ourselves as an influence or a command trying to get us to behave in a certain way. And that is just what we do find inside ourselves . . . something which is directing the universe and which appears in me as a law urging me to do right and making me feel responsible and uncomfortable when I do wrong."

The universal moral law, according to Lewis, finds expression not only in the Old and the New Testaments but also in our conscience. This law, Lewis thinks, is one of the many signposts pointing to the Creator. Lewis says we have two sources of evidence for the existence of this Creator: "One is the universe He has made . . . the other is that Moral Law which He has put into our minds." The moral law is better evidence because "it is inside information . . . you find out more about God from the Moral Law than from the universe in general just as you find out more about a man by listening to his conversation than by looking at a house he has built."

Lewis agrees with German philosopher Immanuel Kant, who pointed to the "moral law within" as a powerful witness to the greatness of God. Perhaps Lewis and Kant had in mind the biblical passages where the Creator says, "I will put my law in their minds, and write it on their hearts" (Jer. 31:33).

Freud expresses confusion over Kant's reference to the moral law: "In a famous pronouncement the philosopher Kant named the existence of the starry heavens and that of the moral law within us as the most powerful witnesses to the greatness of God." But Freud doubts the starry heavens have anything to do "with the question of whether one human creature loves another or kills him." He thinks it "strange" that Kant would use the heavens above and the moral law within as evidence for God's existence.

But, Freud says, on second thought the dictum by Kant "touches on a great psychological truth." In Freud's worldview God is simply a projection of parental authority—and if you accept that, then Kant's statement makes sense. We associate parents with our creation and with teaching us right and wrong. Freud asserts that "the same father (or parental agency) which gave the child life and guarded him against its perils, taught him as well what he might do and what he must leave undone . . . the child is brought up to a knowledge of his social duties by a system of loving rewards and punishments."

Freud asserts that as children become adults, their sense of right and wrong comes simply from what they have been taught by their parents, that "their parents' prohibitions and demands persist within them as a moral conscience." Eventually they introduce this whole system of rewards and punishments "unaltered into their religion."

Lewis agrees that we learn the moral law, in part, from our parents and teachers, and that this helps develop our conscience. But this does not mean that the moral law is simply "a human invention." Lewis explains that our parents and teachers did not make up this law any more than they made up the multiplication tables which they also teach us. He points out that some of what our parents and teachers teach us "are mere conventions which might have been different—we learn to keep to the left of the road, but it might just have been the rule to keep to the right—and others of them, like mathematics, are real truths." Mores or customs change with time; morals and the moral law hold firm.

Freud, however, asserts that ethics and morals come from human need and experience. The idea of a universal moral law as proposed by philosophers is "in conflict with reason." He writes that "ethics are not based on a moral world order but on the inescapable exigencies of human cohabitation." In other words, our moral code comes from what humans find to be useful and expedient. It is ironic that Lewis contrasted ethics with traffic laws; Freud wrote that "ethics are a kind of highway code for traffic among mankind." That is, they change with time and culture.

Lewis argues that this is one point about which empirical evidence exists. He says the moral law is basically the same in all cultures. Though some differences occur from one culture to another, the differences, says Lewis, "are not really that great . . . you can recognize the same law running through them all." Lewis insists that since the beginning of recorded history people have been aware of a law that they felt they ought to obey. "All the human beings that history has heard of acknowledge some kind of morality; that is, they feel towards certain proposed actions the experiences expressed by the words 'I ought' or 'I ought not.'" And they usually fail to live up to this law. Lewis writes: "First . . . human beings, all over the earth, have this curious idea that they ought to behave in a certain way, and cannot really get rid of it. Secondly . . . they do not in fact behave in that way . . . These two facts are the foundation of all clear thinking about ourselves and the universe we live in."

Lewis compared the moral teachings of the ancient Egyptians, Babylonians, Hindus, Chinese, Greeks, and Romans and found "how very like they are to each other and to our own . . . Think of a country where people were admired for running away in battle, or where a man felt proud of double-crossing all the people who had been kindest to him . . . Men have differed as regards what people you ought to be unselfish to—whether it was only your own family, or your fellow countrymen, or everyone. But they have always agreed that you ought not to put yourself first. Selfishness has never been admired."

This moral law has long been recognized and referred to as the Tao, or Natural Law, or First Principles of Practical Reason, or Traditional Morality. Lewis says that throughout history people took for granted that everyone knew the moral law by nature. He reminds us that during the last world war we took for granted that the Nazis knew what they did was wrong. They knew the moral law and knew they broke it. We tried them and found them guilty. "What was the sense in saying the enemy were in the wrong," Lewis asks, "unless Right is a real thing which the Nazis at bottom knew as well as we did and ought to have practiced?"

Lewis points out that although the moral law does not change over time or from culture to culture, the sensitivity to the law, and how a culture or an individual expresses the law, may vary. For example, the German nation under the Nazi regime obviously ignored the law and practiced a morality the rest of the world considered abominable. Lewis claims that when we assert that the moral ideas of one culture are better than those of another, we are using the moral law to make that judgment. "The moment you say that one set of moral ideas can be better than another," Lewis writes "you are, in fact, measuring them both by a standard, saying that one of them conforms to that standard more nearly than the other . . . the standard that measures two things is something different from either. You are in fact comparing them both with some Real Morality, admitting there is such a thing as a real Right, independent of what people think, and that some people's ideas get nearer to that real Right than others." Lewis concludes that "if your moral ideas can be truer, and those of the Nazis less true, there must be something—some Real Morality—for them to be true about."

Some individuals possess, perhaps because of background and training, a more developed conscience than others—a more informed understanding of the moral law. Lewis says that before his changed worldview, his conscience, compared with other young men he knew, was not well developed. "When I came first to the University," Lewis recalls in *The Problem of Pain,* "I was as nearly without a moral conscience as a boy could be. Some faint distaste for cruelty and for meanness about money was my utmost reach—of chastity, truthfulness, and self-sacrifice I thought as a baboon thinks of classical music." He noticed in some of his classmates a greater awareness of the moral law and a greater desire to follow it.

Freud also acknowledges that people differ in the development of their conscience. He states that if God *did* provide us the starry heavens above and the moral law within, He did an especially poor job with the moral law. He observes that "the stars are indeed magnificent, but as regards conscience God has done an uneven and careless piece of work, for a large majority of men have brought along with them only a modest amount of it or scarcely enough to be worth mentioning."

Freud did not include himself in that "large majority." In a letter to Dr. James Jackson Putnam in Boston, who apparently embraced the concept of a universal moral law, Freud wrote: "I was grieved that you should believe that I possibly could consider your idealistic views as nonsense because they differ from mine. I am not so intolerant as to wish to make a law out of a deficiency in my own make-up. I feel no need for a higher moral synthesis in the same way I have no ear for music. But I do not consider myself a better man because of that . . . I respect you and your views . . . Although I am resigned to the fact that I am a God-forsaken incredulous Jew I am not proud of it and I do not look down on others. I can only say with Faust, 'There have to be odd fellows like that, too.'" Eight years later Freud wrote in a letter to his friend Pfister that "ethics are remote from me . . . I do not break my head very much about good and evil." He said that he did not consider most people worth much "no matter whether they publicly subscribe to this or that ethical doctrine or none at all."

Freud believed that education and establishing the "dictatorship of reason" would be the only solution to solving the cruel and immoral behavior that characterizes human history. "Our best hope for the future," he proclaims, "is that intellect—the scientific spirit, reason—may in process of time establish a dictatorship in the mental life of man." In a letter to Albert Einstein, who had written to Freud asking what could be done to protect mankind from war, Freud responds: "The ideal condition of things would of course be a community of men who had subordinated their instinctual life to the dictatorship of reason."

Yet Freud observed the rise of the Nazis within Germany, one of the most educated nations in the world, and he knew the terror of the SS troops, one of the most highly educated fighting forces in history. He also noticed that the increased knowledge of psychoanalysts generally did not make them more moral than other professional groups. "That psychoanalysis has not made the analysts themselves better, nobler, or of stronger character remains a disappointment for me," Freud confessed in another letter to Putnam. "Perhaps I was wrong to expect it."

As with the origins of belief, Freud formulated a theory of how conscience develops. He believed that during a child's development, "at about the age of five," an important change takes place. The child internalizes the part of his parents that tells him what to do and what to avoid doing, and this internalized part of the parents becomes his conscience, a part of what Freud calls the superego. In his last expository work, *An Outline of Psychoanalysis,* Freud writes: "A portion of the external world has, at least partially, been abandoned as an object and has instead, by identification, been taken into the ego and thus become an integral part of the internal world." He explains that "this new mental agency continues to carry on the functions which have hitherto been performed by the [parents] . . . it observes the ego, gives it orders, judges it and threatens it with punishments, exactly like the parents whose place it has taken . . . we call this agency the super-ego and are aware of it in its judicial functions as our conscience."

Freud sums up this process by noting that "it is in keeping with the course of human development that external coercion gradually becomes internalized; for a special mental agency, the super-ego, takes it over and includes it among its commandments. Every child presents this process of transformation to us; only by that means does it become a moral and social being."

Freud observed clinically that guilt sometimes played an important role in illness. Sometimes the guilt is unconscious. "If a patient of ours is suffering from a sense of guilt, as though he had committed a serious crime, we do not recommend him to disregard his qualms of conscience and do not emphasize his undoubted innocence; he himself has often tried to do so without success. What we do is to remind him that such a strong and persistent feeling must after all be based on something real, which it may perhaps be possible to discover."

Nonetheless, despite such sensible pragmatism, Freud's arguments about guilt, superego, and internalization have attracted criticism. Lewis was only one critic. Lewis noted that throughout history all cultures, even the pagan cultures, were aware of a moral law and of a failure to live up to it. In their writings, they expressed fear of eternal punishment. "When the apostles preached, they could assume even in their Pagan hearers a real consciousness of deserving the Divine anger," Lewis writes in *The Problem of Pain*. Our culture, Lewis believes, has lost that sensitivity. One reason for this loss "is the effect of Psychoanalysis on the public mind." "The doctrines of repressions and inhibitions" imply that "the sense of Shame is a dangerous and mischievous thing." Lewis writes, "We are told to 'get things out in the open' . . . on the ground that these 'things' are very natural and we need not be ashamed."

So we tend to accept uncivil behavior—"cowardice, lying, envy, unchastity"—more readily than many earlier cultures. Within this context, Lewis says that the biblical concept of the universal need for atonement and redemption makes little sense. That is, the biblical story makes no sense until "you have realized that there is a real Moral Law, and a Power behind the law, and that you have broken that law and put yourself wrong with that Power."

Freud had to consider his own behavior by a different standard. Indeed, his actions somewhat belied his arguments. He compared his own conduct not against a universal law, but with the moral conduct of others. He liked the comparison. In a letter written in his late fifties to Dr. Putnam, Freud writes: "I consider myself to be a very moral person who can subscribe to the excellent maxim of Th. Visher: 'What is moral is self-evident.' I believe that in a sense of justice and consideration for others, in disliking making others suffer or taking advantage of them, I can measure myself with the best people I have known. I have never done anything mean or malicious and cannot trace any temptation to do so." Freud quickly adds that he obtains no "satisfaction in concluding I am better than most other people." He also points out that, although he stood for a much freer sexuality, he himself did not exercise that freedom; he adhered to the traditional biblical sexual code.

This is a remarkable letter. When Freud said he believes in "the excellent maxim" of "What is moral is self-evident," Lewis would argue he was inadvertently stating support for a moral law. When he acted differently from what he argued, as a monogamous man urging more open and freer sexuality, he apparently saw no contradiction between the free sexuality he professed and the strict code he practiced.

To Lewis, Freud's claim that morality is "self-evident" is telling: "I believe that the primary moral principles on which all others depend are rationally perceived. We 'just see' that there is no reason why my neighbour's happiness should be sacrificed to my own, as we 'just see' that things which are equal to the same thing are equal to one another. If we cannot prove either axiom, that is not because they are irrational but because they are self-evident and all proofs depend on them. Their intrinsic reasonableness shines by its own light. It is because all morality is based on such self-evident principles that we say to a man, when we would recall him to right conduct, 'be reasonable.'"

In a different context, Lewis commented on Freud's comparison of his own behavior to others'. When Freud makes statements such as "I consider myself to be a very moral person . . . I can measure myself with the best people I have known . . . I am better than most other people," he falls into a category that Lewis describes in *The Screwtape Letters*. In an address at a dinner for young devils in training, Screwtape, a very experienced devil, gives advice on how to help people (their patients) on the road to hell. He tells what advantage they (the devils) have when a person compares himself with others and develops the I'm-as-good-as-you attitude.

"The first and most obvious advantage," says Screwtape, "is that you thus induce him to enthrone at the centre of his life a good solid, resounding lie." The lie is not only a lie in fact—no one person is precisely equal to all others in kindness, honesty, and good sense any more than they are all equal in height and weight. The real lie, Lewis says through his character Screwtape, is to the patient himself: "He does not believe it himself . . . No man who says *I'm as good as you* believes it. He would never say it if he did." Screwtape points out that a person who knows he is superior in an area never needs to point that out to others. He merely accepts it.

Screwtape says that "the claim to equality, outside the strictly political field, is made only by those who feel themselves to be in some way inferior." A person's need to tell others that he is superior expresses "the itching, smarting, writhing awareness of an inferiority which the patient refuses to accept."

What motivated Freud to tell others in writing that he was "better than most other people"? Did Freud suffer from feelings of inferiority or low self-esteem? Psychiatrists have long been aware that one classical symptom of depression is a feeling of worthlessness. There is strong evidence that Freud struggled most of his life with clinical depression. He makes frequent mention of this in his letters, and he took cocaine for a number of years to find relief.

Freud also used his clinical observations on severely depressed patients to argue against a universal moral law. He observed that some patients who experience periods of excessive guilt during their depression find that their guilt lessens or disappears as they recover. When a person is depressed, "his super-ego becomes over-severe, abuses the poor ego, humiliates it and ill-treats it, threatens it with the direst punishments, reproaches it for actions in the remotest past which had been taken lightly at the time—as though it had spent the whole interval in collecting accusations and had only been waiting for its present access of strength in order to bring them up and make a condemnatory judgment on their basis. The super-ego applies the strictest moral standard to the helpless ego which is at its mercy; in general it represents the claims of morality, and we realize all at once that our moral sense of guilt is the expression of the tension between the ego and the super-ego."

Furthermore, "after a certain number of months the whole moral fuss is over, the criticism of the super-ego is silent, the ego is rehabilitated and again enjoys all the rights of man till the next attack." The observation is striking: "It is a most remarkable experience to see morality, which is supposed to have been given us by God and thus deeply implanted in us, functioning as a periodic phenomenon." Indeed, Freud was not wrong. We now know depressed patients often suffer pathological guilt, sometimes for an imagined deed they have not in reality committed. A patient may, for example, have lost a younger sibling through death—a sibling toward whom he may have harbored negative feelings. A sense of guilt, as if the patient caused the death, may surface during an emotional illness but disappear when the patient recovers.

Freud extended his observations from the ill to the healthy. He noted, as did Lewis, a "sense of guilt" that appeared to be present in everyone. But because he did not believe in a universal moral law, he formulated an alternative theory to explain guilt, by explaining the origins of organized religion and of ethical precepts. Freud was familiar with the findings of anthropologists that indicated that primitive peoples lived in clans and had an animal that served as an emblem or symbol (i.e., totem) of the clan. These primitive tribes had certain prohibitions—"not to kill the totem and not to have sexual relations with any woman of the same totem-clan." Freud knew of a "conjecture" by Charles Darwin "that men originally lived in hordes, each under the domination of a single powerful, violent and jealous male."

In a famous passage in *Totem and Taboo,* Freud explained that he had had a "vision": "The father of the primal horde, since he was an unlimited despot, had seized all the women for himself; his sons, being dangerous to him as rivals, had been killed or driven away. One day, however, the sons came together . . . to kill and devour their father, who had been their enemy but also their ideal." Freud imagined that this killing of the father is the deed "from which sprang man's sense of guilt (or 'original sin') and which was the beginning . . . of religion and of ethical restrictions." Quoting from Faust who paraphrased the Gospel of John, Freud wrote: "'in the beginning was the Deed.'"

Freud developed his theory further by conjecturing that the clan members substituted a totem—usually an animal, for the primal father—and eventually "the primal father, at once feared and hated, revered and envied, became the prototype of God himself." He asserted that "the totem-feast was the commemoration of the fearful deed" and that this sheds light on the practice of Communion in which "the totem meal still survives with but little distortion." Guilt over this act of parricide has been transmitted from one generation to the next and accounts for the 'sense of guilt' observed among all people. People feel guilty, according to Freud, not because they break the moral law, but because they have inherited guilt over the killing of the primal father.

Depending on one's worldview, this work is either an extraordinary and daring attempt to rewrite human history, or it is a matter of pure fantasy. However, even on its own terms, Freud realized a problem. If the killing of the primal father was the beginning of all ethical restrictions, and if his definition of conscience as an internalization of these restrictions holds true, then the sons who killed their father would not yet feel guilty. They had not yet developed a conscience.

Lewis also saw this flaw in Freud's hypothesis. He pointed out that "attempts to resolve the moral experience into something else always presuppose the very thing they are trying to explain—as when a famous psychoanalyst deduces it from a prehistoric parricide. If the parricide produced a sense of guilt, that was because men felt that they ought not to have committed it: if they did not so feel, it could produce no sense of guilt."

Freud responds with a semantic shift. He said that the sons who killed their father felt "remorse," not guilt. He explains, in *Civilization and Its Discontents*, "when one has a sense of guilt after having committed a misdeed . . . the feeling should more properly be called remorse. It relates only to a deed that has been done, and, of course, it presupposes that a conscience—the readiness to feel guilty—was already in existence before the deed took place. Remorse of this sort can, therefore, never help us to discover the origin of *conscience* and of the sense of guilt in general." Freud then asked, "If a conscience and a sense of guilt were not, as we presupposed, in existence before the deed (the killing of the father) . . . where, in this case, did the remorse come from?" His answer: "This remorse was the result of the primordial ambivalence of feeling towards the father. His sons hated him, but they loved him, too. After their hatred had been satisfied by their act of aggression, their love came to the fore in their remorse for the deed." Freud then added that "there is no doubt that this case should explain the secret of the sense of guilt to us and put an end to our difficulties. And I believe it does."

If we continue to have difficulty with Freud's reasoning here, we join many of Freud's biographers, and Freud himself. Freud expressed doubts about his conclusions soon after finishing *Totem and Taboo.* "I have reverted very much from my original high estimate of the work, and am on the whole critical of it," he wrote to several of his colleagues. Freud feared a negative reaction to the book; he was right. The book met with "complete disbelief as one more personal phantasy of Freud's . . . anthropologists united in discounting his conclusions and in maintaining that he had misunderstood the evidence."

To make matters worse, Freud's whole hypothesis—or as he put it, his "vision"—rested on a conjecture by Darwin that primitive, prehistoric people lived in a horde governed by a polygamous and violent, monopolistic male. Further research has failed to support this hypothesis. In addition, Freud's theory depends on the notion that acquired characteristics can be transmitted from one generation to the next (one generation passing the feeling of guilt to the next): modern genetics has discredited this notion as well.

Why did Freud write a book about which he had such doubts? We can only conjecture. Peter Gay wrote that "it is highly plausible that some of the impulses guiding Freud's arguments in *Totem and Taboo* emerged from his hidden life; in some respects the book represents a round in his never finished wrestling bout with Jacob Freud." Gay also mentions that Freud realized he was "publishing scientific fantasies." If Freud is, indeed, still "wrestling" with the first authority in his life, might he also be wrestling with the notion of an Ultimate Authority? Was he driven by a need to defy and prove the Lawmaker did not exist? Freud wrote to a colleague that his essay "would serve to make a sharp distinction between us and all . . . religiosity."

Freud argued that not only does moral truth come from human sources, but attributing this truth to God is unwise and "dangerous." He wrote, "The ethical demands on which religion seeks to lay stress need, rather, to be given another basis; for they are indispensable to human society and it is dangerous to link obedience to them with religious faith."

Why dangerous? Because Freud believed that as people became more knowledgeable they would eventually turn away from their religious faith. He wrote that as "the treasures of knowledge become accessible, the more widespread is the falling-away from religious belief." If the masses no longer believe in God, what will motivate them to live moral lives? "If the sole reason why you must not kill your neighbor is because God has forbidden it and will severely punish you for it in this or the next life—then, when you learn that there is no God and that you need not fear His punishment, you will certainly kill your neighbor without hesitation, and you can only be prevented from doing so by mundane force."

Freud proposed an argument for enlightened self-interest as a basis for social order. He asserted that "civilization has little to fear from educated people," who live ethical lives because reason tells them it is in their best interest to do so. (Freud wrote this in 1927 before the Nazi rise in educated Germany.) He warned, however, that "it is another matter with the great mass of uneducated." They needed to be given reasons for why they ought to follow basic moral precepts. For example, Freud believed that if the masses were told not to kill "in the interest of their communal existence" they would not. This, however, appears to contradict his strong conviction that passion governed the masses more than reason.

He asserted that "it would be an undoubted advantage if we were to leave God out altogether and honestly admit the purely human origin of the regulations and precepts of civilization." "Along with their pretended sanctity, these commandments and laws would lose their rigidity and unchangeableness as well." As people became more educated, they would understand that these rules were made "to serve their interests . . . and they would adopt a more friendly attitude toward them."

Lewis, however, believed that ignoring the moral law makes it difficult for people to come to know the Lawmaker. After he rejected his atheism, Lewis wrote in a letter to a friend that "Christ promises forgiveness of sins: But what is that to those who, since they do not know the law of nature, do not know that they have sinned? Who will take medicine unless he knows he is in the grip of disease? Moral relativity is the enemy we have to overcome before we tackle Atheism."

When a culture ignores the moral law, Lewis said, such spiritual concepts of the Old and New Testaments as atonement and redemption make little sense. Without a law to transgress and a Lawmaker to whom one is accountable, there is little awareness of how far short one falls in keeping that law and, therefore, little need for forgiveness or redemption. Without acknowledgment of the moral law and an awareness of one's failure to keep that law, we merely compare ourselves with others, especially those who fail more than we do. This in turn leads to pride, or self-conceit, what Lewis calls "the utmost evil" and "the great sin." Whereas Freud spoke of the need to set up "the dictatorship of Reason," Lewis warned of setting up the "dictatorship of Pride."

When Freud compared himself with others, he concluded he was "better than most other people." If, however, he had compared himself with how he measured up to the two great commandments of the Old and New Testaments, he might not have fared as well. He openly spoke of "loving one's neighbor as oneself" as foolish and "impossible."

Both Freud and Lewis recognized that people who adhere most closely to the moral law, for example St. Paul, appear to be most conscious of how far short they fall in keeping the law. But Freud gave an entirely different interpretation of this observation from that of Lewis. Freud noted that "the more virtuous a man is" the more severe is his conscience and thus "it is precisely those people who have carried saintliness [or holiness] furthest who reproach themselves with the worst sinfulness." Freud explained this by saying the lack of instinctual gratification in these individuals makes them more conscious of their *need* for gratification—and thus leaves them feeling more guilty. "When saints call themselves sinners, they are not so wrong, considering the temptations to instinctual satisfaction to which they are exposed in a specially high degree—since, as is well-known, temptations are merely increased by constant frustration, whereas an occasional satisfaction of them causes them to diminish, at least for the time being."

Lewis gave a different interpretation. He noted that "when a man is getting better he understands more and more clearly the evil that is still left in him. When a man is getting worse, he understands his own badness less and less. A moderately bad man knows he is not very good: a thoroughly bad man thinks he is all right . . . Good people know about both good and evil: bad people do not know about either." Lewis says the more we struggle with our bad impulses, the better we know them. The more we give in to them, the less we understand them. He writes, "Virtue—even attempted virtue—brings light; indulgence brings fog."

When Freud examined his own behavior, he was puzzled about the source of his concept of right and wrong. He acknowledged some force within him that motivated him to act morally. Apparently his theory of the superego did not provide an adequate answer. His official biographer and colleague Ernest Jones wrote that "Freud himself was constantly puzzled by this very problem—a moral attitude was so deeply implanted as to seem part of his original nature. He never had any doubt about the right course of conduct."

In a letter to Dr. Putnam, Freud wrote: "When I ask myself why I have always behaved honorably, ready to spare others and to be kind wherever possible, and why I did not give up doing so when I observed that in that way one harms oneself and becomes an anvil because other people are brutal and untrustworthy, then, it is true, I have no answer. Sensible it certainly was not." Then Freud acknowledged that when he looks within himself, there does appear to be evidence for a moral law. He admitted to Putnam that "one could cite just my case for your view that an impulsion toward the ideal forms an essential part of our constitution."

Freud added, however, that under certain conditions he would be able to find "quite natural psychological explanations" for what motivated people to behave morally. He concluded: "But, as I said, I know nothing about it all. Why I—and incidentally my six adult children also—have to be thoroughly decent human beings is quite incomprehensible to me."

Perhaps, Freud's life speaks more loudly than his words. Perhaps his recognition of an "impulsion" within himself to be "thoroughly decent" may be a clear indication that, to quote St. Paul, "the law is written on their hearts." Or, as some scientists have argued recently, this "impulsion" to "be decent" may be an adaptive mechanism that entered the gene pool without divine assistance. Both Lewis and Freud tried to obey the moral law, but only Freud rated his performance by comparing himself with others, concluding that he was "better than most other people." Lewis compared his performance with what the moral law demanded. He was "appalled" by "the terrible things" he found out "about my own character." This made him realize his need for outside help and proved to be one of many steps in his rejection of atheism and his transition to a spiritual worldview.

4

THE GREAT
TRANSITION

Which Road to Reality?

Both Lewis and Freud agreed on the most important question concerning the spiritual worldview: Is it true? Freud admitted that embracing the "fairy tales" of religious faith might bring one consolation. But he insisted that in the long run it could only create difficulty: "Its consolations deserve no trust. Experience teaches us that the world is no nursery." This raises another central question: Does it work? Does the spiritual worldview hinder functioning or enhance it? Does it provide resources that make our few days on this planet more meaningful? Freud argues that because it is not true, it can't work. Basing one's life on an illusion, on a false premise, will make living more difficult. Only the truth can help us confront the harsh realities of life. Lewis, however, argues that the most important reality concerns our relationship with the Person who made us. Until that relationship is established, no accomplishment, no fame or fortune will ever satisfy us. Who is right?

Before looking further into the arguments and lives of these renowned intellectuals, let's consider Lewis's change of worldview. Is there anything to be learned from this transition?

It happened when he was thirty-one years old. The change revolutionized his life, infused his mind with purpose and meaning, and dramatically increased his productivity; it also radically altered his values, his image of himself, and his relationships to others. This experience not only turned Lewis *around,* but turned him *outward*—from a focus on himself to a focus on others.

Even his temperament changed. People who knew him before and after his conversion write about his becoming more settled, with an inner quietness and tranquility. A buoyant cheerfulness replaced his pessimism and despair. On the last days before he died, those who were with Lewis spoke of his "cheerfulness" and "calmness."

Lewis referred to this experience as "my conversion." Webster's defines conversion as "an experience associated with a definite and decisive adoption of religious faith." The term conversion occurs infrequently in the Scriptures. In the Old Testament it refers to the people of Israel turning from idolatry to the true God, "the Father of Abraham, Isaac and Jacob." In the New Testament, it is synonymous with being "born again." In the third chapter of the Gospel According to St. John, Jesus tells a Jewish ruler named Nicodemus, "Except a man be born again, he cannot see the kingdom of God." When the puzzled Nicodemus asks how a person can enter again into his mother's womb to experience rebirth, Jesus explains the second birth is not physical, but "of the spirit." As one's physical birth begins one's relationship with parents, one's spiritual birth begins one's relationship with the Creator.

According to a recent Gallup poll, about eight out of ten adult Americans profess faith in a personal God, and about half of them report having a conversion experience. Many prominent men and women from the apostle Paul, Augustine, Blaise Pascal, Jonathan Edwards, David Livingstone, Dorothy Day, and Leo Tolstoy to more modern writers such as Malcolm Muggeridge, Eldridge Cleaver, and Charles Colson—all describe in their writings spiritual experiences that radically transformed their lives. To understand this significant part of our population, we need insight into the process of conversion. How does it happen? What actually takes place in the individual? As a psychiatrist, I have had a long-standing clinical interest in these experiences.

Freud expressed doubt about them, especially the claim that they formed the basis for insight into the spiritual worldview. "I . . . once . . . was blind, but now I see," wrote John Newton after his conversion, in the famous hymn "Amazing Grace." Newton, the former British slave trader, who, with William Wilberforce, became a seminal figure in the abolition of slavery in Great Britain, wrote this hymn some fifty years before Freud's birth, and it may have been known to Freud. If a conversion experience is necessary to "see" spiritually, Freud wonders about all those who do not have this experience. He asks, "If the truth of religious doctrines is dependent on an inner experience which bears witness to that truth, what is one to do about the many people who do not have this rare experience?" In other words, Freud asks, "What about me?"

Freud appears to accept these inner experiences when they occur in people he knows and admires. For example, he never questions his close friend Oskar Pfister about the possibility of self-deception, of harboring an illusion. And Freud makes little mention of the famous conversion experience of St. Paul, whom he quotes frequently and classifies among "the great thinkers": "I have always had a special sympathy for St. Paul as a genuinely Jewish character. Is he not the only one who stands completely in the light of history?"

Paul describes his experience—perhaps the most dramatic and famous of all conversions—in Acts 22: "About noon . . . suddenly a bright light from heaven flashed around me. I fell to the ground and heard a voice . . ." If one begins with Freud's assumption that God does not exist, then the experience of Paul can only be explained as an expression of pathology, a case of visual and auditory hallucinations. Indeed, some modern neurologists have attributed his conversion experience to a seizure disorder known as temporal lobe epilepsy.

In an interview published in 1927, Freud mentioned his lack of faith and indifference to an afterlife. In response, an American physician wrote Freud of a recent experience in which "God made it clear to my soul that the Bible was His Word, that the teachings about Jesus Christ were true, and that Jesus was our only hope. After such a clear revelation I accepted the Bible as God's word and Jesus Christ as my personal Savior. Since then God has revealed Himself to me by many infallible proofs . . . I beg you as a brother physician to give thought to this most important matter, and I can assure you, if you look into this subject with an open mind, God will reveal the *truth* to your soul . . ." Freud wrote back that "God had not done so much for me. He had never allowed me to hear an inner voice; and if, in view of my age, he did not make haste, it would not be my fault if I remained to the end of my life what I now was—'an infidel Jew.'"

Shortly afterward, Freud wrote an article titled "A Religious Experience" in which he psychoanalyzed the experience of the American physician, concluding that he suffered from "a hallucinatory psychosis." Freud wonders if this case throws "any light at all on the psychology of conversion in general." He admits, however, that "by no means" does this explain "every case of conversion." Perhaps Freud's different attitude toward people like St. Paul reflects a tacit acknowledgment that some of these experiences may be genuine and others pathologic. Or it may be simply one of the contradictions in Freud stemming from his deep ambivalence toward the spiritual worldview.

The field of psychiatry, strongly influenced by Freud, has tended until relatively recently to ignore the spiritual dimension of a person, and to dismiss all faith as "neurotically determined," "an illusion," "a projection of childhood wishes," "a hallucinatory psychosis," etc. During the past several years, however, physicians increasingly recognize the importance of understanding the spiritual dimension of their patients. At the Annual Meeting of the American Psychiatric Association held in May of 2000, no less than thirteen of the proceedings focused on spiritual issues, the highest number of such events in the history of the organization.

Several years ago I conducted a research project exploring Harvard University students who, while undergraduates, experienced what they referred to as "religious conversion." I interviewed these students as well as people who knew them before and after their conversion. Were these experiences an expression of pathology, i.e., isolating and destructive, or were they adaptive and constructive? Did these experiences impair or enhance functioning? Results published in the *American Journal of Psychiatry* stated that each subject described "a marked improvement in ego functioning, [including] a radical change in life style with an abrupt halt in the use of drugs, alcohol, and cigarettes; improved impulse control, with adoption of a strict sexual code demanding chastity or marriage with fidelity; improved academic performance; enhanced self-image and greater access to inner feelings; an increased capacity for establishing 'close, satisfying relationships'; improved communication with parents, though most parents at first expressed some degree of alarm over the student's rather sudden, intense religious interest; a positive change in affect, with a lessening of 'existential despair'; and a decrease in preoccupation with the passage of time and apprehension over death."

The question remains, however, how do these experiences occur? What causes these dramatic changes in individuals? How did

C. S. Lewis, a gifted, highly intelligent, critical, militant atheist, and a respected faculty member in perhaps the most prestigious university in the world, come to embrace a worldview so in conflict with his atheism? What led to that experience that so radically transformed his life—his temperament, motivation, relationships, productivity, and his very purpose? What led him not only to embrace the spiritual worldview, but to spend the rest of his life defining it, defending it, and becoming its "most influential spokesman"? What led Lewis to his firm conviction, not only that an Intelligence exists beyond the universe, but that that very Being stepped into human history?

Beforehand, Lewis had been even more certain of his atheism than was Freud. Freud wavered in his atheism as an undergraduate at the University of Vienna; Lewis, at Oxford, never wavered. He met and liked people in the clergy, but writes, "Though I liked clergymen as I liked bears, I had as little wish to be in the church as in the zoo." The notion of an Ultimate Authority who might interfere in his life made him feel nauseated: "There was no region even in the innermost depth of one's soul . . . which one could surround with a barbed wire fence and guard with a notice 'No Admittance.' And that was what I wanted; some area, however small, of which I could say to all other beings, 'This is my business and mine only.'" Lewis recognized in himself a deep-seated wish that God not exist.

Lewis wrote in a letter that the transforming change in his life was "very gradual and intellectual . . . and not simple." First, throughout his life, from the time he was a boy living in Belfast to his conversion in his early thirties, he periodically experienced a sense of intense longing for some place or person. He struggled for years to understand it. Lewis recalled that when eight years old, an intense desire "suddenly arose in me without warning, and as if from the depth not of years but of centuries . . . It was a sensation, of course, of desire, but desire for what?" Then, as suddenly as it ap-

peared, "the desire was gone . . . the whole world turned common-
place again, or only stirred by a longing for the longing that had just
ceased. It had taken only a moment of time; and in a certain sense
everything else that had ever happened to me was insignificant in
comparison." Lewis described this longing as "an unsatisfied desire
which is itself more desirable than any other satisfaction . . . I call it
Joy . . . I doubt whether anyone who has tasted it, would ever, if both
were in his power, exchange it for all the pleasures in the world."
And he carefully distinguished this desire from wishful thinking. He
writes: "Such longing is in itself the very reverse of wishful thinking:
it is more like thoughtful wishing."

Although Lewis described this experience as "the central story of
my life," he eventually came to realize that no human relationship
could ever satisfy this longing. Joy was a "pointer to something other
and outer," a signpost pointing to the Creator. After his great transition to faith, the experience of Joy "nearly lost all interest for me."
He explains that "when we are lost in the woods the sight of a signpost is a great matter. He who first sees it cries 'Look.' The whole
party gathers round and stares. But when we have found the road
and are passing signposts every few miles, we shall not stop and
stare."

Lewis's friends also played a critical role in his transition. When
Lewis was a young Oxford don, a few of his close friends, people he
admired, rejected their materialist worldview and became what he
called "thoroughgoing supernaturalists." Lewis thought it was all
"arrant nonsense" and felt there was no danger of his being "taken
in." Yet he experienced a "loneliness and sense of being deserted"
by these friends. Then he met other faculty that he admired, especially Professor H. V. V. Dyson and Professor J. R. R. Tolkien. Both
men were devout believers and both were to play an important role
in Lewis's great transition. Lewis writes that these strange people
"began to pop up on every side."

Lewis became aware that all the authors he most admired, both ancient and modern, embraced the spiritual worldview—Plato, Virgil, Dante, Johnson, Spenser, Milton, and more modern writers like George MacDonald and G. K. Chesterton. The materialists he read seemed by comparison "a little thin." (To be sure, Plato's spiritualism differed from Chesterton's; but in a world divided between materialists and spiritualists, he could only be classified among the latter.)

Then two events happened in quick succession. First, Lewis read G. K. Chesterton's *Everlasting Man,* a book that profoundly impressed him with arguments he later used in his own writings. Chesterton was a prolific British author, journalist, poet, and literary critic. Lewis first encountered his writings when nineteen years old and serving in the army. He became ill with trench fever and, while recovering in the hospital, read a book of Chesterton's essays. Lewis could not understand his positive reaction to Chesterton's spiritualism. He notes: "My pessimism, my atheism, and my hatred of sentiment would have made him to me the least congenial of all authors." Lewis then adds: "It would almost seem that Providence . . . quite overrules our previous tastes when it decides to bring two minds together."

In an interview in 1963, Lewis acknowledged that "the contemporary book that helped me most is Chesterton's *The Everlasting Man."* Elsewhere in his autobiography, he explained: "I did not know what I was letting myself in for. A young man who wishes to remain a sound Atheist cannot be too careful of his reading." Although "Chesterton had more sense than all the other moderns put together," he suffered from that same "kink" as most of the other authors Lewis admired: Chesterton was a believer.

Then a second event happened that had "a shattering impact." One of the most militant atheists among the Oxford faculty, T. D. Weldon, sat in Lewis's room one evening and remarked that the historical authenticity of the Gospels was surprisingly sound. This deeply disturbed Lewis. He immediately understood the implications. If this "hardest boiled of all the atheists I ever knew" thought the Gospels true, where did that leave him? Where could he turn? "Was there no escape?" He had considered the New Testament's stories to be myth, not historical fact. If they were true, he realized all other truth faded in significance. Did this mean his whole life was headed in the wrong direction?

Lewis remembered an incident that happened several years earlier—on the first day he arrived at Oxford as a teenager. He left the train station carrying his bags and began to walk in the direction of the college, anticipating his first glimpse of the "fabled cluster of spires and towers" he had heard and dreamed of for so many years. As he walked and headed into open country, he could see no sign of the great university. When he turned around, he noticed the majestic college spires and towers on the opposite side of the town and realized he was headed in the wrong direction. Lewis wrote many years later in his autobiography, "I did not see to what extent this little adventure was an allegory of my whole life."

Lewis writes that he began to feel his "Adversary"—the One he wanted desperately not to exist—closing in on him. He felt hounded. Most of the great writers he admired and many of his closest friends were believers. "The fox had been dislodged . . . and was now running in the open . . . bedraggled and weary, hounds barely a field behind. And nearly everyone was now (one way or another) in the pack." Lewis wondered if they might be right. He realized he could use his will to "open the door or keep it shut."

He then made one of the most fateful decisions of his life. Lewis decided to open his mind and examine the evidence. "I was going up Headington Hill on top of a bus . . . I became aware that I was holding something at bay, or shutting something out . . . I could open the door or keep it shut . . . The choice appeared to be momentous but it was strangely unemotional . . . I chose to open . . . I felt as if I were a man of snow at long last beginning to melt . . ." When he made that decision, he began to feel the presence of Him whom he had desperately wanted not to meet.

Finally, Lewis surrendered. "You must picture me alone in that room in Magdalen, night after night, feeling, whenever my mind lifted even for a second from my work, the steady, unrelenting approach of Him whom I so earnestly desired not to meet. That which I greatly feared had at last come upon me. In the Trinity term . . . I gave in, and admitted that God was God and knelt and prayed: perhaps, that night the most dejected and reluctant convert in all England."

This first phase in the transition, Lewis explains, "was only to Theism, pure and simple . . . I knew nothing yet about the Incarnation . . . The God to whom I surrendered was sheerly nonhuman." Lewis experienced no personal relationship with this God, and at times, when he prayed, he felt he was "posting letters to a nonexistent address."

Once he accepted, with considerable resistance, the presence of an Intelligence beyond the universe, Lewis concluded that this Being demanded complete surrender and obedience: ". . . the demand was simply 'all' . . . God was to be obeyed simply because He was God . . . because of what He is in Himself . . . If you ask why we should obey God, in the last resort the answer is, 'I am.'"

At this time Lewis expressed confusion about the doctrines of the New Testament. He found that it was difficult to "believe something one doesn't understand." Lewis also wondered about the relevance of the Gospel story to modern life. "What I couldn't understand was how the life and death of Someone Else (whoever he was) 2000 years ago could help us here and now . . ." He found expressions like "'propitiation,' 'sacrifice' and 'the blood of the Lamb' either silly or shocking." He wrote: "My puzzle was the whole doctrine of redemption."

So he began reading the New Testament in Greek. His experience teaching philosophy made him aware of "the perplexing multiplicity of 'religions'" with conflicting claims. How could he possibly know which one contained the truth? Yet the comment by the "hard boiled Atheist" T. D. Weldon concerning the historical authenticity of the Gospels haunted Lewis. As he read the New Testament, he was struck by it. Lewis had spent his life reading ancient manuscripts. As an atheist, he, like Freud, considered the New Testament story simply another of the great myths. He knew well the ancient myths and legends—especially Norse mythology—and they moved him deeply. As a young adolescent, Lewis came upon the book *Siegfried and the Twilight of the Gods,* and it rekindled the experience of joy that had been missing for many years. Many of these myths, such as those of Balder, Adonis, and Bacchus, contained stories similar to the one in the Bible—of a god coming to earth, dying to save his people, and rising again from the dead. Lewis had always considered the New Testament story simply another one of these myths.

But the Gospels, Lewis noted, did not contain the rich, imaginative writings of these talented, ancient writers. They appeared to be simple eyewitness accounts of historical events, primarily by Jews who were clearly unfamiliar with the great myths of the pagan world around them. Lewis writes: "I was by now too experienced in literary criticism to regard the Gospels as myths. They had not the mythical taste." He observes that they were different from anything else in literature. "If ever myth had become fact, had been incarnated, it would be just like this." In his book *Miracles,* Lewis explains that God sometimes uses myth to foretell what will eventually occur in history: ". . . the truth first appears in *mythical* form, and then by a long process of condensing or focusing finally becomes incarnate as history." Lewis felt that as the truth became historical reality it becomes more simple, "more prosaic," than the myth and is "less rich in many kinds of the imaginative beauties of the Pagan mythologies." "Now the story of Christ is simply a true myth: a myth working on us in the same way as the others, but with this tremendous difference that it really happened . . . ," writes Lewis to Greeves.

He noted both the style and content of the Gospels: "Now as a literary historian, I am perfectly convinced that whatever else the Gospels are they are not legends. I have read a great deal of legend (myth) and I am quite clear that they are not the same sort of thing. They are not artistic enough to be legends. From an imaginative point of view they are clumsy, they don't work . . . Most of the life of Jesus is totally unknown to us . . . and no people building up a legend would allow that to be so."

His concept of the Central Figure in these documents began to change. As an atheist, Lewis had dismissed Jesus of Nazareth as a "Hebrew Philosopher," another great moral teacher. Now he began to see this figure in a different light: ". . . as real, as recognizable, through all that depth of time, as Plato's Socrates or Boswell's Johnson . . . yet also numinous, lit by a light from beyond the world, a god. But if a god—we are no longer polytheists—then not a god, but God. Here and here only in all time the myth must have become fact; the Word flesh; God, Man." Lewis began to realize that this Person made unique claims about himself—claims that if true ruled out the possibility of his being a great moral teacher. First, Lewis points out that Jesus made the "appalling claim" to be the Messiah, to be God. He quotes Jesus Christ saying, "I am begotten of the One God, before Abraham was, I am"; Lewis continues: ". . . and remember what the words 'I am' were in Hebrew. They were the name of God, which must not be spoken by any human being, the name which it was death to utter." As a philologist, Lewis focuses on passages in the New Testament that refer to Christ as "begotten, not created" and "only begotten son." Lewis explains that "to beget is to become the father of: to create is to make . . . What God begets is God; just as what man begets is man. What God creates is not God;

just as what man makes is not man. That is why men are not Sons of God in the sense that Christ is."

Lewis noticed that this Person also claimed to forgive sins, to forgive what people did to others. He wrote later: "Now unless the speaker is God, this is really so preposterous as to be comic. We can all understand how a man forgives offences against himself . . . But what should we make of a man . . . who announced that he forgave you for treading on other men's toes and stealing other men's money?" Even Freud seemed to realize the uniqueness of this claim. In a letter to Oskar Pfister, Freud writes: "And now, just suppose I said to a patient: 'I, Professor Sigmund Freud, forgive thee thy sins.' What a fool I should make of myself."

Lewis argues that the claim of Jesus to be the Messiah and to forgive sins rules out the possibility of his being simply a great moral teacher. Here he was influenced by Chesterton. In *The Everlasting Man,* Chesterton pointed out that no great moral teacher ever claimed to be God—not Mohammed, not Micah, not Malachi, or Confucius, or Plato, or Moses, or Buddha: "Not one of them ever made that claim . . . and the greater the man is, the less likely he is to make the very greatest claim." Lewis expands on Chesterton's point by writing that "if you had gone to Buddha and asked him 'Are you the son of Bramah?' he would have said, 'My son, you are still in the vale of illusion.' If you had gone to Socrates and asked, 'Are you Zeus?' he would have laughed at you. If you had gone to Mohammed and asked, 'Are you Allah?' he would first have rent his clothes and then cut your head off . . . The idea of a great moral teacher saying what Christ said is out of the question."

The claim of Jesus Christ to be God and to have the authority to forgive sins left only one of three possibilities: he was either deluded or deliberately attempting to deceive his followers for some ulterior purpose, or he was who he claimed to be. As Lewis continued his reading of the New Testament documents, he agreed with Chesterton that the evidence weighed against this Person being evil or psychotic. (Psychiatrists do indeed see people who claim to be God, but they are invariably severely impaired in their functioning and have a distorted concept of reality.) For Lewis the eyewitness accounts of the New Testament did not reflect the teachings of a lunatic. He notes "the general agreement that in the teaching of this Man and of His immediate followers, moral truth is exhibited at its purest and best . . . it is full of wisdom and shrewdness . . . the product of a sane mind." Later he closed a chapter in his most widely read book with "A man who was merely a man and said the things Jesus said would not be a great moral teacher. He would either be a lunatic . . . or else he would be the Devil of Hell. You must make your choice . . . You can shut him up for a fool, you can spit at Him and kill Him as a demon; or you can fall at His feet and call Him Lord and God. But let us not come with any patronizing nonsense about His being a great human teacher. He has not left that open to us. He did not intend to."

Chesterton profoundly influenced Lewis's acceptance of "the Incarnation," the astounding conviction that the Creator of the universe actually stepped into human history. Chesterton writes that the New Testament story "is nothing less than the loud assertion that this mysterious maker of the world has visited his world in person. It declares that really and even recently, or right in the middle of historic times, there did walk into the world this original invisible being; about whom the thinkers make theories and the mythologists hand down myths; the Man Who Made the World. That such a higher personality exists beyond all things had indeed always been implied by the best thinkers, as well as by all the most beautiful legends. But nothing of this sort had ever been implied in any of them . . . The most that any religious prophet had said was that he was the true servant of such a being . . . The most that any primitive myth had ever suggested was that the Creator was present at the

Creation. But that the Creator was present . . . in the detailed daily life of the Roman Empire—that is something utterly unlike anything else in nature. It is the one great startling statement that man has made since he spoke his first articulate word . . . it makes nothing but dust and nonsense of comparative religion." The word "Gospel" means good news. Chesterton notes that it is "news that seems too good to be true."

The news is good because it offers a way out of the despair of trying to keep the moral law and failing—as Lewis did. As he continued to read the Bible seriously, he noted that none of the main characters (except one) kept the moral law. Adam blamed Eve for his disobedience—the Fall, which marked the separation of the human race from the Creator and the beginning of disease and death; Abraham lied about his relationship to his wife Sarah; David committed adultery and murder; even the apostle Peter denied knowing Jesus. All this drove home the point that no one except God Himself could keep the moral law. Transgression of the law separated us from God. All needed atonement—to be reconciled to Him. The New Testament affirmed that God sent His "only begotten Son" to make this reconciliation possible—to redeem us. Lewis began to realize that all of the pagan myths about a dying god, the prophesies of the Hebrew Scriptures, and even the pattern of vegetable life— "it must belittle itself into something hard, small and deathlike, it must fall into the ground: thence the new life reascends"—all point to that moment in history when the Creator Himself would come to earth, die, and rise again. All this to free humanity from the consequences of the Fall—to redeem the world. Lewis began to "see" what previously had appeared "silly or shocking." The pieces of the puzzle were coming together.

One might ask how Lewis, as an atheist, a brilliant scholar who spent a good part of his life in the Oxford libraries, could have avoided reading the New Testament documents—considered among the most influential works in the history of civilization. Lewis certainly knew more books had been written about Jesus Christ than about anyone else in history, that He appeared in the writings of Roman and Jewish historians and therefore was more than a myth. Indeed, all events in Western history are recorded as happening before or after His birth. Perhaps part of the answer is that during his years as an atheist Lewis describes in himself a "willful blindness."

On the evening of September 19, 1931, perhaps the most significant in his life, Lewis invited two close friends—Dyson and Tolkien—for dinner. They began discussing myth and metaphor. After dinner they strolled the Oxford campus, along beautiful Addison's Walk. This mile-long path under magnificent beech trees cuts through open fields of flowers and is often visited by deer. The men talked late into the night on this warm, still evening, and as Lewis would later recall, a sudden rush of wind caused the first leaves to fall. The three men stood in the dark and listened. Perhaps this came to have symbolic meaning for Lewis, who had been reading in the Gospel According to St. John: "The wind blows wherever it pleases. You hear its sound, but you cannot tell where it comes from or where it is going. So it is with everyone born of the Spirit" (John 3:8). The discussion continued until the clock in Magdalen Tower struck three in the morning. Tolkien, who apparently didn't realize how late it was, hurried home to his wife. Lewis and Dyson continued for another hour.

Twelve days after that evening, Lewis wrote to Arthur Greeves: "I have just passed on . . . to definitely believing in Christ. I will try to explain this another time. My long night talk with Dyson and Tolkien had a good deal to do with it." And in other letters: ". . . the intellectual side of my conversion was *not* simple"; "Dyson and Tolkien were the immediate human causes of my conversion." "Conversions happen in all sorts of different ways: some sharp and catastrophic (like St. Paul, St. Augustine, or Bunyan), some very gradual and intellectual (like my own)."

But how exactly did this take place? He writes that he knows *"when"* it happened but not exactly *"how."* He was on a motorcycle heading to the zoo. He writes: "When we set out I did not believe that Jesus Christ is the Son of God, and when we reached the Zoo I did. Yet I had not exactly spent the journey in thought. Nor in great emotion . . ." He then uses a rather striking yet familiar metaphor: "It was more like when a man, after a long sleep, still lying motionless in bed, becomes aware that he is now awake."

Certainly we all experience, almost every day of our lives, without knowing exactly how, the transition from the unreal world of sleep and dreams to the world of being awake. We know when we awake, as Lewis knew *when* he came to believe in Jesus Christ. He knew what people and events influenced that process just as we know what events—the daylight, the alarm clock, and others—influence when we awake. But *how* the actual process of his change from unbelief to belief occurred—like our process of change from sleep to wakefulness—remains largely undescribed by the articulate Lewis.

Once Lewis made the conscious decision to overcome his "willful blindness" and examine the evidence, and the second decision to surrender his will, only then did he pass from what he described as the darkness of unbelief and into the light of reality. He awakened.

Lewis insists that his conversion was primarily "intellectual" and gives a long, detailed description of the thought processes involved. On the motorcycle headed for the zoo, Lewis is careful to explain, "I had not exactly spent the journey . . . in great emotion . . . 'Emotional' is perhaps the last word we can apply to some of the most important events."

As a psychiatrist, I find it difficult to believe that these events were entirely unemotional, even for Lewis. We feel more easily than we think, and our feelings often control our decisions and behavior more than our thoughts. Perhaps, because of the traumatic experiences of his early life, Lewis found his feelings less accessible. There is considerable evidence for this in Lewis's autobiography. For example, he comments: ". . . the ups and downs of my father's emotional life . . . bred in me, long before I was able to give it a name, a certain distrust or dislike of emotion as something uncomfortable and embarrassing and even dangerous."

Nevertheless, Lewis's intellect certainly played a significant role in his conversion. He realized his lack of knowledge formed the basis of his unbelief. As Lewis explained in a letter written shortly after his transition, "What has been holding me back . . . has not been so much a difficulty in believing as a difficulty in knowing . . . you can't believe a thing while you are ignorant what the thing is." Only after reading the New Testament did he acquire the knowledge and begin to understand what eventually formed the basis of his faith.

There are many similarities between Lewis's transition and the conversion experiences of the undergraduate students I have researched. First, all the experiences occurred within the context of a modern, liberal university where the climate tended to be hostile to such experiences. Second, both Lewis and the students observed in the lives of people they admired some quality they found missing in their own lives. Lewis observed this in the lives of the great writers as well as certain members of the Oxford faculty; the Harvard students, in the lives of other students. They were clearly influenced by their peers. Third, both Lewis and each of the students made a conscious exertion of their wills to open their minds and examine the evidence. Lewis began to read the New Testament in Greek; the students tended to join Bible study groups on campus. They became convinced of the historical reliability of these documents and came to understand the Central Figure not as one who died two thousand years ago, but as "a living reality" who made unique claims about Himself and with whom they had a personal relationship.

Fourth, both Lewis and each of the students, after their conversion, found their new faith enhanced their functioning. They reported positive changes in their relationships, their image of themselves, their temperament, and their productivity. People who knew Lewis and those who knew the students before and after their transition confirmed these changes.

But could all of these changes be explained psychologically? Could Lewis and these students have experienced some kind of emotional breakdown? If Freud placed Lewis on his couch, would he have found evidence for "obsessional neurosis" or "hallucinatory psychosis"? The evidence weighs against this possibility. Emotional illness, as understood by Freud (and most dynamically oriented psychiatrists today), is caused by unconscious conflicts that seriously impair the functioning of patients in important areas of their lives. Psychiatrists determine whether a patient needs treatment by the degree of impairment in functioning. If Freud analyzed Lewis, the evidence suggests that he would not have dismissed him as dysfunctional; rather, Freud would have admired him—his intellect and his literary skills—as he did St. Paul and his close friend Oskar Pfister. As a skilled clinician, Freud would have observed that the transition Lewis experienced matured him emotionally and did not impair, but enhanced, his functioning. Perhaps he might have concluded, as the noted psychoanalyst Erik Erikson did, that the person who, like Lewis, experiences a spiritual transition "is always older, or in early years suddenly becomes older, than . . . his parents and teachers, and focuses in a precocious way on what it takes others a lifetime to gain a mere inkling of: the questions of how to escape corruption in living and how in death to give meaning to life."

PART TWO

HOW SHOULD
WE LIVE?

~5~

HAPPINESS

What Is the Source of Our Greatest Enjoyment in Life?

The previous chapters focused on questions concerning our philosophy of life—on belief and unbelief, and on the transition between these two states. But there are many—perhaps countless—related questions. Belief and unbelief reflect two utterly distinct worldviews, so they offer very different answers to how to face life and death, love and loss, even sexuality. On each of these questions, Freud and Lewis formulated highly articulate and often conflicting answers.

No aspect of life is more desired, more elusive, and more perplexing than happiness. People wish and strive for what they believe will make them happy—good health, attractive looks, an ideal marriage, children, a comfortable home, success, fame, financial independence—the list goes on and on. Not everyone who attains these goals, however, finds happiness. Unhappiness appears to be at least as prevalent as happiness. One does not need to be a psychiatrist to be aware that an astounding number of Americans suffer from clinical depression—a sustained form of unhappiness—and a significant number decide to end their unhappiness by committing suicide. (In the United States, more than a quarter of a million people attempt to end their lives every twelve months, and about 30,000 succeed.)

I often ask my classes whether or not, from their observation and experience, people around them are happy. Invariably they answer no. Invariably, I express surprise. I point out that, compared with most people in the world, they possess everything—youth, health, intelligence, abundant food, clothes, a comfortable place to live, education, a promising future, etc. What in the world causes them to be unhappy? The typical answer is the lack of meaningful relationships. The students point out that everyone around them appears to be consumed with their success. When I ask what they think their colleagues consider success and what they observe to be the life goals their environment instills, the answer is "fame and fortune."

What is happiness? How does one define it? The great minds of the past have attempted to define this all-important human experience for many centuries. Some philosophers have concluded that happiness is an illusive goal that one never reaches. "Man is never happy, but spends his whole life striving after something he thinks will make him so," writes Arthur Schopenhauer, the famous German philosopher, whose writings influenced Freud. Other definitions reflect specific philosophies of life. "What is happiness?" asks Friedrich Nietzsche, another who influenced Freud. He answers: "The feeling that power increases—that resistance is overcome."

Although Freud and Lewis describe human experience and emotion with considerable accuracy, they define happiness in strikingly different ways. At first this may seem surprising; after all, even if their worldviews led them to seek happiness in different ways, why should they define the mood itself differently? Yet on closer inspection, Freud's view of happiness emerges as fundamental to his materialist view of the world, and certainly Lewis's definition reflects his spiritual life. The contrast is fascinating.

When we turn to modern dictionaries, the concept of happiness is anything but clear. One common definition implies that happiness is a state determined by external circumstances—i.e., "characterized by luck or good fortune" (*American Heritage Dictionary*). A second describes happiness as an emotional state, a feeling, a positive mood—e.g., "expressing the mood of one who is pleased or delighted" (*Webster's Collegiate Dictionary*) or "any condition of good spirits, temporary or sustained" (*American Heritage Dictionary*). Synonyms of "happy" include "glad," "cheerful," "lighthearted," "joyful," and "joyous." These same dictionaries tell us the opposite of happiness is "sadness." And sadness, when experienced over a sustained period of time is a primary symptom of depression, the most prevalent emotional illness in our culture. Recent studies indicate that some 30 percent—more than 75 million Americans—will develop clinical depression during their lifetime and seek treatment. Researchers believe that because most people with depression do not seek help, the actual number who experience depression is considerably higher.

In the widely read and widely quoted *Civilization and Its Discontents,* Freud writes that when you observe what people "show by their behavior to be the purpose and intention of their lives . . . the answer to this can hardly be in doubt. They strive after happiness; they want to become happy and to remain so." Freud also observes that "unhappiness is much less difficult to experience" than happiness. Whether or not we agree, most of us would probably admit that, during our brief journey on this planet, happiness plays an important role in determining the quality of our lives. We would probably also agree, as the recent research on depression indicates, that most people do not appear to be happy for at least part of their lives.

Can either Freud or Lewis enlighten our understanding of happiness so that we can experience it more in our lives?

Freud equates happiness with pleasure, specifically the pleasure that comes from satisfying our sexual needs. He writes, "Happiness . . . is a problem of satisfying a person's instinctual wishes . . . What we call happiness in the strictest sense comes from the (preferably sudden) satisfaction of needs which have been damned up to a high degree . . ." He adds: ". . . sexual (genital) love . . . affords . . . the strongest experiences of satisfaction . . . [and provides] the prototype of all happiness." This "pleasure principle," writes Freud, "dominates the operation of the mental apparatus from the start."

He gives several reasons why it is so difficult to be happy. First, he mentions the many sources of pain: illness, aging, the destructive forces of nature, and, most painful of all, our relations to other people. Second, he points out that because we experience sexual pleasure only as "an episodic phenomenon"—that is, only after the sexual desire has reached a certain intensity—we can experience happiness only for brief periods of time. "We are so made," explains Freud "that we can derive intense enjoyment only from a contrast and very little from a state of things. Thus our possibilities of happiness are already restricted by our constitution."

In addition, our culture imposes restrictions and prohibitions on the expression of our instinctual sexual needs that further limit our pleasure and thus our capacity for happiness. When we break these rules, most of us, though not all, experience guilt which makes us feel less than happy. Freud explains that our parents first impose these social restrictions and we obey them out of fear of losing their love. Later, this parental authority becomes internalized into our conscience, the superego.

Freud asks, perhaps with tongue in cheek, "If one imagines its [civilization's] prohibitions lifted—if, then, one may take any woman one pleases as a sexual object, if one may without hesitation kill one's rival for her love or anyone else who stands in one's way, if, too, one can carry off any of the other man's belongings without asking—how splendid, what a string of satisfactions life would be!" Freud realizes that everyone else "has exactly the same wishes as I have and will treat me with no more consideration than I treat him. And so in reality only one person could be made 'unrestrictively' happy by such a removal of the restrictions . . . and he would be a dictator who has seized all the means to power." (One wonders, however, if Hitler and other dictators considered themselves to be happy.) So Freud agrees that, as a culture, we need these prohibitions to control our sexual and aggressive instincts and, thus, to protect us from one another. The price we pay for this protection is a marked decrease in our capacity to experience happiness.

Freud explains still another reason for our unhappiness. Because sexual love "has given us our most intense experience of an overwhelming sensation of pleasure and has thus furnished us with a pattern for our search for happiness," people tend to seek their happiness primarily in love relationships. But Freud warns that when someone succeeds in finding his main source of happiness in a love relationship, he has "made himself dependent in a most dangerous way on a portion of the external world, namely, his chosen loveobject, and exposed himself to extreme suffering if he should be rejected by that object or should lose it through unfaithfulness or death." As any poet would agree, "we are never so defenseless against suffering as when we love, never so helplessly unhappy as when we have lost our loved object or its love."

Freud acknowledges that we can obtain a degree of pleasure from creative work, what he calls the "sublimation of the instincts." But the pleasure or happiness "of this kind, such as an artist's joy in creating . . . or a scientist's in solving problems or discovering truths . . . is mild as compared with that derived from the sating of crude and primary instinctual impulses; it does not convulse our physical being." In addition, not everyone can be involved in creative work; not everyone possesses creative gifts. Nevertheless, Freud explains that work generally could act as a "powerful deflection" from our unhappiness. He assumes Voltaire has this in mind when, in *Candide,* he advises one to cultivate one's garden. But Freud quickly cautions that "as a path to happiness, work is not highly prized by men. They do not strive after it as they do other possibilities of satisfaction. The great majority of people only work under the stress of necessity . . ." Work, for most people, fails to provide happiness.

Not even the advances of science and technology and "the lengthening of the average life" in Freud's day had succeeded in making people happier. (Nor has it in ours.) As a matter of fact, Freud believes, these advances have contributed to our unhappiness. "Men have gained control over the forces of nature to such an extent that . . . they would have no difficulty exterminating one another to the last man. They know this, and hence comes a large part of their current unrest, their unhappiness and their mood of anxiety."

Whereas happiness appears to be very difficult to attain in this life, "unhappiness is much less difficult to experience." Freud explains: "We are threatened with suffering from three directions: from our own body, which is doomed to decay and dissolution and which cannot even do without pain and anxiety as warning signals; from the external world, which may rage against us with overwhelming and merciless forces of destruction; and finally from our relations to other men. The suffering which comes from this last source is perhaps more painful to us than any other."

Freud dismisses out of hand the large number of people who find that spiritual resources help free them from this "unrest," "unhappiness," and "anxiety." He calls religious faith "an attempt to procure a certainty of happiness and a protection against suffering through a delusional remolding of reality . . . and no one, needless to say, who shares a delusion ever recognizes it as such."

Nevertheless, Freud acknowledges that one's worldview can not only lessen unhappiness, but can also influence the degree of happiness one experiences. He expresses envy that his worldview offers little in this regard. In *Moses and Monotheism*, Freud states sarcastically: "How we who have little belief envy those who are convinced of the existence of a Supreme Power . . . How comprehensive, exhaustive, and final are the doctrines of the believers compared with the labored, poor and patchy attempts at explanation which are the best we can produce." He notes that believers claim to possess an awareness of how they ought to behave. "The Divine Spirit . . . has implanted within the soul of men the knowledge of this ideal and at the same time the urge to strive toward it." He acknowledges that how well they live up to this ideal influences their emotional state. Referring to the concept of a universal moral law, Freud says that "their emotional life is measured by the distance from their ideal. It affords them high gratification when they . . . so to speak, come nearer to it; and they are punished by severe distress when . . . they have moved further away from it." But once again Freud dismisses this view. "All this is so simply and unshakably established," he states sardonically. He quickly adds, "We can only regret it if certain experiences of life and observations of nature have made it impossible to accept the hypothesis of such a Supreme Being." And Freud wonders where this widespread belief in a Supreme Being "obtained its immense power, which overwhelms reason and science." Freud ultimately concludes, ". . . one feels inclined to say that the intention that man should be 'happy' is not included in the plan of 'Creation.'"

Lewis believes the plan of creation did indeed provide for our happiness. But something went wrong with the plan. Because most of our suffering comes from other human beings—Lewis surmises three-fourths of our suffering falls into this category—we need to ask what causes humans to inflict such misery on others. He ex-

plains: "God created things which had free will. That means creatures which can go either wrong or right. Some people think they
can imagine a creature which was free but had no possibility of going wrong; I cannot. If a thing is free to be good it is also free to be
bad. And free will is what has made evil possible. The more intelligent and more gifted the person God creates, the greater the capacity to love and to be a positive force in the universe, but also, if
that person rebels, the greater capacity to cause evil, to inflict pain
and to cause unhappiness. Our remote ancestors rebelled and used
their free will to transgress the moral law . . . and to become their
own masters . . . to invent some sort of happiness for themselves,
apart from God."

Lewis asks: "Why, then, did God give them free will?" Why in the
world would God give us freedom to choose if He knew people
would use that freedom to cause so much frustration in themselves
and so much misery in others? "Because free will, though it makes
evil possible, is also the only thing that makes possible any love or
goodness or joy worth having." Without free will, we would be ro-
bots, and God obviously preferred to relate not to machines, but to
human beings. Lewis asserts that "the happiness which God designs
for His higher creatures is the happiness of being freely, voluntarily
united to Him and to each other in an ecstasy of love and delight
compared with which the most rapturous love between a man and a
woman on this earth is mere milk and water. And for that they must
be free."

Lewis asserts that the primary purpose of our lives—the reason
for our existence on this planet—is to establish a relationship with
the Person who placed us here. Until that relationship is established, all of our attempts to attain happiness—our quest for recognition, for money, for power, for the perfect marriage or the ideal
friendship, for all that we spend our lives seeking—will always fall
short, will never quite satisfy the longing, fill the void, quell the rest-

lessness, or make us happy. Lewis explains that "God designed the
human machine to run on Himself. He Himself is the fuel our spirits were designed to burn, or the food our spirits were designed to
feed on . . . God cannot give us happiness and peace apart from
Himself, because it is not there. There is no such thing."

Lewis disagrees with Freud that "sexual (genital)" satisfaction
provides the strongest experiences of pleasure and is thus the prototype of all happiness. In *God in the Dock*, Lewis argues that happiness even in a marriage depends on considerably more that sexual
compatibility. "When two people achieve lasting happiness, this is
not solely because they are great lovers but because they are also—
I must put it crudely—good people; controlled, loyal, fair-minded,
mutually adaptable people."

Lewis also argues that, although we have a right to seek happiness—to pursue it, as Americans say—we have no right to happiness
itself. "This sounds to me as odd as a right to good luck . . . we depend for a very great deal of our happiness or misery on circumstances outside our control. A right to happiness doesn't, for me,
make much more sense than a right to be six feet tall, or to have a
millionaire for your father or to get good weather whenever you
want to have a picnic." Although Lewis believes that all forms of
pleasure, fun, happiness, and joy come from God, who gives these
freely for all to enjoy, he admits that these earthly pleasures never
completely satisfy us. "We have plenty of fun, and some ecstasy,"
Lewis writes, but they never quite satisfy our yearnings. God with-
holds from us "the settled happiness and security which we all desire." Otherwise, Lewis says, we would think this world our home
rather than a place we are passing through. He writes that the Creator "refreshes us on the journey with some pleasant Inns, but will
not encourage us to mistake them for our home."

Earthly pleasures and earthly sources of happiness, though given
by God to be enjoyed fully, pose a certain danger, Lewis believes,

when they become the primary purpose of our lives. They may not only mislead us into thinking this world our permanent residence, but may also detract from our relationship with God. Lewis warns that although "all pleasure and happiness is in its own nature good, and God wishes us to enjoy it, He does not, however, wish us to enjoy it without relation to Him, still less to prefer it to Him." Lewis keeps emphasizing a basic principle of the spiritual life: when one's relationship to God is given first place, everything else, including our earthly loves and pleasures, increases. In a letter to a friend Lewis writes: "When I have learned to love God better than my earthly dearest, I shall love my earthly dearest better than I do now. In so far as I learn to love my earthly dearest at the expense of God and *instead* of God, I shall be moving towards that state in which I shall not love my earthly dearest at all. When first things are put first, second things are not suppressed but increased."

Last, but not least, Lewis emphasized that no pleasure on earth can substitute for or satisfy the profound need and desire that we have for a relationship with the Person who made us. Lewis believed that if we seek first this relationship, we will attain it and a good measure of happiness as well. But if we seek first our happiness, we will obtain neither a relationship with the Creator nor our happiness. "Indeed the best thing about happiness itself," Lewis writes, "is that it liberates you from thinking about happiness—as the greatest pleasure that money can give us is to make it unnecessary to think about money . . ."

Lewis quotes a verse in the New Testament that states, "Thou hast created all things, and for thy pleasure they are and were created." He then observes that "we were made not primarily that we may love God (though we were made for that too) but that God may love us, that we may become objects in which the Divine love may rest 'well pleased.'" To become an object God can love may require alteration. Some of our unhappy or painful experiences work to change us into beings God can love and find pleasure in. Lewis writes, "when we are such as He can love without impediment, we shall in fact be happy." Lewis keeps stressing that all of our efforts to find the profound, settled, lasting happiness we desire apart from a relationship with the Creator will be frustrating. He explains that humans are made for that relationship: "The place for which He designs them in His scheme of things is the place they are made for. When they reach it their nature is fulfilled and their happiness attained . . . the anguish is over." Lewis concludes that "God gives what He has, not what He has not: He gives the happiness that there is, not the happiness that is not. To be God—to be like God and to share His goodness in creaturely response—to be miserable—these are the only three alternatives. If we will not learn to eat the only food that the universe grows—the only food that any possible universe ever can grow—then we must starve eternally."

✿   ✿   ✿

Freud's materialism makes him pessimistic concerning the possibility of attaining happiness; as an atheist, Lewis shared Freud's pessimistic outlook. For Freud, the nature of physical pleasure is fleeting, making general unhappiness unavoidable. He saw the future as dark and ominous. Lewis, after his conversion, became optimistic and saw the future filled with hope. Which one was right? Their biographies shed light on this question.

Both Freud and Lewis—before Lewis experienced his change of worldview—speak often in their letters and their autobiographies of their pessimism, gloom, and general state of unhappiness. Both experienced early losses in their lives. (Research has shown that loss of a parent or surrogate parent early in life predisposes one to clinical depression.) Freud wrote often of his "bouts of depression." Friends of Lewis spoke of a "Celtic melancholy" in him before his conversion.

When a young teenager, Freud exchanged many letters with his friend Eduard Silberstein. Apparently, Silberstein commented on Freud's despondent mood. As with many depressed people, Freud did not see himself as depressed and resisted the notion. "You do me an injustice when you call my mood gloomy and sad," Freud wrote when he was sixteen years old. He insisted he was really light-hearted and only in "unguarded moments am I seized by that forlorn mood." Yet within six months he wrote a letter to a friend and referred to his despondency as "my miserable life."

Perhaps one of these unguarded moments occurred after Freud experienced disappointment in love. Although he refers to Gisela Fluss many years later as "my first love," we have little information concerning how well he actually knew her and how much of the relationship occurred in his adolescent daydreams. Apparently, about three years later, he heard she was to marry someone else. Freud wrote a letter to Silberstein enclosing a long poem titled "Epithalamium." The poem appears to be an attempt to overcome the pain and sorrow of the loss by making her sound undesirable and by mentioning all that he did not like about her. However, more disturbing, Freud also included in his letter, perhaps inadvertently, a sheet of notes he wrote while writing the first draft of the poem. The notes mention how enraged he is when he thinks of "the faithful bride in another man's arms," "abominable despair," "I rage, pain sears my breast." Even more disturbing are the many references to suicide: "Send me forthwith two potassium cyanides . . . five drops of ether . . . hemlock . . . arsenic, all white and pure . . ." This may just be an exaggerated teenage response to what he later referred to as a "flirtation"—but perhaps it is not exaggerated in someone struggling with depression.

Many letters written in his twenties refer to his depression. When twenty-six, he mentions in a letter to his fiancée Martha Bernays that his friends "have lifted me out of my despondency."

A few years later, Freud found another means of obtaining relief. Early in 1884, when he was twenty-eight years old, Freud began experimenting with a new drug called cocaine. His letters indicate that he had been notably depressed during the preceding year. In August of 1884 he writes to his fiancée, "I have experienced during the past fourteen months only three or four happy days . . . And that is too little for a human being who is still young and yet has never felt young." He began to take cocaine a few weeks before and found that it lifted his depression. In the letters he refers to himself as "a big wild man who has cocaine in his body. In my last severe depression I took coca again and a small dose lifted me to the heights in a wonderful fashion."

Six months later he mentions the drug again in a letter to Martha: "I take very small doses of it regularly against depression and against indigestion, and with the most brilliant success." A few months later he begins a letter with "Today you may miss the note of melancholy to which you will have grown accustomed in my letters from Paris."

Drugs, of course, were not the only answer for Freud. Sometimes he used his work to help lift his mood. In a letter to Fliess, Freud writes that "I mastered my depression with the help of a special diet in intellectual matters." But he remained, at heart, a pessimist capable of dark humor. At age forty-four, Freud shared with Fliess his "new realization of the nature of 'happiness': one has to assume happiness when fate does not carry out all its threats simultaneously." Much later, in a letter to his physician, Freud commented on how elusive happiness is: ". . . you think you already have it in your grasp and it is always gone again." At eighty, near the end of his life, he could still sound morose: "My mood is bad, little pleases me, my self-criticism has grown much more acute. I would diagnose it as senile depression in anyone else."

In addition to sadness, other characteristics of depression involve feelings of hopelessness and helplessness, a negative interpretation of life with frequent thoughts of death, and a pessimistic view of the future. In fact, some authorities believe that negative thinking and pessimism not only characterize depression but actually *cause* it. (Certain forms of psychotherapy, especially cognitive behavior therapy, aim at changing these negative thought patterns as a means of treating depression.) Freud evidenced each of these traits of depression. We will focus here on his intense negativity and dire pessimism.

Pessimism pervades much of Freud's writing. In a letter to his colleague Karl Abraham, Freud writes that "life bears too heavily on me. I talk very little about this because I know that others would take such statements as complaints and signs of depression." Another letter to Abraham, written some fifteen years before Freud's death, reveals both his preoccupation with death and his pessimism. "Though I am supposed to be on the way to recovery, there is deep inside a pessimistic conviction that the end of my life is near. That feeds on the torments from my scar [from his surgery for cancer of the jaw] which never cease. There is a sort of senile depression which centers in a conflict between an irrational love of life and a more sensible resignation . . ."

Freud's pessimism is expressed not only in his letters, but in his expository and philosophical works as well. For example, in *Civilization and Its Discontents*, written when in his seventies, Freud concludes pessimistically, "What good to us is a long life if it is difficult and barren of joys, and if it is so full of misery that we can only welcome death as a deliverer?"

Freud appeared to be aware of the relationship between his worldview and his pessimism. In a letter to Oskar Pfister, he defended it by writing, "I am neither a self-tormentor nor am I cussed and, if I could, I should gladly do as others and bestow upon mankind a rosy future, and I should find it much more beautiful and consoling if we could count on such a thing. But this seems to me to be yet another instance of illusion (wish fulfillment) in conflict with truth. The question is not what belief is more pleasing or more comfortable or more advantageous to life, but of what may approximate more closely to the puzzling reality that lies outside us . . . to me my pessimism seems a conclusion, while the optimism of my opponents seems an a priori assumption." Freud drives home the point that his theories and philosophy are based on sound logic. "I have concluded a marriage of reason with my gloomy theories, while others live with theirs in a love-match." He says of his opponents: "I hope they will gain greater happiness from this than I." Freud appeared to know his worldview offered little hope for happiness, but he felt powerless to do anything about it.

C. S. Lewis also suffered from depression during the first half of his life. The loss of his mother, rejection by his father, and the cruelty of the headmaster at his first boarding school all played a role in it. His late childhood years were painful ones that contributed to the sorrow and unhappiness of his profound loss. Only at fifteen, when studying under Mr. Kirkpatrick at Great Bookham, did Lewis experience some semblance of happiness. In a letter to his friend Greeves, Lewis writes: "Strange indeed is my position, suddenly whirled from a state of abject terrorism, misery and hopelessness at Malvern, to a comfort and prosperity far above the average. If you envy my present situation, you must always remember that after so many years of unhappiness there should be something by way of compensation. All I hope is that there will not come a corresponding depression after this . . ."

There is also considerable evidence that Lewis shared Freud's pessimism and gloom before his conversion. Lewis speaks of this pessimism in his autobiography, letters, and other writings. In *Surprised by Joy*, he mentions that as a young child he "had the gloomiest anticipation of adult life." Some of this gloomy outlook he attributes to his father, who "represented adult life as one of incessant drudgery under the continual threat of financial ruin." So his idea of what lay ahead of him once he left school was "work, work, work, then we die." When discussing the many obstacles to his embracing a spiritual worldview as an adolescent, he writes: "Working against my faith, there was in me a deeply ingrained pessimism; a pessimism, by that time, much more of intellect than of temper . . . I had very definitely formed the opinion that the universe was, in the main, a rather regrettable institution . . . a menacing and unfriendly place."

Lewis makes a distinction here. He realizes his pessimism resulted more from his thinking than from his feeling, more from how he thought about and viewed the world. Why then did he think so negatively? He gives several reasons—a physical handicap that made playing sport difficult and, of course, the death of his mother. "As to the sources of my pessimism," Lewis writes, "the reader will remember that, though in many ways most fortunate, yet I had very early in life met a great dismay."

Lewis describes how, at that early age, his pessimism influenced his whole outlook on the future as "a settled expectation that everything would do what you did not want it to do. Whatever you wanted to remain straight, would bend; whatever you tried to bend would fly back to the straight; all knots which you wished to be firm would come untied; all knots you wanted to untie would remain firm. It is not possible to put it into language without making it comic, and I have indeed no wish to see it (now) except as something comic. But it is perhaps just these early experiences which are so fugitive and, to an adult, so grotesque, that give the mind its earliest bias, its habitual sense of what is or is not plausible."

As a young adolescent, Lewis wrote a tragedy called *Loki Bound*. Loki, the hero, was (as he later realized) "a projection of myself; he voiced that sense of priggish superiority whereby I was, unfortunately, beginning to compensate myself for my unhappiness." The hero was in conflict with Odin because "Odin had created a world though Loki had clearly warned him that this was a wanton cruelty. Why should creatures have the burden of existence forced on them without their consent?" Lewis realized he was expressing here his own anger and pessimism. "I was at this time living, like so many Atheists . . . in a whirl of contradictions. I maintained God did not exist. I was also angry with God for not existing. I was equally angry with Him for creating a world." He resented being placed on this earth and exposed to all its horrors without his consent. Yet he never felt the "horror of nonentity, of annihilation." Not death but life depressed him. Only after his conversion, when he "began to know what life really is and what would have been lost by missing it," did this change.

The long and short of it, for Lewis, was summed up in a quote from Lucretius:

Had God designed the world, it would not be
A world so frail and faulty as we see.

Did Lewis's atheism precede pessimism, or was it the reverse? Did they perhaps reinforce each other? In a letter written almost thirty years after witnessing the horrors of war, he lists the personal experiences that led to his pessimism and that, in turn, formed the basis of his atheism: "The early loss of my mother, great unhappiness at school, and the shadow of the last war and presently the experience of it, had given me a very pessimistic view of existence. My atheism was based on it: and it still seems to me that far the strongest card in our enemies' hand is the actual course of the world: and that, quite apart from particular evils like wars and revolutions. The inherent 'vanity' of the 'creature,' the fact that life preys on life, that all beauty and happiness is produced only to be destroyed—this was what stuck in my gullet."

Lewis gives the most detailed picture of how he viewed the world before his conversion in his classic work on human suffering, *The Problem of Pain.* "When I was an atheist, if anyone asked

me 'why do you not believe in God?' my reply would run something like this . . ." First, the starkness of the universe: "the greatest part of it consists of empty space, completely dark and
unimaginably cold . . . all the forms of life live only by preying
upon one another . . . The creatures cause pain by being born, and
live by inflicting pain and in pain they mostly die." Next, in the
"most complex creatures, Man, yet another quality appears, which
we call reason, whereby he is enabled to foresee his own pain
which henceforth is preceded with acute mental suffering, and to
foresee his own death while keenly desiring permanence." This
human history is "a record of crime, war, disease, and terror with
just sufficient happiness interposed to give . . . an agonized apprehension of losing it." In short, "If you ask me to believe that this is
the work of a benevolent and omnipotent spirit, I reply that all the
evidence points in the opposite direction."

The many biographers of Lewis, as well as his close friends, emphasize how profoundly his change of worldview altered his life, in
particular his capacity to experience happiness. Before his transition, Lewis had not "the slightest hint . . . that there ever had been
or ever would be any connection between God and Joy." Lewis had
not yet recognized that the deep yearning he called "Joy" was a desire for a relationship with the Person who made him. After his conversion, Lewis found happiness in his newly established relationship
with the Creator and the many new friendships he formed.

The quality of our relationships is a pretty fair barometer of our
emotional health. Happiness or unhappiness is a reflection of our
mood that, in turn, influences how we relate to others. A depressed
person is not only gloomy and pessimistic, but also angry, irritable,
and hopeless—not qualities that make for good relationships. This
may give us some understanding of the stormy relationships
throughout Freud's life and the very few close relationships in the
first half of Lewis's life. After his conversion, Lewis enjoyed many

close friendships. He wrote: "To believe and to pray were the beginning of extroversion. I had been, as they say, 'taken out of myself.'"

Nothing brought Lewis more enjoyment than sitting around a fire with a group of close friends engaged in good discussion, or taking long walks with them through the English countryside. "My happiest hours," Lewis wrote, "are spent with three or four old friends in old clothes tramping together and putting up in small pubs—or else sitting up till the small hours in someone's college rooms, talking nonsense, poetry, theology, metaphysics over beer, tea, and pipes. There's no sound I like better than . . . laughter." In another letter to his friend Greeves, Lewis writes: "friendship is the greatest of worldly goods. Certainly to me it is the chief happiness of life. If I had to give a piece of advice to a young man about a place to live, I think I shd. say, 'sacrifice almost everything to live where you can be near your friends.' I know I am v. fortunate in that respect . . ." And Lewis found an overwhelming happiness in his marriage that can best be appreciated by reading his wife's letters and Lewis's book about her death, *A Grief Observed*. Lewis changed from a wary introvert with very few close relationships to a personable extrovert with scores of close friends and colleagues. George Sayer, a biographer who knew Lewis for some thirty years, and Owen Barfield, a close friend for over forty years, describe Lewis after his transition. "He was unusually cheerful, and took an almost boyish delight" in life. They describe him as "great fun, an extremely witty and amusing companion . . . considerate . . . more concerned with the welfare of his friends than with himself."

Why the change? As a psychiatrist, I suggest three factors: First, as Lewis began to read the Old and New Testaments seriously, he noted a new method of establishing his identity, of coming to terms with his "real personality." This process, Lewis writes, involves losing yourself in your relationship to the Creator. "Until you have given up yourself to Him," Lewis writes, "you will not have a real self." In particular, Lewis paid attention to the New Testament verse "Whoever loses his life for my sake will find it." He turned outward instead of inward to "find himself."

Second, his understanding of Agape—of loving one's neighbor by wanting the best for him and exercising one's will to act accordingly—also took Lewis outside of himself. He developed a capacity to step out of his own needs sufficiently to become aware of the needs of others and to exercise his will to meet those needs.

Third, Lewis's new worldview changed his valuation of people. Death no longer marked the end of life, but only the end of the first chapter in a book that went on without end. Every human being, he now believed, would live forever—outliving every organization, every state, every civilization on earth. "There are no *ordinary* people," Lewis reminded his audience in an address given at Oxford. He encouraged them "to remember that the dullest and most uninteresting person you talk to may one day be a creature which if you saw it now, you would be strongly tempted to worship." No one ever talks to "a mere mortal . . . it is immortals whom we joke with, work with, marry, snub, and exploit—immortal horrors or everlasting splendors . . . your neighbor is the holiest object presented to your senses."

People, in Lewis's new view, transcend in time and significance everything else on earth. This forced him to set new priorities in his life—the first priority given to his relationship with the Creator, the second priority, to his relationship with others. The importance of keeping our priorities in order is a recurrent theme in his writings.

Happiness and Ambition

Is fame or the desire for fame related to happiness? If contentment is an important aspect of happiness, then the lack of recognition may be a source of unhappiness in one who yearns to be famous.

Some writers have implied that fame itself is an obstacle to happiness. Thomas Jefferson in a letter to John Adams wrote, "He is happiest of whom the world says least, good or bad."

The need for recognition provided a strong motivation for Freud and for Lewis before his transition. Freud had always openly expressed his desire to be famous. After his conversion Lewis expressed the strong conviction that the need to be famous, the desire to be more well known than others, had provided a spiritual stumbling block in his earlier years.

When Freud began an analysis of himself in his forties, he observed a long-standing, intense desire to be famous, to be known as a great man. In his *Interpretation of Dreams,* Freud tells of an event he heard repeated often in his childhood. At his birth "an old peasant woman had prophesied to my mother, happy over her first-born, that she had given the world a great man." Freud thought this story, repeated over and over as he was growing up, could have been responsible in part for his yearning.

Freud recalled a second incident from his childhood that he thought related to his need to be famous. When seven or eight years old, Freud had an accident in his parents' bedroom. He urinated on the floor. His father exploded in anger and commented that the boy would never amount to anything. This embarrassment haunted Freud for years and recurred in his dreams. Freud thought this "must have been a terrible blow to my ambition." He noticed that "allusions to this scene keep constantly recurring in my dreams and are regularly linked with enumerations of my achievements and successes." Freud speculated that his need for fame and greatness may have been motivated by a desire to say to his father and to the world, "You see, I have amounted to something after all."

When Freud was seventeen years old, he wrote to his friend Emil Fluss and suggested that Fluss save the letters he received from Freud, implying that someday Freud would be famous. "And now I advise you as a friend . . . ," Freud writes, "to preserve them—have them bound—take good care of them—one never knows."

About twelve years later, Freud made a decision that he thought would frustrate future biographers, reflecting again his thoughts of someday being famous. "I have just carried out one resolution which one group of people, as yet unborn and fated to misfortune, will feel acutely. Since you can't guess whom I mean I will tell you: they are my biographers," Freud wrote in a letter to his fiancée. He explained: "I have destroyed all my diaries of the past fourteen years, with letters, scientific notes and the manuscripts of my publications. Only family letters were spared. Yours, my dear one, were never in danger." Freud appears confident, even at this early stage of his career, and still in his twenties, that people someday will want to write about him, "Let the biographers chafe; we won't make it too easy for them. Let each one of them believe he is right in his 'Conception of the Development of the Hero': even now I enjoy the thought of how they will all go astray." What did the papers reveal about Freud that he wanted destroyed? He did not specify except to write that they included "all my thoughts and feelings about the world in general, and in particular how it concerned me . . . I cannot leave here and cannot die before ridding myself of the disturbing thought of who might come by the old papers."

When one of his colleagues met with success and received recognition, Freud referred to him as a "great man with a great invention" but then added regretfully, "Oh, they have all outstripped me in fame."

When Freud entered his fifties, he appeared to lose interest in what others thought of him. "What those others say now is a matter of indifference," he wrote in a letter to his colleague Sándor Ferenczi. And he appeared to realize that fame could have negative effects: "We shall all of us get more gratitude and posthumous fame from psychoanalysis than would be good for us now while we are in the midst of the work." In another letter to Ferenczi, Freud made clear that though he may have strongly desired fame, he harbored doubts about ever receiving it: "I certainly do not work because of the expectation of any reward or fame; in view of the inevitable ingratitude of humanity I do not expect anything either for my children later."

Nevertheless, lack of recognition and especially the criticism he encountered from others bothered Freud throughout his life. When writing his autobiography at almost eighty he related a rather strange story blaming his fiancée for the long delay in becoming famous. After describing his years of education and his settling down in Vienna to set up a medical practice, he suddenly adds: "I may here go back a little and explain how it was the fault of my fiancée that I was not already famous at that early age." Freud said that he had obtained "from Merck some of what was then the little-known alkaloid cocaine." He began to do research on the drug, when "an opportunity arose for making a journey to visit my fiancée, from whom I had been parted for two years." Before leaving to visit her, Freud suggested to a friend that he should investigate the "anaesthetizing properties" of cocaine for the eye. This resulted in someone other than Freud becoming "the discoverer of local anesthesia by cocaine, which has become so important for minor surgery; but I bore my fiancée no grudge for the interruption of my work."

In this same autobiography Freud expresses the bitterness he feels toward those who ridiculed his work and delayed his receiving the recognition he felt he deserved. Freud wrote that "German science will not have cause to be proud of those who represented it . . . for the degree of arrogance which they displayed, for their conscienceless contempt of logic, and for the coarseness and bad taste of their attacks there could be no excuse." He acknowledges that, after so many years have passed, it may be "childish of me to give free rein to such feelings as these now." But he then adds, "it none the less hurt deeply."

In 1917, Freud was nominated for a Nobel Prize but did not receive it. In his journal that year he noted, "No Nobel Prize." He apparently hoped he might receive it at a future date. As late as 1930, he again noted, "Definitely passed over for the Nobel Prize."

C. S. Lewis also dreamed of being famous—but only *before* his transition. In an essay written in 1941, he mentions "dreams of success, fame, love, and the like . . . I have had dozens of them . . . dreams in which I said clever things . . . fought battles, and generally forced the world to acknowledge what a remarkable person I was." Before his transition Lewis harbored all of the snobbery, pride, and arrogance bred into those attending the elite boarding schools in England and the prestigious universities. His diary, his autobiography, and letters show this clearly. Lewis writes of his school experience: "I have never seen a community so competitive, so full of snobbery and flunkeyism, a ruling class so selfish and so class conscious, or a proletariat so fawning."

Shortly before his changed worldview, Lewis began to examine himself seriously for the first time. He didn't like what he observed. "What I found appalled me: a zoo of lusts, a bedlam of ambitions," he writes in *Surprised by Joy*. This may perhaps have contributed to a realization of a need for help outside of himself and to his eventual conversion. During the years of his transition he writes to his friend Greeves: "I have found out ludicrous and terrible things about my own character . . . Sitting by, watching the rising thoughts . . . as they pop up . . . one of every three is a thought of self-admiration . . . I catch myself posturing before the mirror, so to speak, all day long. I pretend I am carefully thinking out what to say to the next pupil (for his good, of course) and then suddenly I am really thinking how frightfully clever I'm going to be and how he will admire me . . . And when you force yourself to stop it, you admire yourself for doing *that.*"

Another letter to Greeves reveals what Lewis considered a related flaw in his character, namely his desire to be recognized as a great writer. "The side of me which longs . . . to be approved as a writer, is not the side of us that is really worth much. And depend upon it, unless God has abandoned us, he will find means to cauterize that side somehow or other. If we can take the pain well and truly now and by it *forever* get over the wish to be distinguished beyond our fellows, well: if not we shall get it again in some other form. And honestly, the being cured, with all the pain, has pleasure too: one creeps home, tired and bruised, into a state of mind that is really restful, when all one's ambitions have been given up."

Although Lewis did not seek fame after his transition, he found it. He found that when he concentrated on writing well and forgot about becoming famous as a writer, he both wrote well and became recognized for it. This may have contributed to his oft-repeated principle that when first things are put first, second things don't decrease, they increase.

Lewis also discovered that fame or the desire for it contained a great danger. He realized the desire for fame was simply the desire to be more known than others and that such a desire was an expression of pride—"the essential vice, the utmost evil." Lewis shares some insightful observations on human nature when he notes "that Pride is essentially competitive—is competitive by its very nature—while the other vices are competitive only, so to speak, by accident. Pride gets no pleasure out of having something, only out of having more of it than the next man . . ." He also notes that "pride . . . has been the chief cause of misery in every nation and every family since the world began . . . pride always means enmity . . . not only between man and man, but enmity to God." Lewis refers to pride as "spiritual cancer: it eats up the very possibility of love, or contentment, or even common sense."

Lewis attempts to clear up some misunderstandings about pride. First, pride does *not* mean self-respect or self-love. Pride means self-conceit, the need to feel superior to others. "A proud man is always looking down on things and on people: and of course, as long as you are looking down, you can not see something above you," he asserts in explaining how pride interferes with one's relationship to God. Second, Lewis explains that "pleasure in being praised is not pride. The child who is patted on the back for doing a lesson well, the woman whose beauty is praised by her lover, the saved soul to whom Christ says 'Well done,' are pleased and ought to be. For here the pleasure lies not in what you are but in the fact that you have pleased someone you wanted (and rightly wanted) to please." No problem there. But the problem develops "when you pass from thinking, 'I have pleased him; all is well,' to thinking, 'What a fine person I must be to have done it.' The more you delight in yourself and the less you delight in the praise, the worse you are becoming. When you delight wholly in yourself and do not care about the praise at all, you have reached bottom."

In his famous scholarly work *A Preface to Paradise Lost,* Lewis explains how pride causes the fall of Adam and Eve. "The fall is simply and solely disobedience—doing what you have been told not to do; and it results from pride—from being too big for your boots, forgetting your place, thinking you are God." Lewis notes, "This Milton states in the very first line of the first book [of *Paradise Lost*] . . . and all his characters reiterate throughout the poem as if it were the subject of a fugue."

Lewis appeared, after his transition, to be alert to the danger of falling into the vice of pride. In a letter he writes: "I am now in my fiftieth year. I feel my zeal for writing, and whatever talent I originally possessed, to be decreasing; nor (I believe) do I please my readers as I used to . . . Perhaps it will be the most wholesome thing for my soul that I lose both fame and skill lest I were to fall into that evil disease, vainglory." Needless to say, Lewis published many of his most popular books during the next twelve years. He lost neither his fame nor his skill.

* * *

All of this discussion about pessimism, ambition, and pride helps us to understand the change in Lewis's *thinking* after his conversion. But what about his *feelings,* his disposition, his mood? Does a change in worldview help change how one *feels*—even for a person suffering from depression?

A number of recent articles in leading medical journals have researched the effects of worldviews in patients suffering from depression. They found those with a spiritual worldview responded more quickly to treatment for their depression than those with a secular worldview. They also found that the stronger the commitment to their spiritual convictions, the more rapid was their response to treatment. How does this work? If one looks critically and objectively at Lewis's worldview, how would his newly formed convictions have helped his depression? Perhaps the most effective way to answer that is to look at the research I did on this topic with Harvard students who like Lewis experienced a dramatic change in worldview.

In these undergraduates who experienced what they called "religious conversion," I was curious to explore whether these transitions, as so many in my field thought, reflected pathology and a futile attempt to resolve severe inner conflict or to escape reality. Many of those students, as with so many today, had struggled with depression.

Before their conversion experience, they referred often to an emptiness and despondency, sometimes calling it existential despair. This depressive mood was partly related to a gap they felt between their social conscience on the one hand and their personal morality—how they actually lived—on the other. They appeared to struggle with the passage of time, with aging and death, as paradoxical as this may seem in this age group. They spoke despairingly of feeling old, of having accomplished little in their lives, and, as students, living a parasitical existence. Yet after their conversion, they spoke of experiencing a sense of forgiveness that apparently helped them become less intolerant of themselves, helped them bridge the gap between what they felt they were and what they thought they ought to be, and provided resources outside themselves that made the future bridging of this gap less hopeless.

Although their spiritual experience did not free them from alterations in mood, they spoke of a "sense of joy" not previously known and a marked decrease in the feeling of utter hopelessness and despair that they had struggled with previously. It may be more than coincidence that Lewis writes in his autobiography that joy was "the central story of my life." Did the newfound faith of these students help with their feelings of worthlessness?

The conversion experience brought about a change in how the students felt about themselves, but not, perhaps, in the way that unbelievers might think. A newfound intense introspection made them more acutely aware—not less—of how far short they fell from the ideal of perfection their faith demanded. Though one would expect this process to widen the gap between what they felt they were and what they thought they ought to be, and thus to increase the agonizing despair that many struggled with before conversion, the opposite appeared to hold true. They spoke of spiritual resources that give strength and renewed hope and that foster a more open, more tolerant, and more loving spirit toward others. They referred frequently to the theological concepts of redemption and forgiveness as being instrumental in reducing their self-hatred.

Freud despaired of finding sustained happiness in his life. He considered those who were optimistic about the future unreasonable and "in conflict with the truth." Throughout his life, Freud suffered from "bouts of depression," asking near the end of his life, "What good to us is a long life if it is difficult and barren of joys, and if it is so full of misery that we can only welcome death as a deliverer?" Lewis shared Freud's pessimism before his conversion, but experienced a radically new happiness in his relationship with the Creator: "How true it all is: the SEEING ONE walks out into joy and happiness unthinkable, where the dull, senseless eyes of the world see only destruction and death." In his *Preface to Paradise Lost* Lewis quotes Addison: "The great moral which reigns in Milton is the most universal and most useful that can be imagined, that obedience to the will of God makes men happy and disobedience makes them miserable."

When we observe Freud's life and the life of Lewis before and after his conversion, we can't help but observe how one's worldview has a profound impact on one's capacity to experience happiness. Lewis stated clearly that his pessimism and gloom were closely related to his atheism. His conversion experience changed his pessimism, gloom, and despair to joy, freedom from the burden of a driving ambition, and many satisfying relationships.

∽6∾

SEX

Is the Pursuit of Pleasure Our Only Purpose?

Freud and Lewis wrote extensively about sexuality. Freud said that when you look at people's behavior, their one purpose in life is to be happy and that "sexual (genital) love . . . [is] the prototype of all happiness." Lewis strongly disagreed. He believed there are other, more lasting sources of happiness. Satisfaction of the desire for sex, like satisfaction of the desire for food, is only one of many God-given pleasures. He considered Freud much too preoccupied with sex. Both Freud and Lewis realized human sexuality can be a source of great pleasure and a vehicle for expressing the tenderest, most sublime feelings, but also a source of pain and of death itself. We observe frequent newspaper articles on the sexual abuse of children, the rape and murder of women, and death caused by sexually transmitted diseases.

Freud and Lewis debated several related questions. Do traditional moral guidelines frustrate our normal, natural desires? Or do they in-

126

crease our pleasure? How is sexuality related to those complicated human experiences we call "love" and "happiness"? The more we learn about the physiology, biochemistry, sociology, and psychology of sexuality, the more, as a culture, we appear both preoccupied with and confused by this powerful, pervasive, and somewhat perplexing instinct. Not only the writings of Freud and Lewis, but also how they expressed their own sexuality sheds light on these questions.

o   o   o

In his last expository work, *An Outline of Psychoanalysis*, written during his last year of life and after his theories were most developed, Freud summarized his principal findings on sexuality:

"a. Sexual life does not begin at puberty, but starts with plain manifestations soon after birth.

b. It is necessary to distinguish sharply between the concepts of 'sexual' and 'genital.' The former is the wider concept and includes many activities that have nothing to do with the genitals.

c. Sexual life comprises the function of obtaining pleasure from zones of the body—a function which is subsequently brought into the service of . . . reproduction."

"According to the popular view," Freud adds, "human sexual life consists essentially in the impulse to bring one's own genitals into contact with those of someone of the opposite sex." Freud writes that his findings "contradicted this view" and therefore "provoked astonishment and denial."

In *An Autobiographical Study*, Freud presents a clear description of the development of his theories. He applied the term "sexual" to almost all human interaction that involves pleasurable feelings, including those of affection: "In the first place sexuality is divorced from its too close connection with the genitals and is regarded as a more comprehensive bodily function, having pleasure as its goal and only secondarily coming to serve the ends of reproduction . . . the sexual impulses are regarded as including all of those merely affectionate and friendly impulses to which usage applies the exceedingly ambiguous word 'love.'"

Failure to understand this broader definition of sex continues, even today, to evoke intense opposition, gross misunderstanding, and inevitable denial of Freud's theories. Perhaps if Freud had used a term less emotionally charged than the word "sex" to describe this broad range of functions, he would have saved himself and the field of psychoanalysis unnecessary conflict and stress. A great deal of the opposition Freud encountered, even from some of his colleagues, focused in particular on Freud's labeling as sexual many early childhood experiences—from the infant sucking at its mother's breast to the affection of a four-year-old girl for her father. Yet the more people reacted to the word "sexual," the more he insisted on using the term. "Anyone who considers sex as something mortifying and humiliating to human nature is at liberty to make use of the more genteel expressions 'Eros' and 'Erotic.'" He adds wistfully: "I might have done so myself from the first and thus have spared myself much opposition."

Why did Freud insist on this term when so many people advised him otherwise? When Carl Jung urged Freud to reconsider, Freud replied that he thought it was more effective to challenge people with a confrontational approach. "We cannot avoid the resistances, so why not rather challenge them at once? In my opinion, attack is the best defense."

The first of Freud's three principal findings asserts that sexuality begins at birth, not at puberty as was the prevailing opinion at that time. Freud once said, "It seems to be my fate to discover only the obvious: that children have sexual feelings, which every nursemaid knows; and that night dreams are just as much a wish-fulfillment as day dreams." Though nursemaids may have known children possess sexual feelings, the medical profession at that time did not believe it. And they expressed shock and disgust once Freud let them in on the secret.

Yet when Freud announced that children possess sexual feelings—feelings sometimes exploited by older children and adults— he did not mean that a two- or three-year-old child had any concept of *adult* sexuality. He meant only that children experience sensual pleasure from various areas of their body at different stages of development. He referred to these stages as "oral," "anal," and "phallic." For example, Freud observed that during the period of development following birth, "all mental activity is centered on the task of providing satisfaction for the needs" of the body and the mind through the mouth. "The first organ to emerge as an erotogenic zone . . . is, from the time of birth onwards, the mouth. To begin with, all physical activity is concentrated on providing satisfaction for the needs of that zone." Freud noted that sucking takes place even after the need for food has been satisfied—thus indicating the presence of a psychological need for the oral pleasure. Freud writes: "Physiology should not be confused with psychology. The baby's obstinate persistence in sucking gives evidence at an early stage of a need for satisfaction which, although it originates from and is instigated by the taking of nourishment, nevertheless strives to obtain pleasure independently of nourishment and for that reason may and should be termed *sexual.*"

Thus, the mouth, to Freud, becomes the first "erotogenic zone." The oral stage is the first phase in "a long complicated process of development before it becomes what we are familiar with as the normal sexual life." The oral stage precedes "the second phase, which we describe as the sadistic-anal phase, because satisfaction is then sought in aggression and excretory function." Freud calls the third phase "the phallic one, which is, as it were, a forerunner of the final form taken by sexual life and already much resembles it."

Difficulty progressing through these stages of sexual development may influence character development and result in certain traits. Freud linked obsessive orderliness, miserliness, and obstinacy with the anal stage, and thus one of many psychoanalytic concepts has infiltrated our language. We often refer to a person with these traits as "anal."

When he was forty-one, in self-analysis, Freud discovered that he loved his mother and had been jealous of his father: the Oedipus complex. As he wrote to a friend, "we can understand the gripping power of Oedipus Rex . . . the Greek legend seizes upon a compulsion which everyone recognizes because he senses its existence within himself. Everyone in the audience was once a budding Oedipus in fantasy and each recoils in horror from the dream fulfillment here transplanted into reality . . ."

In his early clinical work, Freud observed that many of his neurotic patients recalled early childhood sexual experiences that appeared to be related to their symptoms. These experiences often involved seduction by older children or adults. Freud eventually realized that, although some of these experiences actually happened— i.e., some patients actually had been abused when children—many of the experiences reflected only childhood fantasies. Exploring these fantasies confirmed Freud's self-analysis; children go through a phase of development in which they experience a preference for the parent of the opposite sex and ambivalent feelings toward the parent of the same sex. The Oedipus complex has become part of everyday language.

Freud's theories include the concept that we possess two basic instincts which create bodily needs or tensions. These tensions make "demands on mental life." He assumed "the existence of only two basic instincts, *Eros* and *the destructive instinct*." The psychic energy of Eros "henceforward we shall speak of as 'libido.'" Because Freud assumes that this energy called libido motivates many human interactions, he refers to these interactions as sexual.

When Freud announced his discoveries, especially his observation that sexuality begins in infancy, he outraged the medical community. Doctors considered these findings utterly absurd and obscene. Freud wrote in his autobiography: "Few of the findings of psychoanalysis have . . . aroused such an outburst of indignation as the assertion that the sexual function starts at the beginning of life . . ." One professor at a German conference of neurologists and psychiatrists declared these matters not fit for scientific meetings as much as for the police. Freud was accused of being "dirty-minded," and the psychoanalytic method was called objectionable and unnecessary. At that time few had ever heard of child sexual abuse, quite the opposite of today. Also, physicians believed that because sexuality began at puberty young children were completely innocent of sexual feelings. To speak of sexuality beginning at birth and clearly present in young children was simply unacceptable. Most professionals considered such talk, Freud said, "'a desecration of the innocence of childhood.'"

Critics accused Freud of being a libertine and using psychoanalysis to abolish traditional morality. A careful reading of his works does not support that conclusion. Quite the opposite: Freud believed in the freedom to *speak* about sex, not the freedom to *act*. Yet Freud's critics thought that even such talk was inappropriate. Freud encouraged his colleagues to expect and confront resistance. He insisted on using the broad definition of sexuality and persisted in demanding the freedom to talk about it. In a letter to his friend and colleague Ernest Jones, he explained: "It has always seemed to me best to behave in such a manner as if the freedom to talk about sexuality were self-evident and calmly face the inevitable resistance."

In his defense, it must be stressed that he emphasized over and over how important it was that children be taught high moral standards and that society enforce these standards to control both aggressive and sexual impulses. As Freud writes in *Civilization and Its Discontents*, "A . . . community is perfectly justified, psychologically" in prohibiting sexual behavior in children "for there would be no prospect of curbing the sexual lusts of adults if the ground had not been prepared for it in childhood."

If he urged prohibitions on behavior, he also thought it healthy to demystify the subject for children. Freud had a great deal to say about enlightening children about sexual matters. He advised parents to inform children "without making more of a secret of sexual life than any other matter which is not yet accessible to their understanding" and to treat sex "like anything else that is worth knowing about." When do you tell them all the facts? Freud says "at the end of elementary school . . . before ten years old." But giving children facts without moral guidelines is inadequate. He asserts that "moral obligations" concerning sexuality should be given at "the period of [religious] confirmation." (Whether he was simply recognizing that his atheism was not widely shared, or whether he was expressing ambivalence about the rule of religious faith in most people's lives, he did not say.) That so many people distorted and misunderstood his concepts drove Freud to distraction. To say that psychoanalysis encouraged people to be immoral, he said, was based on sheer ignorance and stupidity. If anything, just the opposite was the case.

He writes: "To believe that psycho-analysis seeks a cure for neurotic disorders by giving a free rein to sexuality is a serious misunderstanding which can only be excused by ignorance. The making conscious of repressed sexual desires in analysis makes it possible, on the contrary, to obtain a mastery over them which the previous repression had been unable to achieve. It can more truly be said that analysis sets the neurotic free from the chains of his sexuality."

Freud persistently opposed any physical contact between the psychoanalyst and the patient and warned that when sexual standards disappear, as happened "in the decline of ancient civilizations, love became worthless and life empty." When he heard of what he considered improper behavior of a colleague with a patient, Freud spared no words. "You have not made a secret of the fact that you kiss your patients and let them kiss you; I had also heard that from a patient of my own," Freud wrote. "Now when you decide to give a full account of your technique and its results you will have to choose between two ways: either you relate this or you conceal it. The latter, as you may well think, is dishonorable. Besides, both ways soon come together. Even if you don't say so yourself it will soon get known, just as I knew it before you told me."

Yet his concern was not that love might be devalued by such relationships. Freud assured his colleague his concern came not from "prudishness or from consideration of bourgeois convention," but on what the long-term impact would have *on the technique of psychoanalysis.* Freud warned: "Now picture what will be the result of publishing your technique. There is no revolutionary who is not driven out of the field by a still more radical one. A number of independent thinkers in matters of technique will say to themselves: why stop at a kiss?" Freud painted a vivid picture of what could then happen, warning that "the younger of our colleagues will perhaps find it hard to stop at the point they originally intended."

Recent research shows that inappropriate sexual involvement between psychiatrists (as well as other physicians) and patients continues and has been openly discussed in the lay press and in recent medical literature. Although changes in sexual mores and other aspects of our culture have contributed to this discussion, the Hippocratic oath and the American Psychiatric Association code of ethics proscribes sexual relationships with patients. Because of the intense emotional interaction between therapist and patient involved in the practice of psychoanalytic psychoptherapy, the therapist may be more vulnerable to temptation than the average practitioner. However, one survey of several hundred physicians reported that "between 5 and 13 percent . . . engaged in erotic behaviors, including and excluding sexual intercourse, with a limited number of patients" and that the psychiatrists in the sample were "least likely to engage in erotic acts, particularly when compared with obstetrician-gynecologists and general practitioners."

Early in his clinical experience Freud became aware of the process of transference, whereby a patient might develop romantic and sexual feelings toward the doctor. When he first began treating neurotic patients, he used hypnotism to help them bring unconscious thoughts into awareness. He found, however, that this method had certain limitations. First, not all patients could be hypnotized. Second, he realized that the success or failure of his treatment depended in large measure on the feelings of the patient for the doctor. These feelings could not be explored or controlled if the patient was under hypnosis. He noted that "the most brilliant results were liable to be suddenly wiped away if my personal relation with the patient became disturbed." Finally an unexpected event persuaded him to give up hypnosis: ". . . one day I had an experience which showed me in the crudest light what I had long expected. One of my most acquiescent patients, with whom hypnotism had enabled me to bring about the most marvellous results, and whom I was engaged in relieving of her suffering by tracing back her attacks of pain to their origins, as she woke up on one occasion, threw her arms round my neck. The unexpected entrance of a servant relieved us from a painful discussion, but from that time onwards there was a tacit understanding between us that the hypnotic treatment should be discontinued." Freud quickly adds: "I was modest enough not to attribute the event to my own irresistible personal attraction, and I felt that I had now grasped the nature of the mysterious element that was at work behind hypnotism." In a paper titled "Further Recommendations on Technique," Freud warns that "it is not a patient's crudely sensual desires which constitute the temptation. These are more likely to repel, and it will call for all the doctor's tolerance if he is to regard them as a natural phenomenon. It is rather, perhaps, a woman's subtler and aim-inhibited wishes which bring with them the danger of making a man forget his technique and his medical task for the sake of a fine experience." He adds that "I do not mean to say that it is always easy for the doctor to keep within the limits prescribed by ethics and technique. Those who are still youngish and not yet bound by strong ties may in particular find it a hard task." In fact, ethics committees have found that complaints of sexual activity have been primarily against older doctors, who may have been more likely to have suffered recent losses.

Freud insisted that psychoanalysis in no way encouraged the breaking of traditional sexual standards. He apparently also realized that if sexual involvement became part of the psychoanalytic process, it would provide ammunition to those who called him a "libertine" intent on destroying the moral structure of society and who charged that psychoanalysis encouraged immoral behavior.

Lewis agreed that psychoanalysis in no way conflicts with the moral law. He explained that we must distinguish clearly between "the actual medical theories and techniques of the psychoanalysts, and the general philosophical view of the world which Freud and some others have gone on to add to this." Lewis said that Freud's materialist philosophy *does* conflict with the biblical worldview. "But psychoanalysis itself," Lewis wrote, "apart from all the philosophical additions that Freud and others have made to it, is not in the least contradictory . . . [and] it would not be a bad thing if every person knew something about it . . ."

Freud began his adult life during the reign of Queen Victoria. He thought that the hypocrisy and prudishness of that era increased the excessive repression that he believed led to neurotic illness. He saw no reason for sexuality to be hushed up. Lewis agreed with Freud that there is nothing forbidden or sinful about sexuality and that we ought to have complete freedom to speak about it. He added that the biblical worldview, especially that based on the New Testament, "thoroughly approves of the body . . . glorifies marriage . . . believes that matter is good, that God himself once took on a human body, that some kind of body is going to be given to us even in Heaven and is going to be an essential part of our happiness, our beauty and our energy." He implied that it is no accident that "nearly all of the greatest love poetry in the world has been produced" by those who embrace this worldview.

Lewis astutely pointed out that we must understand what Freud means when he speaks of excessive repression leading to neurotic symptoms. We must not, Lewis writes, confuse the term "repression" with "suppression"—as so many in our culture tend to do. The word "repression" is a technical term that refers to an unconscious process that, when excessive, may give rise to symptoms. Excessive repression, Lewis accurately points out, usually occurs early in life, and when it happens, we are unaware of its happening. "Repressed sexuality does not appear to the patient to be sexuality at all." Suppression, on the other hand, is the conscious control of one's impulses. By confusing the two, many in our culture concluded that any control of sexual impulses is unhealthy. Lewis argued that this is nonsense. In reality, *lack* of control is what is unhealthy. Lewis writes: "Surrender to all our desires obviously leads to . . . disease, jealousy, lies, concealment and everything that is the reverse of health . . . For any happiness, even in this world, quite a lot of restraint is going to be necessary . . ."

The media has contributed to the confusion in our culture between repression and suppression. "Poster after poster, film after film, novel after novel," Lewis notes, "associate the idea of sexual indulgence with the ideas of health, normality, youth, frankness and good humor." He claims this association gives a false impression and is a lie. "Like all powerful lies," Lewis explains, "it is based on a truth . . . that sex in itself . . . is 'normal' and 'healthy' . . . The lie consists in the suggestion that any sexual act to which you are tempted at the moment is also healthy and normal." Lewis adds that human sexuality, like gravity or any other aspect of our universe, cannot in itself be moral or immoral. Sexuality, like the rest of the universe, is given by God and therefore good. How people express their sexuality, on the other hand, can be moral or immoral.

Lewis goes beyond Freud to argue that people who control their sexual impulses understand their sexuality *more* than people who fail at controlling them. "Virtue—even attempted virtue—brings light; indulgence brings fog."

Lewis also disagrees with Freud's notion that the reluctance to talk about sex has caused so much of the difficulty we have with it. Lewis writes: "We have been told . . . that sex has become a mess because it was hushed up . . . that if only we abandon the silly old Victorian idea of hushing it up, everything in the garden will be lovely. It is not true." He points out that for the past several decades "sex has not been hushed up. It has been chattered about all day long . . . I think it is the other way round. I think the human race originally hushed it up because it had become such a mess."

Perhaps if Freud and Lewis were living today, both would agree that talking about sex has not decreased the mess—we *have* been chatting about it day and night in movies, novels, and television programs. Yet our pain and the confusion about love and sex continues—with every other marriage ending in divorce, a large number of out-of-wedlock pregnancies, sexually transmitted diseases, and so forth. And sexual scandals have never entirely left politics—in America, and in much of Europe as well.

Lewis and Freud also differed over whether or not clear guidelines for behavior are essential. Discussing the sexual code based on the Hebrew Scriptures and the New Testament, Lewis declares: "There is no getting away from it: the . . . rule is, 'Either marriage, with complete faithfulness to your partner or else total abstinence.'" Freud appeared to resist this strict code, though he himself and his family followed it. Does this strict standard increase the pleasure and fulfillment of sex and decrease its confusion and pain?

Lewis agreed with Freud that most people find this rule anything but easy. Lewis writes: "This is so difficult and so contrary to our instinct that either the rule is wrong or our sexual instinct, as it now is, has gone wrong." Lewis believed that the instinct had gone wrong. He gave several illustrations of why he thinks sexual appetite had grown "in ludicrous and preposterous excess of its function." Comparing it with the appetite for food, he writes: "You can get a large audience together for a strip-tease act—that is to watch a girl undress on the stage. Now suppose you came to a country where you could fill a theater by simply bringing a covered plate onto the stage and then slowly lifting the cover so as to let every one see, just before the lights went out, that it contained a mutton chop or a bit of bacon, would you not think that in that country something had gone wrong with food? And would not anyone who had grown up in a different world think there was something equally queer about the state of the sex instinct among us?" Lewis believed that the exploitation of the sexual instinct, created to give us great pleasure, had intensified the instinct beyond what it was intended to be. The resulting lack of control has contributed to sexuality being more a source of pain than of pleasure for many.

Unlike Freud, who considered all forms of love as expressions of sexuality, Lewis made a clear distinction between Eros, the romantic feeling between a couple in love, and sexuality. The physical, sexual act he referred to as Venus, after the Roman goddess of love. "By Eros, I mean of course that state which we call 'being in love,'" writes Lewis in his book *The Four Loves*. He distinguished *being in love* from the physical act of sex. "The carnal or animal sexual element within Eros, I intend (following an old usage) to call Venus. And I mean by Venus what is sexual not in some cryptic or rarefied sense—but in a perfectly obvious sense; what is known to be sexual by those who experience it; what could be proved to be sexual by the simplest observations."

Lewis took a strong stand against the popular notion that being in love could make an immoral sexual act moral. If a sexual relationship, for example, is adulterous, being in love does not make it less so. "I am not at all subscribing to the popular idea that . . . the absence or presence of Eros [being in love] . . . makes the sexual act 'impure' or 'pure,' degraded or fine, unlawful or lawful." Lewis reminds his readers that in many successful marriages in the past the partners were chosen by parents and sexual intercourse occurred between couples who were not in love. "This act, like any other, is justified (or not) by far more prosaic and definable criteria; by the keeping or breaking of promises, by justice or injustice, by charity or selfishness, by obedience or disobedience."

Does sexual attraction always serve to bring a couple together so that, as they come to know each other, they eventually "fall in love"? Lewis believes that more often they fall in love first and then find themselves sexually attracted. "There may be those who have first felt mere sexual appetite for a woman and then gone on at a later stage to 'fall in love with her.' But I doubt if this is at all common," Lewis writes in his *Four Loves*. "Very often what comes first is simply a delighted pre-occupation with the Beloved—a general, unspecified pre-occupation with her in her totality. A man in this state really hasn't leisure to think of sex. He is too busy thinking of a person." Lewis states that a man in love wants "not a woman, but one particular woman. In some mysterious but quite indisputable fashion the lover desires the Beloved herself, not the pleasure she can give." Lewis sums up with: "Sexual desire . . . wants *it*, the *thing in itself*; Eros [being in love] wants the Beloved."

Lewis writes that being in love leads one to desire the other person apart from any need that person can meet, even the need for sexual gratification. Sexual desire is a fact about ourselves; it focuses on oneself, whereas being in love (Eros) is about another, focused on the Beloved. "For one of the first things Eros does is to obliterate the distinction between giving and receiving." Perhaps this happens because falling in love causes a couple to feel they have become one. Lewis quotes his colleague Charles Williams: "Love you? I *am* you." (Freud makes this same observation when he writes: "At the height of being in love the boundary between ego and object threatens to melt away. Against all the evidence of his senses, a man who is in love declares that 'I' and 'you' are one, and is prepared to behave as if it were a fact."

Lewis makes the interesting observation that our culture tends to be too serious about sex. This may, at first, appear to contradict his description above that, despite a great deal of discussion and preoccupation with sex, the current state of sexuality is "a mess." Lewis, however, refers here to attitude. "Our advertisements, at their sexiest, paint the whole business in terms of the rapt, the intense, the swoony-devout; seldom a hint of gaiety . . . nothing is more needed than a roar of old-fashioned laughter."

Lewis wonders what makes Freud so serious and so preoccupied with sex. "I am sometimes tempted to wonder whether Freudianism is not a great school of prudery and hypocrisy. The suggestion that we are 'shocked' by such interpretations, or that a disgusted recoil is the cause of our resistance, sounds to me like nonsense. I can speak, of course, only for my own sex, and class, and I readily admit that the Viennese ladies who came to consult Freud may have had either chaster or sillier minds than our own: but I can confidently assert that neither I nor anyone I have ever met suffers from such shrinking nausea in the presence of sexual phenomena as the theory seems to demand."

Lewis agrees that sex involves serious aspects of our lives: the obligations involved in being a parent, the spiritual implications, etc. But Lewis says we tend to forget the comic, humorous side to sexuality. He reminds us that Aphrodite, the Greek goddess of love, is always laughing. Lewis states that Venus is "a mocking, mischievous spirit . . . [who] makes games of us."

Lewis reminds lovers that often, when external circumstances are perfect for making love, sexual desire will suddenly leave one or both of them. On the other hand "whenever the overt act is impossible and even glances cannot be exchanged—in trains, in shops, and at . . . parties—she [Venus] will assail them with all her force . . ." Although this leads to great frustration, Lewis observes that "sensible lovers will laugh." Lewis sees humor in our sexual desire being influenced by "such mundane factors as weather, health, diet, circulation and digestion." Comedy cannot help but result. "It is not for nothing that every language and literature in the world is full of jokes about sex," writes Lewis. Although many are "dull or disgusting," Lewis says they serve to keep people from taking sex too seriously, of making a god of it. Lewis warns: "Banish play and laughter from the bed of love and you may let in a false goddess."

Perhaps the greatest contribution Lewis makes to understanding sexuality and love is his clear distinction between being in love and love in its deeper, more mature form. I always tell my Harvard students that if they learn nothing more than to understand clearly this distinction, they may save themselves a lifetime of unnecessary stress.

Half of all marriages end in divorce. From my clinical practice of many years and my research on young adults who come from divorced families, I can say unequivocally that a great deal of the unhappiness in our society results from failure to understand the distinction between being in love (Eros) and loving in the deeper sense (Agape). The majority of couples that come to my office contemplating divorce come because one of them has fallen in love with someone else. That person claims they no longer are in love with their spouse. The husband (or the wife) met someone at work and came to feel those wonderful feelings that were once felt toward the spouse—of being in love. Mistaking the feeling of being in love as the only basis for a relationship and the only source of real happiness, the person sees no reason for staying in the marriage. He (or she) fails to realize that the feeling of being in love in the new relationship will also inevitably change, so that he may find himself once more in love with yet another person. A high percentage of second marriages end in divorce.

Lewis believes divorce is like the amputation of a limb, considered only as a last, lifesaving resort. But should two people stay together if they are no longer in love? Lewis gives "several, sound social reasons" for doing so. First, "to provide a home for the children." Second, "to protect the woman . . . from being dropped whenever the man is tired of her."

The third reason Lewis gives is, based on my clinical experience, the most insightful and most helpful of all. The state of being in love is a significant, wonderful human experience. Lewis writes that this "glorious state . . . helps make us generous and courageous . . . opens our eyes, not only to the beauty of the beloved but to all beauty . . . and is the great conqueror of lust." But Lewis makes the startling statement that being in love does not last, nor is it intended to last. "Being in love is a good thing . . . it is a noble feeling, but it is still a feeling . . . no feeling can be relied on to last to its full intensity . . . feelings come and go."

He explains that the "state of being in love" involves a kind of intensity and excitement that, if it persisted, would interfere with sleep, work, and appetite. The intense feeling of being in love ought to change to a deeper, more comfortable and mature kind of love based on the will as well as on feeling. Lewis explains that "ceasing to be 'in love' need not mean ceasing to love . . . Love in this second sense—love as distinct from 'being in love'—is not merely a feeling. It is a deep unity, maintained by the will and deliberately strengthened by habit . . ." Lewis says a couple can "retain this love even when each would easily, if they allowed themselves, be 'in love' with someone else." Lewis asserts that being in love brings people together and motivates them to promise fidelity; the quieter, deeper, more mature love helps them keep their promise.

Both Freud and Lewis agree that for the well-being of both the individual and society, sexual impulses need to be controlled. Their reasons, however, differ considerably. Freud argues that civilization imposes certain restrictions on the individual to maintain social order. This causes the individual to be discontent and less than happy. Lewis argues that the moral law comes from a Creator who loves us and desires our happiness. Following that law will help us to love more effectively and, therefore, to be more happy. A look at how they controlled their own sexual impulses before and after their marriages sheds some light on both arguments.

The Sexual Life of Freud

Freud lived his sexual life, most of his biographers agree, in strict compliance to the traditional code of "sex within marriage with complete fidelity—or abstinence." Although he fought for greater freedom in sexual expression, his own conduct, as far as we know, adhered closely to this code. "I stand for an incomparably freer sexual life, although I myself have made very little use of such freedom . . . ," Freud wrote to Dr. Putnam in Boston.

We know little of Freud's romantic daydreams or sexual feelings until he was sixteen years of age. At that time he developed his "first love." During a visit to Freiberg, where the Freuds lived before moving to Vienna, Freud met a young woman named Gisela Fluss, a year younger than he and the sister of a friend. Freud first became infatuated with the girl's mother, Frau Fluss, and wrote at great length of her intelligence and charm and how well she treated him. He then fell in love with Gisela. Because of Freud's shyness and timidity, the relationship developed only in Freud's mind. He apparently never even spoke to her. After a few days, she went away to school. He continued to daydream about her and referred to her and to her mother in letters to his friend Silberstein. He wondered if he had transferred his feelings from the mother to the daughter— perhaps already anticipating some of his later theories.

Freud also mentioned his infatuation with Gisela to his fiancée some ten years later. "Did I ever tell you that Gisela was my first love when I was but 16 years old?" Freud confessed to Martha, his fiancée. "No? Well, then you can have a good laugh at me, firstly on account of my taste and also because I never spoke a meaningful, much less an amiable word to the child. Looking back, I would say that seeing my old hometown again had made me feel sentimental."

Because Freud shared little of the details of his early life, we know relatively little of his early sexual thoughts and experiences. What we do know indicates that because of his shyness and timidity, his involvement was limited to observations and to fantasies. When he was nineteen, Freud visited Trieste and was very conscious of the attractive young women he saw on the streets. "I felt that the city was inhabited by none but Italian goddesses, and I was filled with apprehension," Freud wrote to his friend Silberstein. In the same letter he expressed a preference for blondes: "In Muggia, however, the women, as I said, are more attractive, mostly blonde, oddly enough, which accords with neither Italian nor Jewish descent . . ."

Paradoxically, Freud, the world-renowned explorer of the psyche, admitted he did not understand the mind of women. His letters indicated he thought of women as more noble and more ethical than men, but his ideas of their role in life and in marriage left much to be desired—even for the period in which he lived. Although he maintained good relationships with a number of professional women whom he liked and admired, he felt a woman's place remained in the home.

Responding to an essay on women by J. S. Mill (which some claim was written by Mill's wife), Freud notes that Mill asserts that women should have careers and that a "married woman could earn as much as her husband." In a letter to his fiancée, Freud writes: "We surely agree that the management of a house, the care and bringing up of children, demands the whole of a human being and almost excludes any earning, even if a simplified household relieves her of dusting, cleaning, cooking, etc. He [Mill] had simply forgotten all that, like everything else concerning the relationship between the sexes."

Freud strongly disagrees with Mill's declaration that the suppression of women is analogous to the suppression of the black population. He writes that "any girl . . . whose hand a man kisses and for whose love he is prepared to dare all, could have set him right." Freud concludes his long letter to Martha by predicting that the basic role of women will never change: "Nature has determined woman's destiny through beauty, charm and sweetness. Law and custom have much to give women that has been withheld from them, but the position of women will surely be what it is: in youth an adored darling and in mature years a loved wife."

Many decades later, Freud said to his colleague and friend Marie Bonaparte that "the great question that has never been answered and which I have not yet been able to answer, despite my thirty years of research into the feminine soul, is 'What does a woman want?'" Perhaps most women today would readily agree that Freud didn't understand.

During his early twenties Freud became absorbed in his studies, and we have no record of romantic involvement until a fateful day in April 1882. On that date, Martha Bernays visited the Freud home to call on one of Freud's sisters. Freud fell in love quickly and began sending Martha a red rose every day with a visiting card in Latin, Spanish, English, or German. In one card he referred to her as a fairy princess from whose lips fell roses and pearls. From then on his favorite term of endearment would be "Princess."

Two months after their first meeting they became engaged. But the road ahead was less than smooth. Martha's mother had serious doubts about Freud and about the relationship. The main objection of Martha's family involved Freud's atheism. Most of her family thought of Freud as a heathen. Freud realized they did not like him. He wrote to Martha: "They would have preferred you to marry an old Rabbi . . . An advantage of your family not liking me is that I get you without any family appendages, which is what I most wish."

Martha's family had social prestige but no money. Freud came from a poor family. His father—who himself needed financial assistance—could not even support Freud during the years of his education. (Freud received financial support from some of his friends, including the physician Josef Breuer, his mentor.) Freud not only lacked money to provide for a wife and family, he would be without income for the many years needed to finish his medical training. This resulted in a four-year engagement. To make the situation worse, Martha's mother insisted her daughter live with her in Hamburg, Germany—reasoning that if the engagement had to be a long one, they had best be apart. Freud's feelings toward his future mother-in-law were less than positive and proved an ongoing source of conflict with his fiancée.

Freud did not have the money to visit Martha, and the four years were frustrating. He wrote her more than nine hundred letters—one almost every day—during these years. In the letters he reveals himself as a passionate and fiercely jealous lover.

Freud once met a young man, a close friend of Martha's, whom Freud believed to have romantic feelings toward her. They argued vehemently. The friend threatened to shoot Freud and then himself if Freud did not treat Martha well. The argument became so intense that both broke down in tears. Later, Freud wrote Martha: "The man who brings tears to my eyes must do a great deal before I forgive him. He is no longer my friend, and woe to him if he becomes my enemy. I am made of harder stuff than he is, and when we match each other he will find he is not my equal . . . I can be ruthless."

Freud expressed intense affection and tenderness in his letters as well. All of them begin with "My sweet, precious darling" or "Princess, my little Princess." But also, at times, he could be so frank as to be unkind. In one letter he wrote: "I know you are not beautiful in a painter's or sculptor's sense; if you insist on strict correctness in the use of words then I must confess you are not beautiful." In another letter Freud reminded Martha not to forget "that 'beauty' only stays a few years and that we have to spend a long life together"; and in another letter that "nature shaped your nose and mouth more characteristically than beautifully, with an almost masculine expression, so unmaidenly in its decisiveness." Candor or cruelty? To rule out the latter, Freud threw her a little bouquet: ". . . if there is any vanity left in your little head I will not conceal from you that some people declare you to be beautiful, even strikingly so. I have no opinion on the matter."

Both of Freud's parents came from devout Jewish families, with rabbis among his relatives. Though their theology did not sink in, their sexual ethics did. Freud did not marry until he was thirty, and most biographers agree he had no sexual experience beforehand. Martha Bernays grew up in a strictly observant Orthodox Jewish family. Sex before or outside of marriage was forbidden. Peter Gay writes that "during their long engagement her virginity remained intact" and they limited their contact to "hugs and kisses." And

Freud's official biographer, Ernest Jones, described Freud as "peculiarly monogamous," arguing that he remained faithful throughout his marriage.

On Easter Sunday 1886, Freud opened a private office to begin his practice in "Nervous Diseases." He worried about being able to make a living. He confessed he could not, at times, afford to take a cab to make house calls.

He tried to borrow money from friends to make his wedding possible and even wrote to Martha's mother begging her to raise a loan from her wealthy sister. The request was turned down. In a rather embarrassing letter, Martha's mother wrote Freud and essentially told him to stop whining and to grow up. "When a man without means or prospect gets engaged to a poor girl he tacitly shoulders a heavy burden for years to come, but he cannot make anyone else responsible for it . . . to run a household without means for it is a curse. It is one I have borne for years, so I can judge. I beg and implore you not to do it . . . wait quietly until you have a settled means of existence . . . At the moment you are like a spoilt child who can't get his own way and cries, in the belief in that way he can get everything."

Freud did, nevertheless, save enough. His fiancée's dowry, wedding presents of cash from her family, and gifts from wealthy friends enabled them to marry on September 13, 1886.

The wedding took place in Wandsbek, Germany. Freud hated religious ceremony and talked Martha into a civil one. Soon after, however, they were informed that Austrian law required a religious ceremony and so a second ceremony was held before a few friends the next day. Freud reluctantly recited the Hebrew responses he quickly memorized. Among the many demands Freud made on Martha during their long engagement were that she was always to take his side in arguments with her family, that she must recognize she belonged to him and not to them, and that she must give up her "religious prejudices." He asserted his authority immediately and forbade her from keeping the Sabbath. She shared with her cousin that "not being allowed to light the Sabbath lights on the first Friday night after my marriage was one of the more upsetting experiences of my life."

Freud fathered six children in eight years. Yet his sexual desire appeared to wane for long periods of time even when in his thirties. In 1893, thirty-seven years old, he wrote to his friend Fleiss that "we are now living in abstinence."

Two years later, after the birth of Anna, his last child, Freud discontinued sexual relations with his wife permanently. Some scholars say the reason was to avoid having more children; at that time no satisfactory contraceptive existed. They also point to a lecture he gave in 1916 in which he stated: "We . . . describe a sexual activity as perverse if it has given up the aim of reproduction and pursues the attainment of pleasure as an aim independent of it." (Sometimes it is hard to fathom how Freud became an international symbol of sexual freedom.)

Other scholars point out that Freud ceased sexual activity not immediately after the birth of his last child, but immediately after the death of his father. They point to the profound reaction of Freud to this loss, which he described as "the most significant event" in his life and one that "revolutionized my soul." They also point to one of Freud's case histories where the patient, after his father's death, "denied himself all enjoyment of women out of a tender sense of guilt." Perhaps Freud suffered in the same way.

In raising his children Freud was a strict and somewhat overprotective father. An interview with Freud's son Oliver revealed that Freud warned his sons of the "dangers" of masturbation. To his peers he wrote, in a paper presented before the Vienna Psychoanalytical Society in 1912, "On the basis of my medical experience, I cannot rule out a permanent reduction in potency as one among the results of masturbation." In another paper Freud wrote that "such substitutive means of sexual satisfaction are by no means harmless; they predispose to the numerous varieties of neuroses and psychoses." In another lecture given at the Vienna Psychiatric Clinic, Freud stated: "You all know the immense aetiological importance attributed by our neurotic patients to their masturbation. They make it responsible for all their troubles and we have the greatest difficulty in persuading them that they are mistaken. In fact, however, we ought to admit to them that they are right, for masturbation is the executive agent of infantile sexuality, from the faulty development of which they are indeed suffering."

Freud thought that a clinical syndrome called neurasthenia, consisting of depression, anxiety, and multiple somatic symptoms, was caused by excessive masturbation. "Whereas true neurasthenia arises from spontaneous emissions or is acquired through masturbation, the factors belonging to the aetiology of anxiety neurosis are such as correspond to a holding back of sexual excitation—such as abstinence when libido is present, unconsummated excitation and, above all, coitus interrruptus." In another paper: "It has become clear to me that various obsessional movements have the meaning of a substitute for the abandoned movements of masturbation."

Freud proved to be an unusually conservative parent in overseeing the social life of his children. When Ernest Jones expressed interest in dating Freud's daughter Anna, Freud wrote a letter politely telling him to stay away. "I thank you very much for your kindness with my little daughter. Perhaps you know her not enough," Freud wrote in July 1914. Freud explained that she was the most gifted and accomplished of his children. He then made a strange statement for one who insisted that sexuality began at birth. "She does not claim to be treated as a woman, being still far away from sexual longings . . . There is an outspoken understanding between me and her that she should not consider marriage or the preliminaries before she gets 2 or 3 years older. I don't think she will break the treaty." Anna was almost nineteen.

Anna Freud never married. I have often wondered why. I found her to be not only highly intelligent, but also warm and personable. When I visited her clinic in London, I sometimes had lunch with her secretary Gina Bon. Once, I asked why Miss Freud had never married. Miss Bon stopped eating, looked at me for a few seconds, and then said, "Don't ever ask that question."

The Sexual Life of C. S. Lewis

How C. S. Lewis expressed his sexuality can be understood, I believe, only in light of the devastating losses of his grandfather, uncle, and mother that he incurred as a nine-year-old boy. When his father sent him away to school, the loss was only compounded. Perhaps the fear of experiencing another loss and reactivating this early, overwhelming trauma kept Lewis from forming any close relationships until he met the woman he married.

Yet he did not lack for desire. "I underwent a violent and wholly successful assault of sexual temptation," Lewis writes in his autobiography, describing vividly the awakening of his sexual urges as a fourteen-year-old adolescent. Before this time, Lewis said he had learned "from another boy" the "mere facts of generation." But at that time he says he was "too young to feel more than a scientific interest in them." Now for the first time he experienced intense desire while observing the movements of a beautiful woman teacher on the dance floor. "She was the first woman I ever 'looked upon to lust after her' . . . a gesture, a tone of voice . . . I was undone." He realized what he felt for this young woman was not "romantic passion." "What I felt for the dancing mistress was sheer appetite; the prose and not the poetry of the flesh." He acknowledged his struggle to control his sexual fantasies, including some of sadomasochism, his self-gratification, and, much later, his intense feelings of guilt. This struggle continued until his transition (or conversion), after which, for the first time, he gained control over these tendencies.

When sixteen years old, Lewis became infatuated with a young Belgian girl whose family had been evacuated to England during the First World War. Lewis wrote to his friend Greeves: "I don't think I have ever been so bucked up about anything in my life, she's an awfully decent sort." In another letter a couple of weeks later, he went into detail about his relationship, closing with: "In any case, it would be impossible now; as she has gone with her mother for a week to visit some other Belgians in Birmingham. But perhaps you are tired of my 'affaires.'" This "affair," however, like Freud's with Gisela Fluss, occurred only in fantasy.

In a letter to Greeves, written sixteen years later when they considered editing these early letters, Lewis decided to "suppress" certain letters—those discussing masturbation, which they referred to as "it," and those discussing the "affair" with the Belgian girl. "I am suppressing . . . all letters that refer to my pretended assignation with the Belgian." Lewis was embarrassed by "that folly" and wondered if his punishment shouldn't include "having [the letters] typed and laid open to posterity." He then added, "I hope this is not really necessary in the case of a sin so old and (I hope) so fully abandoned."

Lewis claimed that as an adolescent he felt no guilt over his sexual thoughts and experiences of self-gratification. "And I may as well say here that the feeling of guilt . . . was a thing which at that time I hardly knew. It took me as long to acquire inhibitions as others (they say) have taken to get rid of them." At eighteen, Lewis entered Oxford University. Whatever restraints he imposed on his sexual life did not arise from his conscience. "When I first came to the University," Lewis later wrote about his early college years, "I was as nearly without a moral conscience as a boy could be." As a soldier, Lewis wrote his friend Greeves that he did not waste his money "on prostitutes, restaurants and tailors, as the gentiles do . . . You will be surprised and, I expect, not a little amused to hear that my views at present are getting almost monastic about all the lusts of the flesh." But he also made it clear that his reasons for refraining from such behavior were not on moral or spiritual grounds. A few weeks later he wrote: "I believe in no God, least of all in one that would punish me for the 'lusts of the flesh.'" What reasons then would Lewis have for avoiding the "lusts of the flesh" at this time in his life? He feared that he might become ill physically or emotionally. Lewis wrote this letter in 1918 when Freud's writings were well known. George Sayer, who knew Lewis for many years, writes in his biography of Lewis that "some doctors said it [masturbation] could lead to insanity as well as to various bodily diseases. The habit caused him more misery than anything else in his early life."

Though we have no details of Lewis's sexual relationships before his transition, we know that he had a robust sexual appetite and felt no moral restraint in satisfying it. Before his conversion he noticed others he admired appeared to live on a higher ethical plane, and he tried to imitate them. He failed—especially, he admitted, in the areas of "lust and anger." Lewis apparently had a temper that he found difficult to control. When he began to examine himself seriously for the first time, he found "what appalled me . . . a zoo of lusts." Without resources outside of himself, he found he could do little to control his impulses.

As a tutor at Oxford, Lewis possessed good looks, good voice, good intelligence, and standing-room-only popularity as a lecturer. He managed, nevertheless, to avoid romantic involvement—even at a time when it was not unusual for tutors to be involved with their woman students. A letter to his father indicated that he tended to use certain defense mechanisms for keeping himself uninvolved with his more attractive students. Such mechanisms didn't always work, however. A close friend and biographer wrote that Lewis gave up teaching a particular female student because he found her so beautiful that "her presence rendered him speechless."

One biographical note asserted that Lewis frequently locked himself in his room when female visitors appeared at the college. Lewis denied this charge. All that we know is that he avoided any romantic involvements. He admitted the fear of being abandoned—a fear present in every child—became intense after his mother's death and must have played a part in this.

People who knew Lewis before and after his transition note the transformation that took place. One prep school classmate recalled Lewis as a "riotously amusing atheist. He was really pretty foul mouthed about it." When he met Lewis after his conversion many years later, he noticed "the complete transformation of character" that had occurred and "was staggered to find him the author of *The Screwtape Letters.*"

When Lewis finally fell in love and enjoyed the full expression of his sexuality, the intensity, passion, and drama of the affair would become known around the world. A London and Broadway play, several books, a television series, and a movie attempt to recapture the love, joy, and pathos of this unusual love story.

How did Lewis finally become involved romantically in light of his many defenses? An American Jewish woman, an author, named Joy Davidman Gresham, read Lewis's books and through those writings experienced a change in worldview from atheism similar to what Lewis had experienced.

Joy Davidman was born in New York City, attended Hunter College, and pursued graduate studies at Columbia University. She made her living as a writer and won the Yale Poetry Award in 1938 for a book of verse, *Letter to a Comrade.* She published two novels. She joined the Communist Party and worked as a film critic and poetry editor for the Communist paper *New Masses*. She also spent time in Hollywood as a scriptwriter for Metro-Goldwyn-Mayer. She met and married William Gresham, like her a member of the Communist Party, an atheist, and a gifted novelist. He had previously been married and divorced.

William Gresham suffered from severe depression, suicidal tendencies, an addiction to alcohol, and a tendency to become involved with other women. Psychiatric treatment relieved the depression but the heavy drinking continued. The marriage proved difficult. Once he called Joy and said he would not be coming home. She felt hopeless and desperate and found herself on her knees crying out to God. In an article describing her conversion, Joy wrote, ". . . the walls of arrogance and cocksureness and self love behind which I had hid from God went down momentarily. And God came in." She had been influenced by the writings of Lewis, and she decided to write to him in early 1950. Lewis found her letters unusually well written and witty.

In September of 1952, Joy boldly decided to travel to London to see if she could meet Lewis. She invited him to lunch. He returned the invitation by asking her to lunch at Oxford. That lunch began a relationship that would, after several years, end in the celebrated love affair.

Lewis found Joy fascinating. Her bold, abrasive bluntness startled and amused him. She shared many interests with him and many likes and dislikes. They shared a profound interest in great literature and in writing. They both hated the city and loved the country. She criticized modern America. Lewis, like Freud, harbored a similarly negative view of America and Americans, and he found Joy's criticism amusing.

In December of 1952, Joy received a letter from her husband requesting a divorce and announcing that he was in love with her cousin Renée Pierce. When Joy returned home, she found them sleeping together and agreed to the divorce. She then moved to London with her two young sons in the summer of 1953. We have no record of how much contact she had with Lewis over the next couple of years. In 1955, Joy and her two boys moved from London to a home in Headington, close to where Lewis lived. She began to help him with his writing and they met frequently.

At this time the Home Office refused to renew Joy's permit to remain in Great Britain, perhaps because of her background as a Communist. Lewis felt pity for her and offered to marry her in a civil ceremony, simply to allow her to stay in England. For several reasons, he did not plan to consummate the marriage. First, he appeared to be unaware of any romantic feelings for Joy. He viewed her as a good friend. Second, he felt a church ceremony impossible because of cannon law forbidding marriage to a divorced person. He wrote Greeves that he thought a real marriage was "from my point of view, adultery, and therefore mustn't happen." The civil ceremony took place privately on April 23, 1956, and Joy and the children stayed in England.

In October of that year an event occurred that would change dramatically the nature of their relationship. Joy became ill with cancer of the bone, which had spread from a primary site in the breast. Lewis wrote his friend Greeves that "she may die in a few months." He felt a responsibility to take her and her children into his home and look after them. He made public their civil marriage. The *Times* of December 24, 1956, announced: "A marriage has taken place between Professor C. S. Lewis, of Magdalene College, Cambridge, and Mrs. Joy Gresham, now a patient in the Churchill Hospital, Oxford. It is requested that no letters be sent."

Perhaps the thought of losing Joy made Lewis realize not only that he loved her, but was deeply in love with her and wanted her fully as his wife. How he obtained permission to marry her within the church, as Joy desired, presents a complicated story, the de-

tails of which we know little. Apparently, Lewis argued that because Bill Gresham had been married before he married Joy, and
his first wife was still living, their marriage was not a true Christian
marriage. An old pupil of Lewis, the Reverend Peter Bide, agreed
and married them at Joy's bedside at the Churchill Hospital at Oxford on April 21, 1957. Lewis's brother Warren wrote in his diary
of the marriage ceremony: "I found it heart-rending, and especially Joy's eagerness for the pitiable consolation of dying under
the same roof as Jack, though to feel pity for anyone so magnifi-
cently brave as Joy is an insult . . . There seems little left to hope
but that there may be no pain at the end."

Joy moved into the Kilns, the home of Lewis. Lewis wrote in
May that "Joy is home . . . hospital can do no more for her . . .
completely bedridden. But thank God, no pain . . . and often in
good spirits." Before Reverend Bide married Joy and Jack Lewis,
he prayed for her recovery, and Jack continued to do so. Then
something happened many considered miraculous. Joy began to
recover, and then to walk. She wrote a friend in June 1957 that
"Jack and I are managing to be surprisingly happy considering the
circumstances." In July they flew to Ireland for a belated honeymoon. Lewis lived with his wife in "sheer happiness and contentment," according to friends who visited them. Once he mentioned
to a friend, "I never expected to have in my sixties, that happiness
that passed me by in my twenties." Joy had, for many years, desired to visit Greece. In April 1960, with another couple, they
spent ten days vacationing there.

When Joy came to England with the hope of meeting C. S. Lewis,
she not only met him, she smashed through all of his defenses, and
simply stepped over the sign that said PLEASE, DO NOT INTERFERE.
They enjoyed three years and four months of bliss. Letters written
by Joy are "brimming over with happiness," according to biographers. She wrote, "You'd think we were a honeymoon couple in our

early twenties," and commented openly on Lewis's sexual prowess. Lewis wrote in *Surprised by Joy:* "For those few years [my wife] and I feasted on love; every mode of it . . . No cranny of heart or body remained unsatisfied."

When we look at how Freud and Lewis expressed their own sexuality, Freud appears to have had a considerably more restricted sexual life than Lewis. Most biographers agree that Freud had no sexual experience before his marriage at thirty. His sexual activity during marriage appears to have lasted only a few years. Can it be possible that the father of the new sexual freedom restricted his own sexuality to only ten of his eighty-three years of life? If so, why? Is Lewis right in accusing Freud of viewing sex as shocking and disgusting—as did the Viennese ladies he treated?

Certainly, Lewis had a more active sexual life than Freud. He enjoyed a late-life sexual vigor with a woman who became first a friend and then a lover. After his conversion, and before his marriage, when he appeared to be able for the first time to control his sexual impulses, he seemed to be more content with himself and with his relationships. Why? Perhaps the Harvard students I researched can give us a clue.

Before their conversion experience, the students described their sexual relationships as less than satisfactory and as contributing little to providing the emotional closeness they desired. They expressed a profound loneliness and a "sense of not belonging." Their sexual behavior by and large appeared to be a desperate attempt to overcome this loneliness. After their conversion experience, they attempted, like Lewis, to live the strict biblical standard of chastity or marriage with complete fidelity. Though this severe restriction conflicted strongly with their past behavior, and with current mores, they found these clear-cut boundaries less confusing than no boundaries at all and helpful in relating to members of the opposite sex "as persons rather than sexual objects."

Had Freud reached a similar personal conviction based on his clinical observations? We can only speculate. Certainly he raised his children with the clear-cut boundaries that he himself embraced, in sharp contrast to his public appeal for "an incomparably freer sexual life." Perhaps he tacitly concluded, as did Lewis, that "for any happiness, even in this world, quite a lot of restraint is going to be necessary."

~❧7❧~

LOVE

Is All Love
Sublimated Sex?

Both Freud and Lewis write prolifically about love. Both realize the word "love" is used carelessly, has many different meanings, and must be clearly defined. We describe our feelings toward our country, our dog, our children, our friends, our parents, or our spouse all with the word "love." We mean something quite different in each instance.

Freud divides all forms of human love into two basic categories: sexual (genital) love, and love in which the sexual desire is unconscious. "The careless way in which language uses the word 'love' has its genetic justification," Freud writes in *Civilization and Its Discontents*. "People give the name 'love' to the relation between a man and a woman whose genital needs have led them to found a family; but they also give the name 'love' to the positive feelings between parents and children, and between the brothers and sisters of a family." Love between a husband and a wife is "genital love"; love be-

160

tween siblings and between children and parents is "aim-inhibited love" or "affection." Libido—the psychic energy of Eros—may be expressed overtly in an erotic relationship, or sublimated and present only in the unconscious: "Love with an inhibited aim was in fact originally fully sensual love, and it is so still in a man's unconscious. Both—fully sensual love, and aim-inhibited love—extend outside the family and create new bonds with people who before were strangers. Genital love leads to the formation of new families, and aim-inhibited love to 'friendships.'"

Love within the family, and friendship, are forms of love that "have not abandoned their directly sexual aims, but they are held back by internal resistances from attaining them; they rest content with certain approximations to satisfaction and for that very reason lead to especially firm and permanent attachments between human beings. To this class belong in particular the affectionate relations between parents and children, which were originally fully sexual, feelings of friendship, and the emotional ties in marriage which had their origin in sexual attraction."

Freud realized the strong resistance people would have toward his labeling all forms of love "sexual." He attempted to head it off. "The nucleus of what we mean by love naturally consists (and this is what the poets sing of) in sexual love with sexual union as its aim. But we do not separate from this—what in any case has a share in the name 'love'—on the one hand, self-love, and on the other, love for parents and children, friendship and love for humanity in general."

To label love for humanity and love between children and parents and between friends as "sexual" evokes scorn and rejection. Why did Freud do it? In his *Group Psychology and the Analysis of the Ego*, he explains: "Our justification lies in the fact that psychoanalytic research has taught us that all these tendencies are an expression of the same instinctual impulses; in the relations between

the sexes these impulses force their way toward sexual union . . ." In
other forms of love, sexual impulses are "diverted from this aim" but
are nevertheless sexual. "By coming to this decision, psycho-analysis
has let loose a storm of indignation, as though it had been guilty of
an act of outrageous innovation. Yet it has done nothing original in
taking love in this 'wider' sense. In its origin, function, and relation
to sexual love, the 'Eros' of the philosopher Plato coincides exactly
with the love-force, the libido of psychoanalysis . . . when the apostle Paul, in his famous epistle to the Corinthians, praises love above
all else, he certainly understands it in the same 'wider' sense." The
quote from 1 Corinthians is given by Freud as: "Though I speak with
the tongues of men and of angels, and have not charity [love], I am
become as sounding brass or a tinkling cymbal." Freud laments that
"this only shows that men do not take their great thinkers seriously,
even when they profess most to admire them." It is not entirely clear
whether Freud was referring to Plato, Paul, or himself.

Freud argued: "I cannot see any merit in being ashamed of sex;
the Greek word 'Eros,' which is to soften the affront, is in the end
nothing more than a translation of our German word Liebe [love]."

So is love really only about sex? Or is this a materialist extreme?
To give credit where it is due, Freud provides a great deal of insight
into the complex nature of all relationships. He helps us understand
why, in all groups—a family, a club, a church, a college, a corporation, an athletic team, a hospital—the primary problems involve not
the task the organization exists to perform, but conflict between
people. One reason for this, he explains, is that all of us harbor negative feelings toward others. These feelings are usually repressed
and unrecognized. They nevertheless, influence our behavior and
create interpersonal conflict.

Freud writes that "almost every intimate emotional relation between two people which lasts for some time—marriage, friendship,
the relations between parents and children—contains a sediment of

feelings of aversion and hostility, which only escapes perception as a result of repression." We see this clearly in the "common wrangles between business partners." This underlying hostility and tendency to look down on others also expresses itself in large groups. "Every time two families become connected by a marriage, each of them thinks itself superior to or of better birth than the other. Of two neighboring towns each is the other's most jealous rival; every little canton looks down upon the others with contempt." Another phrase bequeathed by Freud is the "narcissism of minor differences." Freud gives geographical national, and racial examples: "The South German cannot endure the North German, the Englishman casts every kind of aspersion upon the Scot, the Spaniard despises the Portuguese." He mentions the "almost insuperable repugnance, such as the Gallic people feel for the German, the Aryan for the Semite, and the white races for the colored."

Freud acknowledges that we don't fully understand why this underlying hostility exists "but it is unmistakable that in this whole connection men give evidence of a readiness for hatred, an aggressiveness the source of which is unknown, and to which one is tempted to ascribe an Elementary character."

Freud also provides insight into how we select our love relationships. He asserts that our early life experiences strongly influence whom we choose to marry as well as our choice of friends. In a 1922 article, Freud wrote, "The nature and quality of the human child's relations to people of his own and the opposite sex have already been laid down in the first six years of his life. He may afterwards develop and transform them in certain directions, but he can no longer get rid of them. The people to whom he is in this way fixed are his parents and his brothers and sisters."

He then makes the startling statement that all of our adult relationships are to some measure determined by these early relationships: "All those whom he gets to know later become substitute figures for these first objects of his feelings . . . His later acquaintances are thus obliged to take over a kind of emotional heritage; they encounter sympathies and antipathies to the production of which they have contributed little. All of his later choices of friendship and love follow upon the basis of the memory-traces left behind by these first prototypes."

Freud eventually developed his theory of *transference,* one that would play a key role in his method of treating emotional disorders and that still today gives us some insight into how we choose both our friends and the person we marry. Feelings in relationships as we now understand them run on a double track. We react and relate to another person not only on the basis of how we consciously experience that person, but also on the basis of our unconscious experience in reference to our past relationships with significant people in infancy and childhood—particularly parents and other family members. We tend to displace our feelings and attitudes from these past figures onto people in the present, especially if someone has features similar to a person in the past. An individual may, therefore, evoke intense feelings in us—strong attraction or strong aversion—totally inappropriate to our knowledge of or experience with that person. This process may, to varying degrees, influence our choice of a friend, roommate, spouse, or employer. We all have the experience of seeing someone we have never met who evokes in us strong feelings. According to the theory of transference, this occurs because something about that person—the gait, the tilt of the head, a laugh, or some other feature—recalls a significant figure in our early childhood. Sometimes a spouse or a superior we work under will provoke in us a reaction far more intense than the circumstances warrant. A gesture or tone of voice may reactivate early negative feelings we experienced toward an important childhood figure.

*   *   *

Although transference reactions occur in all relationships, they occur most frequently and most intensely in relationships with authority. This happens especially in doctor-patient relationships, partly because patients often view the doctor as an authority figure and tend to displace onto him feelings once directed toward their parents, the first authorities in their lives. "[T]he patient sees in [the doctor] the return, the reincarnation, of some important figure out of his childhood or past, and consequently transfers on to him feelings and reactions which undoubtedly applied to this prototype. The fact of transference soon proves to be a factor of undreamt-of importance." Freud realized that the positive feelings of the patient for the doctor ("positive" transference) provided a strong motivating force for the patient to improve. In a letter to Jung discussing the basis of psychoanalytic work, Freud wrote: "Essentially, one might say, the cure is effected by love." With the development of his concept of transference, Freud made a fundamental contribution to our understanding of all human relationships.

Nonetheless, Lewis thought Freud's understanding of love and relationships was incomplete. C. S. Lewis drew on the great literature for his discussion of love. His approach is more detailed than Freud's clinical approach. He focused a considerable part of his scholarly work on human love. His books *The Allegory of Love* and *The Four Loves* are classics.

Lewis first divides all love into two broad categories. One is a love based on need; the other is a love free of need. In *The Four Loves*, Lewis writes: "The first distinction I made was therefore between what I called Gift-love and Need-love. The typical example of Gift-love would be that love which moves a man to work and plan and save for the future well-being of his family which he will die without sharing or seeing; of the second, that which sends a lonely or frightened child to its mother's arms." "Need-love says of a woman 'I cannot live without her'; Gift-love longs to give her happiness, comfort, protection—if possible, wealth."

Like Freud, Lewis quotes the New Testament that "God is love" and warns that we must be careful not to translate that into "love is God." Lewis makes an interesting observation that every form of human love can become a form of idolatry and cause one to commit unloving acts in its name. He writes that love "begins to be a demon the moment he begins to be a god." People tend to do things their conscience would never otherwise allow, all in the name of love. "Every human love, at its height, has a tendency to claim for itself a divine authority. Its voice tends to sound as if it were the will of God Himself." Lewis writes in *The Four Loves:* "Love for a woman may cause a man to break his vows and neglect his wife and children, love of country may cause a person to commit unthinkable atrocities and love of the church may motivate people actually to do evil." "If ever the book which I am not going to write is written," Lewis declares with his usual candor, "it must be the full confession by Christendom of Christendom's specific contribution to the sum of human cruelty and treachery . . . We have shouted the name of Christ and enacted the service of Moloch."

Lewis divides human love further into four categories—following the Greek tradition: (1) Storge, affection between members of a family; (2) Philia, friendship; (3) Eros, romantic love between people "in love"; and (4) Agape, the love one has toward God and one's neighbor. In a letter to a friend, Lewis defines these different forms further: "'Charity' means love. It is called Agape in the New Testament to distinguish it from Eros (sexual love), Storge (family affection) and Philia (friendship) . . . there are four kinds of love, all good in their proper place, but Agape is the best because it is the kind God has for us and is good in all circumstances. There are people I mustn't feel Eros towards, and people I can't feel Storge or Philia for; but I can practice Agape to God . . . Man and Beast, to the good and the bad, the old and the young, the far and the near. You see Agape is all giving, not getting . . . Giving money is only 'one' way of showing charity; to give time and toil is far better and (for most of us) harder."

Storge is that form of human love we call "affection." The Greeks used the term originally to refer to affection within the family. "My Greek Lexicon defines *storge* as 'affection, especially of parents to offspring'; but also of offspring to parents," writes Lewis. "And that, I have no doubt, is the original form of the thing as well as the central meaning of the word." We can feel affection for people outside the family as well. The main criterion appears to be a comfortable familiarity. We may feel affection toward a person with whom we share no interests, and therefore toward people not our friends. We feel affection, Lewis says, toward people merely because we have known them a long time and are familiar and comfortable with them. He captures these feelings in descriptive language: "Affection almost slinks or seeps through our lives. It lives with humble, un-dress, private things: soft slippers, old clothes, old jokes, the thump of a sleepy dog's tail on the kitchen floor, the sound of a sewing machine . . ."

Lewis notes that affection is expressed appropriately in comfortable, private, quiet settings—not in public ones. When expressed in public, affection can make others uncomfortable. Lewis says that "affection would not be affection if it was loudly and frequently expressed; to produce it in public is like getting your household furniture out for a move. It did very well in its place, but it looks shabby or tawdry or grotesque in the sunshine."

Lewis also describes affection as modest. "People can be proud of being 'in love,' or of friendship," he explains. "Affection is modest—even furtive and shame-faced . . . It usually needs absence or bereavement to set us praising those to whom only Affection binds us. We take them for granted: and this taking for granted, which is an outrage in erotic love, is here right and proper up to a point. It fits the comfortable, quiet nature of the feeling."

Affection can accompany other forms of love. We can feel affection for a friend. "To make a friend is not the same as to become affectionate . . . But when your friend has become an old friend, all those things about him which had originally nothing to do with the friendship become familiar and dear with familiarity."

Affection extends far beyond the family and can blend with other forms of love. Affection is and should be a part of Eros. Sexual love without affection would be cold and uninviting. Affection, Lewis writes, is the least discriminating of the loves: ". . . almost anyone can become an object of affection; the ugly, the stupid, even the exasperating . . . I have seen it felt for an imbecile not only by his parents but by his brothers . . . It ignores even the barriers of species. We see it not only between dog and man but, more surprisingly between dog and cat."

Lewis offers an interesting warning concerning relationships based on affection and familiarity. They can pose a danger because they can tempt one to take liberties. "Affection is an affair of old clothes, and ease, of the unguarded moment, of liberties which would be ill-bred if we took them with strangers." But Lewis warns that "the more intimate the occasion, the less the formalization; but not therefore the less need of courtesy. On the contrary, Affection at its best practices a courtesy which is incomparably more subtle, sensitive, and deep than the public kind . . . You can say 'Shut up. I want to read.' You can do anything in the right tone and at the right moment—the tone and moment which are not intended to, and will not, hurt. The better the Affection the more unerringly it knows which these are (every love has its 'art of love')."

Of course, families often fail to practice courtesy. "Who has not been the embarrassed guest at family meals where the father or mother treated their grown-up offspring with an incivility which, offered to any other young people, would simply have terminated the acquaintance? Dogmatic assertions on matters which the children understand and their elders don't, ruthless interruptions, flat contradictions, ridicule of things the young take seriously."

Lewis believes that the love we call affection gives us a large share of our happiness on this earth—if "there is common sense and give and take and 'decency' . . . Affection is responsible for nine-tenths of whatever solid and durable happiness there is in our natural lives."

Lewis joins Freud in warning that all forms of human love "carry in them the seeds of hate." If one has a need to be needed and that need is not met by the child or parent, the need can become more and more demanding and the frustration can turn the love into hate. Lewis warns: "It was of erotic love that the Roman poet said, 'I love and hate,' but other kinds of love admit the same mixture. They carry in them the seeds of hatred. If Affection is made the absolute sovereign of a human life the seeds will germinate. Love, having become a god, becomes a demon." Though on the surface Freud and Lewis seem to agree, Lewis does not suggest that sexuality is central or even peripheral to Storge.

*   *   *

When Lewis considers Philia, or friendship, he disagrees with Freud even more strongly. He sees no basis for considering friendship as a form of repressed sexuality. Freud called it "aim-inhibited" love, but Lewis described four very different characteristics of friendship:

a. It is the least necessary of the various forms of love: "Without Eros none of us would have been begotten and without Affection none of us would have been reared; but we can live and breed without Friendship. The species, biologically considered, has no need of it."

b. It is the least natural of the loves: "the least instinctive, organic, biological, gregarious and necessary. It has least commerce with our nerves; there is nothing throaty about it; nothing that quickens the pulse or turns you red and pale."

c. It is the least appreciated in our modern culture: Friendship "is essentially between individuals; the moment two men are friends they have in some degree drawn apart from the herd . . . The pack or herd—the community—may even dislike and distrust it." Leaders of groups and organizations "feel uneasy when close and strong friendships arise between little knots of their subjects . . . that outlook which values the collective above the individual necessarily disparages Friendship; it is a relation between men at their highest level of individuality."

d. It is different from erotic love but can deepen and enhance it. Lewis says that viewing all love as sexual is nonsense.

Referring to Freud's definition of friendship, Lewis writes that those who see friendship "only as a disguise or elaboration of Eros betray the fact that they never had a friend . . . though we can have erotic love and friendship for the same person . . . nothing is less like a friendship than a love affair . . . Lovers are normally face to face absorbed in each other; friends side by side absorbed in some common interest." But lovers may also become friends and friends lovers.

When two people of the opposite sex meet and find they share a common interest, "the friendship which arises between them will very easily pass—may pass in the first half-hour—into erotic love."

And it may happen the other way around. Two people who fall in love and are sexually attracted may find they share a deep-seated common interest. They then may become friends, in the true sense of friendship, as well as lovers. The difference in their relationship is that in erotic love they are focused only on themselves, but as friends they eagerly share with others the interest that binds them together.

Lewis states that the union of Eros and friendship "so far from obliterating the distinction between the two loves, puts it in a clearer light. If one who was first, in the deep and full sense, your Friend, is then gradually or suddenly revealed as also your lover you will certainly not want to share the Beloved's erotic love with any third. But you will have no jealousy at all about sharing the Friendship. Nothing so enriches an erotic love as the discovery that the Beloved can deeply, truly and spontaneously enter into Friendship with the Friends you already had: to feel that not only are we two united by erotic love but we three or four or five are all travelers on the same quest, have all a common vision."

In his discussion of Philia, Lewis gives us a clue as to how he felt about his own friends. He writes that in a group of friends each holds the other in such respect that he feels "in his secret heart humbled before all the rest. Sometimes he wonders what he is doing there among his betters. He is lucky beyond desert to be in such company."

Lewis had many close friends that he met with regularly for long walks and stimulating conversation. He writes that the pleasure of friendship is greatest "when the whole group is together, each bringing out all that is best, wisest, or funniest in all the others. Those are the golden sessions; when four or five of us after a hard day's walking have come to our inn; when our slippers are on, our feet spread out towards the blaze and our drinks at our elbows; when the whole world, and something beyond the world, opens itself to our minds as we talk; and no one has any claim on or any responsibility for another, but all are freemen and equals as if we had first met an hour ago, while at the same time an Affection mellowed by the years enfolds us. Life—natural life—has no better gift to give. Who could have deserved it?"

Lewis believed that friendship carries certain dangers. Sometimes we desire to be included within a group of people not because we share a deep-seated interest with them, but simply because we see them as part of an "in group." If a group exists not on the basis of shared interests, as with true friendship, but "for the sake of the pleasures of conceit and superiority," then that group falls into the danger of "pride . . . the danger to which Friendships are naturally liable."

Such groups attract people who join for reasons other than the shared interests that form the basis of real friendships. "The snob wishes to attach himself to some group because it is already regarded as an 'elite'; friends are in danger of coming to regard themselves as an 'elite' because they are already attached . . ." "Pride," Lewis points out, "is the utmost evil . . . the essential vice . . . the complete anti-God state of mind . . . the pleasure of being above the rest . . . always looking down on people."

In every group of people—at home, school, college, hospital, law firm, or corporation—there exists what Lewis calls "The Inner Ring." Lewis asserts that everyone at some time in their lives struggles with "the desire to be inside the local Ring, and the terror of being left outside." The fear of being left out, of not being part of the important circle, causes considerable stress and unhappiness. To be accepted by the people we think important, to be part of the Inner Ring, we often do things against our better judgment. Lewis writes: "Freud would say, no doubt, that the whole thing is a subterfuge of the sexual impulse. I wonder whether the shoe is not sometimes on the other foot. I wonder whether, in ages of promiscuity, many a virginity has not been lost less in obedience to Venus than in obedience to the lure of the caucus. For of course, when promiscuity is the fashion, the chaste are outsiders. They are ignorant of something that other people know . . . As for lighter matters, the number who first smoked or first got drunk for a similar reason is probably very large."

Lewis makes clear that he believes wherever people live and work, Inner Rings will form and are not in themselves evil. Only the desire to be in them is. He then gives an example of how a thing may in itself be morally neutral but the desire for it immoral: "The painless death of a pious relative at an advanced age is not an evil. But an earnest desire for her death is not reckoned a proper feeling, and the law frowns on even the gentlest attempt to expedite her departure."

What motivates us to desire the Inner Ring? Lewis lists several reasons, including the desire for "power, money, liberty to break the rules, avoidance of routine duties," but most of all, "the delicious sense of secret intimacy." Lewis warns that "of all the passions, the passion for the Inner Ring is most skillful of all in making a person . . . do very bad things." And Lewis observes that the greater the fear of being an outsider, the more likely one will remain an outsider. "Until you conquer the fear of being an outsider, an outsider you will remain." He adds that "the quest of the Inner Ring will break your hearts unless you break it."

Lewis offers insight into how to gain acceptance in the world of work independent of any Inner Ring: "If in your working hours you make the work your end, you will presently find yourself all unawares inside the only circle in your profession that really matters. You will be one of the sound craftsmen, and other sound craftsmen will know it."

And similarly: "If in your spare time you consort simply with the people you like, you will again find that you have come unawares to a real inside: that you are indeed snug and safe at the center of something which, seen from without, would look exactly like an Inner Ring." But there is a major difference from the usual Inner Ring: "Its secrecy is accidental, and its exclusiveness a by-product, and no one was led thither by the lure of the esoteric: for it is only four or five people who like one another meeting to do things that they like." Lewis calls this type of ring "friendship." He concludes that friendship "causes perhaps half of all the happiness in the world, and no Inner Ringer can ever have it."

To illustrate how Eros, Affection, and Philia can overlap and blend with one another, Lewis points to the kiss. Lewis reminds us that "at most times and places all three of them had in common, as their expression, the kiss. In modern England Friendship no longer uses it, but Affection and Eros do." Lewis says we don't know whether the kiss started as an expression of one or the other. He adds: "To be sure, you may say that the kiss of Affection differs from the kiss of Eros. Yes; but not all kisses between lovers are lovers' kisses."

✿   ✿   ✿

Freud and Lewis both write about one aspect of love with considerable intensity. This form of human love, referred to in both the Hebrew Scriptures and the New Testament, involves a basic precept of the spiritual worldview that Freud attacks: "Love your neighbor as yourself."

Freud realized the existence of a form of human love that didn't quite fit his classification. Some people commit their entire lives to serving others with no obvious selfish motivation. He decided their unselfishness was somehow born out of a desire to protect themselves. Since investing emotion in a "love-object" carries risks, Freud believed that some people have the capacity to "protect themselves against the loss of the object by directing their love, not to single objects, but to all men alike . . . a universal love of mankind . . . What they bring about in themselves in this way is a state of evenly suspended, steadfast, affectionate feeling, which has little external resemblance of . . . genital love, from which it is nevertheless derived. Perhaps St. Francis of Assisi went furthest in thus exploiting love for the benefit of an inner feeling of happiness." Freud asserts that the difficulty with this kind of "universal love" is that "not all men are worthy of love."

Indeed, for Freud, the great commandment to "Love your neighbor as yourself" is absurd. His sledgehammer attacks on religion were not simply directed at "the miracles" and "the doctrines," but also this teaching. Freud says this precept "is known throughout the world and is undoubtedly older than Christianity, which puts it forward as its proudest claim." (Indeed, it originated in the book of Leviticus [19:18] in the Hebrew scriptures.)

Freud says this commandment, along with "love your enemies," absolutely bewilders him. He simply cannot understand it. He asks: "Why should we do it? What good will it do us? But, above all, how shall we achieve it? How can it be possible? My love is something valuable to me which I ought not to throw away without reflection . . . If I love someone, he must deserve it in some way . . . He deserves it if he is so like me in important ways that I can love myself in him; and he deserves it if he is so much more perfect than myself that I can love my ideal of my own self in him . . . But if he is a stranger to me and if he cannot attract me by any worth of his own or any significance that he may already have acquired for my emotional life, it will be hard for me to love him. Indeed, I should be wrong to do so, for my love is valued by all my own people as a sign of my preferring them, and it is an injustice to them if I put a stranger on a par with them."

Furthermore, Freud writes, when he thinks about it, his neighbor has no love for him and often does him harm. "If it will do him any good," Freud asserts, "he has no hesitation in injuring me . . . he thinks nothing of jeering at me, insulting me, slandering me and showing his superior power; and the more secure he feels and the more helpless I am, the more certainly I can expect expect him to behave like this to me." Freud concludes, "I must honestly confess that [my neighbor] has more claim to my hostility and even my hatred." Freud says he could understand this commandment if it stated "Love your neighbor as your neighbor loves you."

Freud warns that people tend to forget that "men are not gentle creatures who want to be loved, and who at the most can defend themselves if they are attacked; they are, on the contrary, creatures among whose instinctual endowments is to be reckoned a powerful share of aggressiveness." He then asks, "What is the point of a precept enunciated with so much solemnity if its fulfillment cannot be recommended as reasonable?" He concludes that "nothing runs so strongly counter to the original nature of man."

Lewis agrees with Freud that this precept runs counter to our original nature. But for that reason we need a new nature, we need to be reborn spiritually, we need "alteration." The key to understanding the precept "to love your neighbor as yourself," Lewis says, is to understand the phrase "as yourself." How do we love ourselves? We love ourselves, says Lewis, by wanting the best for ourselves and acting accordingly, even when we don't like ourselves. Everything we do, from the time we arise in the morning to the time we go to bed at night, eating, exercising, bathing, working, is all done because we want the best for ourselves. And we use our will to carry out these activities, whether we feel like doing them or not.

Lewis writes: "I have not exactly got a feeling of fondness or affection for myself, and I do not even always enjoy my own society. So apparently 'Love your neighbor' does not mean 'feel fond of him.' Indeed, I can look at some of the things I have done with horror and loathing. So apparently I am allowed to loathe and hate some of the things my enemies do." He then recalls teachers telling him it was important to "hate the bad man's actions but not the . . . man." He always thought this a silly distinction: "How could you hate what a man did and not hate the man?" Years later, Lewis realized there was one person to whom he had been doing that all his life—namely, himself. He writes: "However I might dislike my own cowardice or greed, I went on loving myself"—i.e., he continued to want or will the best for himself.

Once Lewis decided to open his mind to exploring the spiritual worldview, he began to read the New Testament in Greek. As he read the two great commandments "Love the Lord your God with all your heart," and "Love your neighbor as yourself," he observed that in both commandments the word for love is Agape. Unlike Eros, Storge, or Philia, which are all based primarily on feeling, Agape is based more on the will. We don't have control over what we feel, but we always have control over our will and, therefore, over what we say and do. And what we say or do determines whether we help or hurt others. Lewis keeps emphasizing that Agape is "a state of the will, which we have naturally about ourselves, and must learn to have about other people."

Agape relates to a basic principle of human relationships. Lewis points out that when you will the best for someone and act accordingly, even toward a person you don't like, you begin to dislike that person less and to like him or her a little more. But the reverse is true as well. "This same spiritual law works terribly in the opposite direction . . . the more cruel you are, the more you will hate; and the more you hate, the more cruel you will become—and so on in a vicious circle for ever." Clinically this principle has been observed time and again. When we inadvertently help someone we don't like, we tend to dislike him or her less; if we do people harm, we dislike them more—perhaps because they make us feel guilty. Although Agape is based primarily on the will, the exercise of this form of love influences our feelings, often by reversing negative feelings into positive ones.

As a clinician, I have observed that Agape is the key to all successful relationships, even those within groups and organizations. In the institutions I have been involved with—hospitals, universities, corporations, and others—I have noticed that the real problems confronting them do not concern their primary task of caring for the sick, educating students, manufacturing a product, or providing a service. Invariably, they suffer from conflicts between people, problems resulting from people acting primarily on feelings of rivalry, jealousy, hatred, revenge, or vindication, rather than on the will. If

Agape determined how we related to others, we could save ourselves and those around us a lot of unnecessary pain. Lewis appeared to have a good grasp of this principle.

◦ ◦ ◦

So much for Lewis and Freud in theory. Their behavior in practice
may be even more revealing of their differences. Freud's life ex-
hibits a pattern of establishing a very close relationship, developing
serious conflict, and then terminating the relationship suddenly.
This happened with Josef Breuer, the mentor who helped and encouraged young Freud as he opened his medical practice; and with
Wilhelm Fliess, his closest friend and confidante during the early
professional years when he worked primarily alone. It also happened with many of his followers, beginning with members of the
discussion group that met on Wednesday evenings at Freud's apart-
ment. (This group eventually became the Vienna Psychoanalytical
Society.)

Freud broke with many of them amid bitter recrimination and
name-calling. Victims included Wilhelm Stekel, Alfred Adler, Carl
Jung, Otto Rank, and Sándor Ferenczi, to name only those better
known. Some of the phrases Freud used to describe his former
colleagues were "an unbearable human being," "a pig," and "a desperate, shameless liar." He said Adler suffered from "paranoid delusions." Several of these colleagues, such as Wilhelm Stekel, Paul
Federn, and Victor Tausk, committed suicide. Looking back on
these fractured relationships Freud attributed them to "personal
differences—jealousy or revenge or some other kind of animosity."

Freud's relationship with Carl Jung presents a well-known example. "He can go jump in the lake; I don't need him and his friendship any more," Freud wrote in a letter after the break. It had
started innocently enough. Jung, a Swiss psychiatrist working under
Dr. Eugen Bleuler, read Freud's *Interpretation of Dreams*, men-

tioned Freud's ideas in a couple of publications, and sent copies to Freud. This began a correspondence that ultimately resulted in a close friendship. Freud liked Jung and decided he would be his successor. Freud often referred to Jung as his "son and heir." Jung became a leader very quickly—chairman of the First International Psychoanalytical Congress and editor of the *Psychoanalytic Yearbook*. This close relationship extended over several years. Freud valued his connection with the Swiss psychiatrists because of their good reputation and because they were Gentiles. Freud feared, because most of his Vienna followers were Jewish, that his new science might incur prejudice. He wrote to his colleague Karl Abraham in 1908, "Our Aryan comrades are really completely indispensable to us, otherwise psychoanalysis would succumb to anti-Semitism."

But disagreements began to emerge between Freud and Jung. It became a father-son struggle for power. Freud explained to James Jackson Putnam: "I must protect myself against people who have called themselves my pupils for many years and who owe everything to my stimulus. Now I must accuse them and reject them. I am not a quarrelsome person." And in a letter to Ernest Jones: "As for Jung I am resolved to give up private relations with him. His friendship is not worth the ink . . . I want him to go his way and have no need of his companionship myself."

The intensity of Freud's hatred and bitterness toward Jung, and his sense of betrayal by him, are fully expressed in a letter to his colleague Ferenczi: "He [Jung] was absolutely crushed, ashamed, and then admitted everything: that he had already feared for a long time that intimacy with me or with others would damage his independence, and for that reason he had decided to withdraw; that he had certainly construed me according to his father complex . . . that he was certainly wrong in being mistrustful; that it hurt him to be judged a complex fool, etc. I spared him nothing at all, told him calmly that a friendship with him couldn't be maintained, that he himself gave rise to the intimacy which he then so cruelly broke off, that things were not at all in order in his relations with men, not just with me but with others as well."

Freud continued: "He was behaving like a drunkard who cries unremittingly: 'Don't think for a minute that I'm drunk' and was under the influence of an unmistakable neurotic reaction. I had deceived myself on one point, in that I had considered him to be a born leader who by means of his authority could spare others many errors; he was not that, he was immature himself and in need of supervision, etc. He totally ceased contradicting me and admitted everything. I think it did him good." Freud elsewhere called Jung "an evil fellow" and accused him of "lies, brutality and anti-Semitic condescension."

When the long and now tense relationship finally ended with bitter recrimination, Freud wrote to Abraham: "So we are at last rid of them, the brutal sanctimonious Jung and his disciples . . . All my life I have been looking for friends who would not exploit and then betray me." When asked why so many left his movement, Freud replied, "Precisely because they too wanted to be Popes."

In writing his autobiography years later, Freud apparently felt the need to defend himself against the charge of having difficulty maintaining close, sustained relationships. He noted that many colleagues left him. But, lest anyone think this "a sign of my intolerance" or that a "special fatality hangs over me," Freud pointed out that many colleagues remained with him. "It is a sufficient answer to point out that in contrast to those who have left me, like Jung, Adler, Stekel, and a few besides, there are a great number of men, like Abraham, Eitingon, Ferenczi, Rank, Jones, Brill, Sachs, Pfister, van Emden, Reik, and others, who have worked with me for some fifteen years in loyal collaboration and for the most part in uninterrupted friendship." Freud concludes with "I think I can say in my defense that an intolerant man, dominated by an arrogant belief in his own infallibility, would never have been able to maintain his hold upon so large a number of intelligent people, especially if he had at his command as few practical attractions as I had." One wonders: if half of Freud's children rejected him, would he point to the other half to prove he had good relations with his family?

What caused so many broken relationships in Freud's life? Friendship, as Lewis pointed out, is based on shared interests, and Freud's colleagues shared many interests. All these early followers not only were psychoanalysts, but also shared Freud's materialist worldview. Why the conflict?

Freud's distrust of and low evaluation of people may have contributed. "The unworthiness of human beings, even of analysts, has always made a deep impression on me," Freud writes to a colleague in Boston when fifty-nine years old. And Freud readily admits that even psychoanalysis could do little to improve human nature. He asks: "[B]ut why should analyzed people be altogether better than others? Analysis makes for *unity*, but not necessarily for *goodness*. I do not agree with Socrates and Putnam that all our faults arise from confusion and ignorance. I think that too heavy a burden is laid on analysis when one asks of it that it should be able to realize every precious ideal."

Other letters to the Swiss pastor Oskar Pfister reflect this attitude: "I do not break my head very much about good and evil, but I have found little that is 'good' about human beings on the whole. In my experience most of them are trash, no matter whether they publicly subscribe to this or that ethical doctrine or none at all." And, a couple of years later, in a letter that has special significance when one realizes the only sustained pleasure in Freud's life was his intellectual work, he wrote: "What personal pleasure is to be derived from analysis I obtained during the years when I was alone, and since others have joined me it has given me more pain than pleasure. The way people accept and distort it has not changed the opinion I formed of them . . . An incurable breach must have come into existence at that time between me and other men."

When he was seventy-three, Freud continued to hold an extremely negative impression of human beings and of human nature. He writes that the "inclination to aggression, which we can detect in ourselves and justly assume to be present in others, is the factor which disturbs our relations with our neighbor." Freud sees his neighbor as someone tempted "to humiliate him, to cause him pain, to torture and to kill him. *Homo homini lupus.* (Man is a wolf to man)." The only solution Freud has to offer is that "each one of us has to give up as illusions the expectations which, in his youth, he pinned upon his fellow men, and . . . learn how much difficulty and pain has been added to his life by their ill-will."

The contrast with Lewis—at least, after his conversion—could not be more striking. Before the change, however, Lewis also struggled with relationships, though in a different way. In his autobiography Lewis describes himself before his change of worldview as introspective, permitting only a very few to enter his life. Because of the severe trauma that Lewis experienced as a nine-year-old—the death of his mother and several other members of his family—Lewis approached relationships cautiously. He realized, perhaps mostly unconsciously, that every close relationship, especially with a woman, could result in the pain of separation and loss, and reactivate all the early trauma. In his autobiography, written when close to sixty years old, he recalls as a young child waking up in the middle of the night to listen for his brother's breathing. If he did not hear the breathing, Lewis suspected his father and brother "had secretly risen while I slept and gone off to America—that I was finally abandoned." In approaching relationships, Lewis adopted the philosophy that "all humans pass away. Do not let your happiness depend on something you may lose . . . I am a safety-first creature. Of all arguments against love none makes so strong an appeal to my nature as 'Careful! this might lead to suffering.'"

We obtain some further idea of Lewis's attitude toward others before his conversion from his autobiography and from his diary that he kept for five years in his early twenties. When he was a teenager, influenced by a young, popular faculty member, Lewis writes that his experience within the boarding school "was gradually teaching me to be a prig or (in the bad sense) a Highbrow." Lewis was highly critical of the English public school system when he looked back on it after his great transition. Lewis criticized the harsh mistreatment students receive there. "Where oppression does not completely and permanently break the spirit, has it not a natural tendency to produce retaliatory pride and contempt? . . . No one is more likely to be arrogant than a lately freed slave." All in all, "school life was a life almost wholly dominated by the social struggle; to get on, to arrive . . ."

His diary offers ample evidence that he was critical, proud, cynical, cruel, and arrogant. Lewis described the maids who helped with the housework as "country girls, lazy, noisy and inefficient." He referred to a visitor as the "woman-with-the-false-eyebrows-who-tells-lies"; to another as "over-educated, affected, vain, flippant and insufferable"; in another guest he noticed "the sucking, squeaking, crunching noises he makes in eating." After a Catholic church service he wrote that "we were royally bored and . . . the priest . . . was about the nastiest little man I have ever seen." Lewis refers to others as "the bitch," "the little ass," "repulsive dago," "childish, naive and retains many obstinate vulgarities," and "a fat, amiable, ugly woman." In short, before his conversion, Lewis preferred to be alone, embracing the arrogance and snobbery inculcated in him by the British boarding school system and possessing none of the kinds of love he would write about extensively and demonstrate in his relationships later.

After the great transition Lewis turned outward. He no longer spent hours focusing on himself—and he no longer kept a diary. He apparently attained inner resources to help him overcome his fear of establishing close relationships and risking repeating the traumatic loss he experienced as a young child. His valuation of people changed dramatically.

Lewis reached out and established a broad range of friends. Many of them—including several Oxford dons—met in a discussion group in Lewis's rooms on Thursday evenings and then again on Tuesdays before lunch. They met for lunch at a tiny little restaurant or pub called the Eagle and Child. This group of Lewis's friends became known as the Inklings. They read manuscripts they were working on to the group. Some famous books—*The Lord of the Rings* and *The Screwtape Letters*—came out of those discussions. They shared jokes and had great fun. There were about eighteen regular Inklings and many others came and went, as their careers would dictate. Lewis had a great wit and contributed his share of jokes. George Sayer writes in his excellent biography of Lewis that the meetings of the Inklings made Lewis "utterly happy."

The Inklings happened to be all male. But Lewis had many female friends that he admired and with whom he kept in close contact. After his conversion, newly convinced that "there are no *ordinary* people," Lewis carried on regular correspondence with scores of people, most of them women. "It isn't chiefly *men* I am kept in touch with by my huge mail: it is *women*," Lewis writes to a friend. "The female, happy or unhappy, agreeing or disagreeing, is by nature a much more *epistolary* animal than the male." Lewis corresponded regularly with the British author Dorothy Sayers, the poet Ruth Pitter, novelist Rose Macaulay, and the Anglo-Saxon scholar Dorothy Whitlock.

Lewis approached his letter writing—as he approached his promise to his friend Paddy Moore to look after his mother and sister—with considerable diligence and faithfulness. He answered every letter sent him, from those by important leaders to those by a child or a widow he did not know. He answered them daily, before undertaking his hectic work schedule. "The mail, you know, is the great hurdle at the beginning of each day's course for me," Lewis writes to this same friend. "I have sometimes had to write letters hard from 8:30 to 11 o'clock before I could start my own work. Mostly to correspondents I have never seen. I expect most of my replies to them are useless: but every now and then people think one has helped them and so one dare not stop answering letters."

Lewis's conversion dramatically altered his assessment of others. He changed from an introvert who, like Freud, was highly critical and distrustful of others, to a person who reached out and appeared to value every human being. Every decision a person makes, Lewis asserts, will take him toward or away from a relationship with the Person who made him, the one relationship for which that individual was created. "All day long we are, in some degree, helping each other to one or other of these destinations."

"He was a deeply kind and charitable man," wrote the legendary drama critic and author Kenneth Tynan, a former student of Lewis's. After meeting with Lewis in a moment of despair, Tynan would later write: "As I listened to him, my problems began to dwindle to their proper proportions; I had entered his room suicidal, and I left it exhilarated." Tynan writes that if ever he were to stray into the camp of Lewis's spiritual worldview, "it would be because of Lewis's argument as expressed in books like 'Miracles.' (He never intruded them into tutorials.)"

Freud, sadly, saw his neighbor as someone inclined "to humiliate him, to cause him pain." His neighbor was someone who needed to earn his trust and his love. He said, when almost sixty years old, that all of his life he had been looking for friends who would not exploit him or betray him. Before his conversion Lewis shared this cautious, defensive approach to people. Afterward, he saw every indi-

vidual as living forever: "You have never talked to a mere mortal."
He adds that "Nations, cultures, arts, civilization—these are mortal." Our relationships with others must be characterized by "a real
and costly love, with deep feeling for the sins in spite of which we
love the sinner" and with "no flippancy, no superiority, no presumption." Lewis's concept of love clearly enriched his life and helped
make him a profoundly different person—a "new creation."

8

PAIN

How Can We Resolve the
Problem of Suffering?

To live life is to suffer pain. No human being escapes the experience of physical or emotional pain. Pain is an intrinsic part of our existence. We cause pain and experience pain from the moment of our birth, and periodically, in one form or another, throughout our lives. Many of us die in pain.

For Freud, and for Lewis before his transition, and for a brief period after, the problem of reconciling the notion of an all-loving, benevolent Creator with human suffering presented the greatest obstacle to acceptance of the spiritual worldview. Indeed, the problem of pain and the related problem of evil have been central conundra for believers throughout history.

Both Freud and Lewis asked, "If God is sovereign, if He really is in charge of the universe and if He really loves me, then how could he allow me to suffer so? Either He does not exist or He is not in control or He doesn't really care." Freud concluded He does not exist. Lewis concluded differently.

People come to my office primarily to find relief from emotional pain. Clinically, emotional pain is often considerably more intolerable than physical pain. Although we may experience long respites from physical pain, we receive little relief from emotional pain. We hover somewhere on a spectrum between a painful state of anxiety and an even more painful state of despondency and despair. Though we experience periods of freedom from these uncomfortable states of mind, they are far too brief. Furthermore, the more aware and more sensitive we are to suffering in the lives of those around us, the more likely we are to live in what Freud refers to as a "state of anxious expectation."

Finally, awareness of our mortality causes pain because our most deep-seated need is for permanence and our most pervasive fear is separation from those we love. The Psalmist tells us that there is wisdom in the awareness that our days are numbered (Psalm 90:12). But in that awareness lies pain as well.

My first encounter with what Lewis calls "the problem of pain" and what Freud calls "the painful riddle of death" occurred when I was a surgical intern on the wards of a large hospital. I witnessed unbearable suffering, watching young children die and hearing the grief-stricken cries of their families. I was haunted and unable to sleep. How could anyone on earth—or in heaven—with the power to prevent this not do so? I came across a copy of *The Problem of Pain* by C. S. Lewis on the table of the hospital library and found it helpful. (Little did I realize it would be a key part of the course I would teach many years later.) Lewis suffered greatly, and came to terms with it. Freud suffered also, both physically and emotionally.

When three years old, Freud lost his beloved nanny. Later in life he lost through death many other loved ones, including a favorite daughter and a beloved grandson. These losses contributed to the depression that Freud suffered throughout his life.

No experience, however, inflicted more emotional pain on Freud than the pervasive anti-Semitism he encountered in Vienna, especially at the University of Vienna. Perhaps only those who have experienced prejudice and bigotry can understand the intense emotional suffering such experiences can have on both a child and an adult. I have learned from friends and colleagues, as well as from my clinical work, the hurt that remains throughout life when one experiences prejudice as a child. One close Jewish friend can still recall vividly hearing other children use the term "Christ killer." From my Afro-American colleagues I have become aware of the more subtle but unmistakably clear expressions of racism that make one feel tolerated but not welcome.

It is clear that Freud experienced anti-Semitism with regularity, and from a young age. In his *Interpretation of Dreams,* Freud wrote that, as a schoolboy, "I began for the first time to understand what it meant to belong to an alien race, and anti-Semitic feelings among the other boys warned me that I must take up a definite position." It was when he was ten or twelve years old that his father told of being bullied on the sidewalk and of meekly submitting.

Freud remembered that "this struck me as unheroic conduct on the part of the big strong man who was holding the little boy by the hand." The great Carthaginian general Hannibal had sworn to his father that he would take vengeance on Rome. "To my youthful mind, Hannibal and Rome symbolized the tenacity of Jewry and the organization of the Catholic Church." Vienna at that time was heavily Catholic and Freud associated Catholicism with anti-Semitism. The Catholic Church would be viewed by Freud for the rest of his life as the enemy.

At seventeen, he entered the University of Vienna. A young adolescent experiences no greater need than to be accepted by his

peers. Many decades later Freud could recall clearly the rejection
he experienced as a college student. "When, in 1872, I first joined
the University, I experienced some appreciable disappointments.
Above all, I found that I was expected to feel myself inferior and an
alien because I was a Jew." His initial reactions were not Hannibal-
esque, but perhaps his long-term resolve did echo the great war-
rior's. "I put up, without much regret, with my non-acceptance into
the community . . . These first impressions at the University, however, had one consequence which was afterwards to prove important; for at an early age I was familiar with the fate of being in the
Opposition and of being put under the ban of the 'compact majority.' The foundations were thus laid for a certain degree of independence of judgment."

Throughout his adult years Freud held a strong conviction that
anti-Semitism caused much of the resistance and antagonism toward psychoanalysis. He acknowledged differences between
"Aryan" and "Jewish" cultures but argued that "there should not be
such a thing as Aryan or Jewish science. Results in science must be
identical, though the presentation of them may vary." Instead, there
was a tendency among many to imply that psychoanalysis resulted
from "Viennese culture." Freud thought this was only a slightly dis-
guised form of anti-Semitism. He wrote in *On the History of the
Psychoanalytic Movement*, "We have all heard of the interesting attempt to explain psycho-analysis as a product of the Vienna mi-
lieu . . . The suggestion is that psycho-analysis, and in particular its
assertion that the neuroses are traceable to disturbances in sexual
life, could only have originated in a town like Vienna—in an atmosphere of sensuality and immorality foreign to other cities—and that
it is simply a reflection, a projection into theory, as it were, of these
peculiar Viennese conditions. Now I am certainly no local patriot;
but this theory about psycho-analysis always seems to me quite ex-
ceptionally senseless—so senseless, in fact, that I have sometimes

been inclined to suppose that the reproach of being a citizen of Vienna is only a euphemistic substitute for another reproach which no one would care to put forward openly."

In a letter to a colleague, Freud made clear his conviction that anti-Semitism lay behind rejection of his theories: "I nurse a suspicion that the suppressed anti-Semitism of the Swiss that spares me is deflected in reinforced form upon you. But I think that we as Jews, if we wish to join in, must develop a bit of masochism, be ready to suffer some wrong. Otherwise there is no hitting it off. Rest assured that, if my name were Oberhuber, in spite of everything my innovations would have met with far less resistance."

As early as 1912, Freud expressed his impatience with the difficulty he encountered in his attempts to insure that psychoanalysis not be considered a Jewish science: "The only serious thing about it is this: Semites and Aryans or anti-Semites, whom I wanted to bring together in the service of psycho-analysis, once again separate like oil and water."

Freud's rejection and ridicule by German physicians and other scientists evoked bitter disappointment. Although he struggled bravely to overcome despair and continue his work as part of "the opposition," he suffered from this rejection throughout his life. When he was almost eighty years old, he wrote, ". . . for the degree of arrogance . . . they displayed, their conscienceless contempt of logic, and for the coarseness and bad taste of their attacks there could be no excuse . . . it nonetheless hurt deeply."

In a paper titled "Analysis of a Phobia in a Five-Year-Old Boy," Freud offers a psychoanalytic interpretation of anti-Semitism: "The castration complex is the deepest unconscious root of anti-Semitism; for even in the nursery little boys hear that a Jew has something cut off his penis—a piece of his penis, they think—and this gives them a right to despise Jews. And there is no stronger unconscious root for the sense of superiority over women."

In *Moses and Monotheism,* written during the last years of his life, he added other reasons, noting that there must be more than one for a "phenomenon of such intensity and permanence." He then attempts to analyze some of them. He mentions that Jews "live for the most part as minorities among other people" and points out that "the communal feeling of groups requires . . . hostility toward some extraneous minority, and the numerical weakness of this excluded minority encourages its suppression."

Another reason: "They [the Jews] defy all oppression . . . the most cruel persecutions have not succeeded in exterminating them, and, indeed . . . on the contrary they show a capacity for holding their own in commercial life and, where they are admitted, for making valuable contributions to every form of cultural activity."

Ultimately, he settles on three "deeper motives" for anti-Semitism: first, people are jealous of the Jews being the chosen people. "I venture to assert that jealousy of the people which declared itself the first-born, favorite child of God the Father, has not yet been surmounted among other peoples, even today: it is as though they thought there was truth in the claim." Second, again, is castration fear: "Among the customs by which the Jews made themselves separate, that of circumcision has made a disagreeable, uncanny impression, which is to be explained, no doubt, by its recalling the dreaded castration."

Third, Freud asserts that because Christianity, which derives from Judaism, had often been imposed on people against their will, anti-Semitism is, in reality, hostility toward Christianity—a hostility then displaced onto the Jews. "We must not forget that all those peoples who excel today in their hatred of Jews became Christians only in late historic times, often driven to it by bloody coercion . . . They have not got over a grudge against the new religion which was imposed on them; but they have displaced the grudge on to the source from which Christianity reached them." Freud reminds his readers that the "fact that the Gospels tell a story which is set among the Jews, and in fact, deals only with Jews has made this displacement easy for them." He concludes that "their hatred of Jews is at bottom a hatred of Christians." To confirm this he points to the hostile treatment by the Nazis of both Christians and Jews.

Nazi hostility was something that Freud knew firsthand. During a visit to Anna Freud's clinic in London on June 23, 1980, I interviewed Paula Fichtl, the maid who served the Freud family for more than half a century. Miss Fichtl shared with me some of the moments of terror of living in Vienna during the Nazi occupation. She told of SS troops coming to the Freud house and taking Miss Freud away for questioning. She said that before Miss Freud left, her father gave her cyanide pills to take if the Nazis decided to torture her.

But Freud did not feel hostility only from Germans and Austrians. In a letter he wrote in his eighties, after his escape from Nazi Austria to England, Freud said of the English: "Basically all are anti-Semites. They are everywhere. Frequently anti-Semitism is latent and hidden, but it is there. Naturally, there are also exceptions . . . But the broad masses are anti-Semitic here as everywhere."

"Don't you think you ought to reserve the columns of your special number [on anti-Semitism] for the utterances of non-Jewish people, less personally involved than myself?" Freud asks in a letter written to the editor of *Time and Tide,* a British publication, only ten months before his death. (The magazine had quoted him.) Freud felt strongly that non-Jewish people should be aware of and speak out against what the editor observed as "a certain growth of anti-Semitism even in this country."

In that letter Freud summarizes his own painful experiences: "I came to Vienna as a child of 4 years from a small town in Moravia. After 78 years of assiduous work I had to leave my home, saw the Scientific Society I had founded dissolved, our institutions de-

stroyed, our Printing Press . . . taken over by the invaders, the books
I had published confiscated or reduced to pulp, my children expelled from their professions."

❋   ❋   ❋

It would not be fair to attribute all of Freud's unhappiness to anti-
Semitism. Freud suffered from bouts of depression, from pho-
bias—especially the fear of death—and from psychosomatic
symptoms. For the last sixteen years of his life, Freud suffered physically from a painful cancer of his palate.

Early in 1923, when sixty-seven years old, Freud noticed a white,
thickened area on the roof of his mouth. As a physician, he recognized these white spots as leukoplakia, found often in heavy smok-
ers. Freud smoked several cigars a day and was heavily addicted to
nicotine. Though he realized these lesions could become cancerous,
he waited a couple of months before consulting with Dr. Felix
Deutsch, a young internist. Freud asked Deutsch to help him "disappear from the world with decency" if his diagnosis offered him
nothing but suffering.

Deutsch diagnosed cancer. Fearing Freud might commit suicide,
Deutsch withheld his diagnosis, saying only that the lesions needed
to be removed surgically and that Freud should cease smoking.
Freud, however, surmised the truth.

"I detected 2 months ago a leukoplastic growth on my jaw and
palate right side, which I had removed on the 20th," Freud wrote to
his colleague Ernest Jones in April 1923. "I am still out of work and
cannot swallow . . . I was assured of the benignity of the matter . . .
My own diagnosis had been epithelioma [cancer] but was not accepted. Smoking is accused as the etiology of this tissue—rebellion."

This first operation did not go well. One of Freud's physicians
would later describe it as a "grotesque nightmare." Freud chose Dr.

Marcus Hajek to perform the surgery. Freud knew him personally. Hajek told Freud the procedure would be a "very slight operation" and that he could go home the same day. To spare his family worry, Freud did not inform them of his surgery.

Hajek performed the operation under local anesthesia in the outpatient clinic of a general teaching hospital with less than adequate facilities. Complications developed.

Freud began to bleed profusely. Deutsch writes: "We drove to the hospital together with the understanding that he would be home immediately after the operation. But he lost more blood than it was foreseen and as an emergency he had to rest on a cot in a tiny room . . . with another patient who, by tragicomic coincidence, I might say, was an imbecile dwarf."

The clinic called Freud's family, who were shocked to learn of the proceedings. When his wife and daughter Anna arrived at the clinic, they found Freud sitting on a kitchen chair, covered with blood. When Mrs. Freud and Anna left for lunch, Freud began to bleed again. He could not speak or call for help and tried to ring a bell. The bell didn't work. The dwarf noticed Freud was in trouble, rushed for help, and perhaps saved Freud's life. Thereafter Anna would not leave Freud alone and during the night noticed Freud was weak from loss of blood and in considerable pain. She and the nurse became alarmed over his condition and the nurse called the house surgeon. The surgeon refused to get out of bed.

One of Freud's physicians wrote many years later that Dr. Hajek "certainly was not qualified" to perform the complicated surgery. Dr. Deutsch eventually placed Freud in the hands of a distinguished oral surgeon named Dr. Hans Pichler, who performed a more radical surgery necessitated by the invasive cancer.

During the remaining years of his life, Freud would undergo some thirty operations—all performed under local anesthesia. After surgeons cut away the roof of Freud's mouth, they inserted a metal

prosthesis to separate his nasal cavity from his mouth. Breathing
and eating became extremely difficult. The toxic effects of numerous X-ray and radium treatments added to the suffering he experienced during the next sixteen years of his life.

Freud came to prefer eating alone. Once he and his daughter
Anna were eating breakfast on a train, visiting with an American
couple they had just met. Suddenly blood spurted from Freud's
mouth, a hard crust of bread having apparently reopened the
wound. Freud nevertheless continued to travel on his vacations and
accepted his suffering with a certain impassivity. At times, however,
his anger would erupt, as when he wrote to his friend Oskar Pfister:
"—let me be impolite for once—how the devil do you reconcile all
that we experience and have come to expect in this world with your
assumption that there is a moral order?" Freud concluded instead
that "obscure, unfeeling and unloving powers determine men's
fate."

※   ※   ※

C. S. Lewis also experienced incredible suffering—both emotional
and physical. If anti-Semitism caused the greatest suffering in
Freud's life, the childhood loss of Lewis's mother, reactivated by the
loss of his beloved wife several decades later, caused the most prolonged and intense suffering in Lewis. When Lewis wrote of his
mother's death that "my father never fully recovered from this loss,"
he could perhaps have said the same for himself.

In his autobiography Lewis recalls the terror he and his brother
felt when informed their mother might die. Children tend to re-
press painful experiences so that their recall of childhood remains
predominantly positive. As they become adults, they tend to forget
the fears common to every child, such as fears of the dark or fears
of being abandoned. They remember their early childhood as
peaceful and blissful.

With Lewis, however, the pain of his mother's death so over-whelmed him that, when writing his autobiography almost a half century later, he recalled it vividly. "For us boys the real bereave-ment had happened before our mother died. We lost her gradually as she was gradually withdrawn from our life into the hands of nurses and delirium and morphia, and our whole existence changed into something alien and menacing."

Looking back, Lewis realized children and adults experience grief differently, causing children to feel isolated and alienated from those around them. "If I may trust my own experience," Lewis wrote, "the sight of adult misery and adult terror has an effect on children which is merely paralyzing and alienating." He and his brother felt more distant from their father and consequently "drew daily closer together . . . two frightened urchins huddled for warmth in a bleak world." He recalled being "taken into the bedroom where my mother lay dead." On observing her corpse he wrote, ". . . my grief was overwhelmed with terror." He reacted with horror "against all the subsequent paraphernalia of coffin, flowers, hearse, and fu-neral." Lewis wrote that with his mother's death all happiness "dis-appeared from my life."

We have already seen how difficult were Lewis's early years at boarding school. But his troubles hardly stopped there. At the age of nineteen, Lewis experienced the terror of being on the front lines during World War I and being wounded by a shell that killed friends nearby. He did not write in detail about these experiences except to say that "my memories of the last war haunted my dreams for years."

Lewis became ill with "trench fever," was admitted to the hospi-tal near the front lines for three weeks, and then returned to the trenches in time for "the great German attack." "Through the win-ter, weariness and water were our chief enemies. I have gone to sleep marching and woken again and found myself marching still.

One walked in the trenches in thigh gum boots with water above the knee; one remembers the icy stream welling up inside the boot when you punctured it on concealed barbed wire." Lewis found that, although he often dreamed of the war, the most horrible aspects of his war experiences tended to fade from memory. He noted "the cold, the smell . . . the horribly smashed men still moving like half-crushed beetles, the sitting or standing corpses, the landscape of sheer earth without a blade of grass, the boots worn day and night till they seemed to grow on your feet—all this shows rarely and faintly in memory." Lewis recalled the first bullet he heard, feeling "not exactly . . . fear" but "a little quavering signal that said, 'This is war. This is what Homer wrote about.'"

While recovering from his wounds in a London hospital, Lewis, according to George Sayer, "suffered intensely from . . . loneliness and depression." Dreams about the war made sleeping difficult.

Today we might diagnose Lewis with post-traumatic stress disorder—not uncommon among young men wounded on the battlefield. Lewis certainly met many of the criteria psychiatrists use today to diagnose the disorder, having had life-threatening experiences; serious injury; and having responded with fear, helplessness, and horror. Recurrent nightmares are also a standard symptom.

Later, Lewis suffered rejection by the faculty at Oxford, who, perhaps because they did not share his worldview or felt jealous of his popularity, failed to offer him a chair. Not until his middle fifties did Cambridge University offer Lewis a chair as professor of medieval and renaissance literature.

His worst loss and source of pain, of course, was his loss of Joy Davidman when he was sixty-two years old. This type of loss Lewis feared and tried to avoid all of his life. He once again experienced the terror of his early childhood. Lewis tried desperately to maintain control of his emotions, perhaps by methods he developed early in life. He used his keen intellect to understand the complexity and intensity of his feelings and to keep from being overwhelmed by them. He recorded on paper all of his thoughts and feelings, trying to understand the complicated process of grief. "No one ever told me that grief felt so much like fear," he writes in *A Grief Observed*. "I am not afraid, but the sensation is like being afraid. The same fluttering in the stomach, the same restlessness, the yawning. I keep on swallowing."

Lewis noted that his grief, at times, felt like being intoxicated or dazed from a blow to the head: ". . . it feels like being mildly drunk, or concussed." It separated him from people, making it difficult to interact with them. "There is a sort of invisible blanket between the world and me. I find it hard to take in what anyone says . . . It is so uninteresting." Yet he does did not desire to be alone. "I want the others to be about me. I dread the moments when the house is empty. If only they would talk to one another and not to me." Lewis describes what I have observed clinically: people in mourning want to be with people without having to talk with them. Family and friends can be helpful by just being there.

To assuage the pain Lewis tried to talk himself into feeling strong and in control. He reminded himself that he had plenty of what are called "resources" and that he functioned fine before his marriage. But then he writes: "One is ashamed to listen to this voice but it seems for a little while to be making out a good case. Then comes a sudden jab of red-hot memory and all this 'common-sense' vanishes like an ant in the mouth of a furnace."

Lewis had two stepchildren who, in trying to cope with the loss of their mother, reminded him of his own childhood reaction to his mother's death. He noted: "I cannot talk to the children about her. The moment I try, there appears on their faces neither grief, nor love, nor fear, nor pity, but the most fatal of all non-conductors, em-barrassment. They look as if I were committing an indecency. They are longing for me to stop. I felt just the same after my own mother's death when my father mentioned her. I can't blame them. It's the way boys are."

Lewis questioned his need to scrutinize his feelings by recording them on paper: "I not only live each endless day in grief, but live each day thinking about living each day in grief. Do these notes merely aggravate that side of it? Merely confirm that monotonous, tread-mill march of the mind round one subject?" He defended himself in the only way possible. "But what am I to do? I must have some drug, and reading isn't a strong enough drug now. By writing it all down (all?—no: one thought in a hundred) I believe I get a little outside it. That's how I defend it."

Lewis worries that his method may encourage feeling sorry for himself: ". . . the bath of self-pity, the wallow, the loathsome sticky-sweet pleasure of indulging it—that disgusts me." And he wonders: "Aren't all these notes the senseless writhings of a man who won't accept the fact that there is nothing we can do with suffering except to suffer it? Who still thinks there is some device (if only he could find it) which will make pain not to be pain. It doesn't really matter whether you grip the arms of the dentist's chair or let your hands lie in your lap. The drill drills on."

As Lewis worked through his grief, he realized how his wife Joy had given his life an intimacy he had never before known. "The most precious gift that marriage gave me was this constant impact of something very close and intimate yet all the time unmistakably other, resistant—in a word, real." He yearned for her return and cried out: "My dear, my dear, come back for one moment." Losing his wife was losing a part of himself: "At present I am learning to get about on crutches. Perhaps I shall presently be given a wooden leg. But I shall never be a biped again."

Lewis differentiates beween physical and emotional suffering: "Grief is like a bomber circling round and dropping its bombs each time the circle brings it overhead; physical pain is like the steady barrage on a trench in World War I, hours of it with no let-up for a moment. Thought is never static; pain often is." Yet the painful thoughts seemed to never end: "How often—will it be for always?— how often will the vast emptiness astonish me like a complete novelty and make me say, 'I never realized my loss till this moment'? The same leg is cut off time after time. The first plunge of the knife into the flesh is felt again and again."

Ultimately, Lewis asked the deepest question, one that many sufferers have anguished over: "Where is God?" He noted that "when you are happy, so happy that you have no sense of needing Him, so happy that you are tempted to feel His claims upon you as an interruption, if you remember yourself and turn to Him with gratitude and praise, you will be—or so it feels—welcomed with open arms." But when Lewis needed Him most, God appeared to be absent. "But go to Him when your need is desperate, when all other help is vain, and what do you find? A door slammed in your face, and a sound of bolting and double bolting on the inside. After that, silence. You may as well turn away. The longer you wait, the more emphatic the silence will become . . . What can this mean? Why is He so present a commander in our time of prosperity and so very absent a help in time of trouble?" A friend reminded him that Jesus of Nazareth, in time of great need, also cried out, "My God, my God, why have you forsaken me?" (Matt. 27:46). Lewis replied, "Does that make it easier to understand?"

Lewis not only wondered about God's presence when he needed Him most but also what all this suffering tells one about Him. "Not that I am (I think) in much danger of ceasing to believe in God. The real danger is of coming to believe such dreadful things about Him. The conclusion I dread is not, 'So there's no God after all,' but, 'So this is what God's really like. Deceive yourself no longer.'"

Lewis struggled to understand how an omnipotent Being who loved him could allow such suffering. He thought perhaps one should think of God as a good, conscientious surgeon: "The kinder and more conscientious he is, the more inexorably he will go on cutting. If he yielded to your entreaties, if he stopped before the operation was complete, all the pain up to that point would have been useless." But Lewis wondered if such pain and suffering is really necessary. His answer: "Well, take your choice. The tortures occur. If they are unnecessary, then there is no God or a bad one. If there is a good God, then these tortures are necessary. For not even a moderately good Being could possibly inflict or permit them if they weren't." Lewis asked: "What do people mean when they say, 'I am not afraid of God because I know He is good?' Have they never even been to a dentist?'"

Though his inquisitve mind forced Lewis to ask a barrage of questions, he never lost his faith. The stage and cinematic versions of *Shadowlands* imply that he did. The reality, based on his letters and the many people who knew him well, attests to his faith being even stronger after Joy's death than before. He asked endless questions only about the Object of his faith.

Lewis recalled the promise of the New Testament that if one knocks, the door will be opened. But he found "only the locked door, the iron curtain, the vacuum, absolute zero." Lewis realized he was not simply knocking on the door; he was, in his desperate need, trying to kick it down. He asked: "Does knocking mean hammering and kicking the door like a maniac?" Finally, Lewis realized that his desperation and his grasping for help may have interfered with his capacity to receive it: "'To him that hath shall be given.' After all, you must have a capacity to receive, or even omnipotence can't give. Perhaps your own passion temporarily destroys the capacity."

God's presence returned gradually like the dawn of a warm summer day. "Turned to God, my mind no longer meets that locked door; turned to H. (Mrs. Lewis) it no longer meets that vacuum—nor all that fuss about my mental image of her. My jottings show something of the process, but not so much as I'd hoped. Perhaps both changes were really not observable. There was no sudden, striking, and emotional transition. Like the warming of a room or the coming of daylight. When you first notice them they have already been going on for some time."

Lewis did not receive answers to all of his questions. But he received what he called "a rather special sort of 'No answer.' It is not the locked door. It is more like a silent, certainly not uncompassionate, gaze. As though He shook His head, not in refusal, but waiving the question. Like, 'Peace, child; you don't understand.'"

As Lewis looked back on his time of mourning, he realized that he made the process more difficult because he focused not on God, but on himself. He realized that God "has not been trying an experiment on my faith or my love in order to find out their quality. He knew it already. It was I who didn't." Perhaps Lewis began to understand through personal experience what he wrote some twenty years before in his *Problem of Pain*: ". . . suffering is not good in itself. What is good in any painful experience is, for the sufferer, his submission to the will of God, and, for the spectators, the compassion aroused and the acts of mercy to which it leads. In the fallen and partially redeemed universe we may distinguish (1) the simple good descending from God, (2) the simple evil produced by rebellious creatures, and (3) the exploitation of that evil by God for His redemptive purpose, which produces (4) the complex good to which accepted suffering and repented sin contribute. Now the fact that God can make complex good out of simple evil does not excuse—though by mercy it may save—those who do the simple evil."

*   *   *

If Lewis finally did reconcile suffering and faith, Freud could not. The suffering in his own life and the lives of those he loved, for him, ruled out the notion of an all-loving, all-powerful Creator. Indeed, the problem of suffering fueled one of Freud's main arguments against the existence of a Creator.

In his paper "A Religious Experience" Freud asserts that "God allows horrors" to occur. He says he will hold God responsible. Similarly, in a letter to Dr. James Jackson Putnam of Boston, Freud expresses his anger and defiance: "I . . . have no dread at all of the Almighty. If we ever were to meet I should have more reproaches to make to Him than He could to me." Those who have suffered much perhaps can understand Freud's anger. But as an atheist, with whom is he angry?

Freud's clinical work made him aware of the universality of suffering. He observed that his patients who became seriously ill emotionally—even psychotic—often did so to escape an intolerably painful reality. When either external or internal reality became too difficult to endure, the patient creates a world of his own. Freud writes in *An Outline of Psychoanalysis:* "We learn from clinical experience . . . that the precipitating cause of the outbreak of a psychosis is either that reality has become intolerably painful or that the instincts have become extraordinarily intensified—both of which, in view of the rival claims made on the ego by the id and the external world, must lead to the same result."

Freud kept trying to identify our primary sources of pain, perhaps in an effort to understand his own suffering. He writes in *The Future of an Illusion:* "There are the elements, which seem to mock at all human control: the earth which quakes and is torn apart and buries all human life and its works; water, which deluges and drowns everything in a turmoil; there are diseases, which we have only recently recognized as attacks on other organisms; and finally there is the painful riddle of death, against which no medicine has yet been found, nor probably will be."

A few years later, in *Civilization and Its Discontents*, he adds another source of pain—namely, other human beings. "The suffering which comes from this last source is perhaps more painful to us than any other." Freud concludes that "life is hard to bear" and often results in "a permanent state of anxious expectation."

Freud used the problem of suffering to attack the premise that God blesses those who obey His will. Look around, Freud says, the good as well as the evil suffer. In "The Question of a *Weltanschauung*," Freud writes: ". . . the pronouncements of religion promising men protection and happiness if they would only fulfill certain ethical requirements [have] . . . shown themselves unworthy of belief. It seems not to be the case that there is a Power in the universe which watches over the well-being of individuals with parental care and brings all their affairs to a happy ending . . . Earthquakes, tidal waves, conflagrations, make no distinction between the virtuous and pious and the scoundrel or unbeliever."

When it comes to relations between people, Freud said, the good often come away with the short end of the stick. "Often enough the violent, cunning or ruthless man seizes the envied good things of the world and the pious man goes away empty. Obscure, unfeeling and unloving powers determine men's fate." Freud argued that the notion that good is rewarded and evil punished by "the government of the universe" just does not square with reality.

Lewis put it differently, suggesting that the "government of the universe" is temporarily in enemy hands. He writes: "One of the things that surprised me when I first read the New Testament seriously was that it talked so much about a Dark Power in the universe—a mighty evil spirit who was held to be the Power behind death and disease and sin . . . we are living in a part of the universe occupied by the rebel . . . Enemy occupied territory—that is what this world is."

Freud's response to this argument is classic. He says people can't reconcile their suffering with their concept of a loving God, so they conjure up a devil to take the blame. But even the concept of a devil doesn't let God off the hook. Freud asks, after all, didn't God create the devil? In *Civilization and Its Discontents*, he writes, "The Devil would be the best way out as an excuse for God . . . But even so, one can hold God responsible for the existence of the Devil just as well as for the existence of the wickedness which the Devil embodies." Lewis agrees that God did create the devil—but that doesn't make God evil or the creator of evil.

Lewis writes: "This Dark Power was created by God, and was good when he was created, and went wrong." He explains the relationship between freedom and the potential for evil. "God created things which had free will. That means creatures which can go either wrong or right. Some people think they can imagine a creature which was free but had no possibility of going wrong. I cannot. If a thing is free to be good, it is also free to be bad. And free will is what has made evil possible." So why allow for free will in the first place? He answers: "Because free will, though it makes evil possible, is also the only thing that makes possible any love or goodness or joy worth having. A world of automata—of creatures that worked like machines—would hardly be worth creating."

But one wonders: did not God know this would happen, that all this evil, this horrible suffering, would result? Lewis writes: "Of course God knew what would happen if they used their freedom the wrong way: apparently He thought it worth the risk."

Lewis, as an atheist, also found himself angry with God. He writes: "My argument against God was that the universe seemed so cruel and unjust. But how had I got this idea of 'just' and 'unjust'? A man does not call a line crooked unless he has some idea of a straight line . . . Thus in the very act of trying to prove that God did not exist—in other words, that the whole of reality was senseless—I found I was forced to assume that one part of reality—namely my idea of justice—was full of sense. Consequently atheism turns out to be too simple . . ." Lewis points out that the

New Testament faith "is not a system into which we have to fit the awkward fact of pain: it is itself one of the awkward facts which have to be fitted into any system we make. In a sense, it creates, rather than solves, the problem of pain, for pain would be no problem unless, side by side with our daily experience of this painful world, we had received what we think a good assurance that ultimate reality is righteous and loving."

Once in a discussion with Anna Freud, I mentioned that her father appeared very interested in the problem of suffering. She agreed. Then she asked: "What do you think? Do you think there is Someone up there who says, 'You get cancer, you get tuberculosis'?" I answered that Oskar Pfister would probably attribute some of the suffering in the world to an Evil Power. She appeared to be interested in that concept and kept coming back to it during the conversation. Like father, like daughter.

Freud and Lewis both write extensively about the devil. Lewis's imaginative satire, *The Screwtape Letters,* presents the correspondence between two devils. Screwtape, the senior of the two, draws on keen psychological insights to instruct his junior nephew on how best to lead humanity astray. The widespread impact of this book surprised Lewis. In a preface to a revised edition published almost twenty years after the first, Lewis notes that "sales were at first (at least by my standards) prodigious, and have continued steady." The book's success contributed to Lewis's appearing on the cover of *Time* magazine. Did Lewis actually believe in devils? He answers: "I do. That is to say, I believe in angels, and I believe that some of these, by the abuse of their free will have become enemies to God and, as a corollary, to us. These we may call devils." He points out that he believes that Satan, "the leader or dictator of devils," is a fallen angel, and therefore "the opposite, not of God, but of Michael," the archangel.

In the index to the *Standard Edition of the Complete Psycholog-*

ical Works of Sigmund Freud (vol. XXIV), one finds scores of entries on the devil.

Scholars have noted Freud's preoccupation and facination with the devil. For example, Freud read Gustave Flaubert's *Temptation of St. Anthony* when in his twenties and described in detail his strong reaction to the book. The literary work that he quoted most frequently was Goethe's *Faust*. The last book Freud reads on the day he chose to die by euthanasia was Balzac's *The Fatal Skin*, where the hero also makes a pact with the devil. In both *Faust* and *The Fatal Skin* the main character, a man of science, depressed over his lack of recognition and success, considers suicide.

Freud perhaps identified not only with these main characters, but also with the devil himself—not as the embodiment of evil but as the ultimate rebel, defiant and refusing to surrender to Authority. When Freud wavered as a college student and wrote to his friend that he was no longer a materialist but not yet a theist, he promised, "I do not intend to surrender." In a letter written when he was thirty, he said, "I was always in vehement opposition to my teachers." And in a letter to his fiancée expressing his worry about their future, he quotes from his favorite literary work, Milton's *Paradise Lost*, not using the words of Adam, Eve, or God but the devil:

Let us consult
What reinforcement we may gain from hope,
If not, what resolution from despair.

Throughout Freud's writings he refers often to the devil, sometimes as a figure of speech, sometimes in quotes from the great literature. For example, in a letter to Jung, Freud stresses how they "were in urgent need of able helpers" in disseminating psychoanalytic theories and then uses a quote from *Faust*: "Although it was the Devil who taught her; He cannot do it by himself."

Did Freud, at some level, feel that he, himself, had made a pact with the devil? Some scholars answer yes to that question. Of course, for Freud it would make no sense to treat the devil as objectively real. A paper Freud wrote in 1923, analyzing a seventeenth-century manuscript describing a case of a painter who made a pact with the devil, explains his views. Freud relates what the devil had to offer the painter: "In return for an immortal soul, the Devil has many things to offer which are highly prized by men: wealth, security from danger, power over mankind and the forces of nature, even magical arts, and, above all else, enjoyment—the enjoyment of beautiful women." Freud points out that the painter "signed a bond with the Devil in order to be freed from a state of depression." The painter's father died and the painter had "fallen into a state of melancholia; whereupon the devil had approached him and asked why he was so downcast and sad, and had promised 'to help him in every way and give him support.'" The painter makes this pact: he will give his soul to the devil if the devil replaces his lost father for nine years.

Freud then gives his psychological explanation for the existence of the devil, an explanation based on his Oedipus complex theory: "To begin with, we know that God is a father-substitute; or, more correctly, that he is an exalted father; or, yet again, that he is a copy of a father as he is seen and experienced in childhood." Freud points out that feelings toward the father are ambivalent, that is comprised of "two sets of emotional impulses . . . opposed to each other: . . . not only impulses of an affectionate and submissive nature, but also hostile and defiant ones. It is our view that the same ambivalence governs the relations of mankind to its Deity . . . The unresolved conflict between, on the one hand, a longing for the father and, on the other, a fear of him and a son's defiance of him, has furnished us with an explanation of important characteristics of religion and decisive vicissitudes in it." The positive feelings reemerge as one's concept of God; and the negative feelings as one's concept of the devil.

*　*　*

Lewis develops his response to the problem of suffering in several of his works, the two most popular being *The Problem of Pain,* a cerebral work dealing with the intellectual aspects of the problem, and *A Grief Observed,* a more emotional, visceral response to the death of his wife.

Lewis possessed an uncanny ability to reduce complicated issues to their very essence. He described the problem with startling clarity. He writes: "If God were good, He would wish to make His creatures perfectly happy, and if God were almighty, He would be able to do what He wished. But the creatures are not happy. Therefore God lacks either goodness, or power, or both." This, Lewis explains, is the problem of pain in its simplest form.

To understand the problem of suffering, Lewis asserts we must first understand what we mean when we use terms like "happy," "good," "almighty," or "omnipotent." If we give these words their popular meaning, Lewis writes, then the "argument is unanswerable." For example, the word "omnipotence" "means the power to do all or everything." We are told in Scripture that "with God all things are possible." But Lewis states that this does not mean that God can do anything. God cannot, for example, answer nonsensical questions—such as how many miles are there in the color blue? Likewise, He cannot do both of two mutually exclusive things; for example, He cannot create creatures with free will and at the same time withhold free will from them. Lewis writes: "Omnipotence means power to do all that is intrinsically possible, not to do the intrinsically impossible. You may attribute miracles to [God], but not nonsense."

Lewis explains that if a creature is to have free will there must be an environment in which there is "the existence of things to choose between." Therefore, some choices will be right, some will be wrong. The choices that defy the moral law—like the choices that defy the law of gravity—will incur pain. Lewis explains that "if mat-

ter is to serve as a neutral field it must have a fixed nature of its own"
and not one that changes at the whim of its inhabitants; "if matter
has a fixed nature and obeys constant laws, not all states of matter
will be equally agreeable to the wishes of a given soul . . ." Lewis
writes, "Try to exclude the possibility of suffering which the order of
nature and the existence of free will involve and you find that you
have excluded life itself."

Lewis warns we must not confuse God's goodness or love with
our concept of kindness. He writes, "Love is something more stern
and splendid than mere kindness . . . There is kindness in love: but
love and kindness are not coterminous, and when kindness is separated from the other elements of love, it involves a certain fundamental indifference to its object, and even something like contempt
of it." Lewis points out that "love, in its own nature, demands the
perfecting of the beloved; that the mere 'kindness' which tolerates
anything except suffering in its object is, in that respect, at the opposite pole from Love."

Kindness, when one thinks about it, may sometimes interfere
with love: for example, our kindness may keep us from sending a
child to the dentist to spare her pain, while our love, our wanting the
best for that child, will insist that she confront the pain now to prevent more later. Lewis insists that "we were made not that we may
love God (though we were made for that too) but that God may love
us, that we may become objects in which the Divine love may rest
'well pleased.'" And to arrive at that state, Lewis says we need "alteration." The "problem of reconciling human suffering with the existence of a God who loves, is only insoluble so long as we attach a
trivial meaning to the word 'love.'" Lewis emphasizes that we must
also change our concept of happiness. He believes the Creator is the
source of all happiness and that most of the unhappiness and misery
experienced over the centuries results from efforts to find happiness apart from that Source. He writes: "And out of that hopeless at-

tempt has come nearly all that we call human history—money, poverty, ambition, war, prostitution, classes, empires, slavery—the long terrible story of man trying to find something other than God which will make him happy." He concludes, "God cannot give us a happiness and peace apart from Himself, because it is not there. There is no such thing."

Last but not least, Lewis agrees with Freud that the pain we experience from other human beings is the cause of most of our suffering. Lewis writes: "When souls become wicked they will certainly use this possibility to hurt one another; and this perhaps accounts for four-fifths of the sufferings of men. It is men, not God, who have produced racks, whips, prisons, slavery, guns, bayonets, and bombs; it is by human avarice or human stupidity, not by the churlishness of nature, that we have poverty and overwork."

As Lewis continued to study the Old and New Testaments, he came to a new understanding of the Creation, the Fall, and the doctrines of Atonement and Redemption. He explained that "God is good; that He made all things good . . . that one of the good things he made, namely, the free will of rational creatures, by its very nature included the possibility of evil: and that creatures, availing themselves of this possibility, have become evil . . . man is now a horror to God and to himself and a creature ill-adapted to the universe—not because God made him so but because he has made himself so by the abuse of his free will."

The abuse of this free will to transgress the will of the Creator is the primary cause of suffering, illness, and death. In a letter written when Lewis was fifty years old, he explains: "I do *not* hold that God 'sends' sickness or war in the sense in which He sends us all good things. Hence in Luke XIII:16, Our Lord clearly attributes a disease not to the action of His Father but to that of Satan. I think you are quite right. All suffering arises from sin."

Lewis says that pain is evil—that God does not produce pain, but will use it to produce good. Many do not acknowledge God until they encounter pain or great danger—for example, when their plane hits turbulence. Lewis writes: ". . . pain insists upon being attended to. God whispers to us in our pleasures, speaks in our conscience, but shouts in our pains: it is His megaphone to rouse a deaf world." But Lewis warns pain may also drive people away from God. He writes: "Pain as God's megaphone is a terrible instrument; it may lead to final and unrepented rebellion." Lewis says God may use pain to help us realize our need for Him but sometimes we respond, not by turning to Him, but by turning our backs on Him. I once heard a medical colleague say, "If God permits that kind of horror, I want nothing to do with Him."

Freud confronted suffering in his own life with what he often referred to as "resignation." In his *Future of an Illusion,* Freud described what life would be like when people rejected the spiritual worldview, perhaps describing what he himself experienced. "They will have to admit to themselves the full extent of their helplessness . . . they can no longer be the centre of the creation, no longer the object of the tender care on the part of the beneficent Providence . . . And, as for the great necessities of Fate, against which there is no help, they will learn to endure them with resignation."

When he tried to comfort others in their suffering, Freud had "no consolatory words"—only the advice to endure the suffering with resignation. In a letter to a friend's wife after she lost her husband, Freud laments "that we have to submit with resignation to the blows of fate you know already; and you will have guessed that to me his loss is particularly painful because, with the selfishness of old age, I think he could easily have been spared for the probably short duration of my own life." When his colleague Ernest Jones lost his only daughter, Freud wrote him a letter saying, "As an unbelieving fatalist, I can only sink into a state of resignation when faced with the horror of death." He reminded Jones that when his grandson Heinele

died, he lost all desire to live: "I became tired of life permanently."
Freud appeared to be acutely aware of his lack of spiritual resources
to draw on during times of crisis. After the death of his daughter Sophie, Freud wrote to a colleague: "I do not know what more there is
to say. It is such a paralyzing event, which can stir no afterthoughts
when one is not a believer . . ." Freud wondered "when my turn will
come" and wished that his life would soon be over.

C. S. Lewis, before his changed worldview, had similar views on
pain. In the introduction to *The Problem of Pain*, Lewis explains:
"When I was an atheist, if anyone had asked me, 'Why do you not
believe in God?' my reply would have run something like this: 'Look
at the universe we live in. By far the greatest part of it consists of
empty space, completely dark and unimaginably cold . . . it is improbable that any planet except the Earth sustains life. And Earth
herself existed without life for millions of years and may exist for
millions more when life has left her. And what is it like while it lasts?
It is so arranged that all the forms of it can live only by preying upon
one another . . . The creatures cause pain by being born, and live by
inflicting pain, and in pain they mostly die.'" Because man is endowed with reason, he can "foresee his own pain" as well as "his own
death" and by "a hundred ingenious contrivances" can inflict more
pain on others; human history "is largely a record of crime, war, disease and terror . . . all civilizations pass away and, even while they
remain, inflict peculiar sufferings of their own . . . the universe is
running down . . . and the race is doomed." Lewis writes that "if you
ask me to believe that this is the work of a benevolent and omnipotent spirit, I reply that all the evidence points in the opposite direction. Either there is no spirit behind the universe, or else a spirit
indifferent to good and evil, or else an evil spirit."

Pain occurs in every life. How we react to it determines how it influences the quality of our lives. If we believe, like Lewis, that a
Supreme Being loves us and ultimately controls our destiny, we may

endure with patience and hope. But if we hold to the materialist worldview, we are left with Freud's exhortation to submit to the harsh realities which confront us. As Freud concludes, "If the believer finally sees himself obliged to speak of God's 'inscrutable decrees,' he is admitting that all that is left to him as a last possible consolation and source of pleasure in his suffering is an unconditional submission. And if he is prepared for that, he could probably have spared himself the detour he has made."

~9~

DEATH

Is Death Our Only Destiny?

Soon after we arrive on this earth, we become aware of the most fundamental fact of our existence—that we won't be here very long. An average lifespan lasts less than 30,000 days. We sleep a third of that time, so the days we experience number less than 20,000. We may try, but we can't ever completely deny our mortality. Reminders keep cropping up: classmates fail to return after a summer break; we drive to work on a beautiful spring day, and a line of cars with lights on and a hearse in front suddenly appears; each day's paper carries numerous obituaries.

Though the Psalmist tells us there is wisdom in numbering our days and realizing this world is not our home, the process of becoming aware is extraordinarily painful. The unbelievable brevity of our lives conflicts with our deep-seated yearning for permanence and with our lifelong fear of being separated from those we love—a fear that haunts us from infancy to old age.

How do we resolve and come to terms with what Freud called "the painful riddle of death"? Socrates said, "The true philosopher is always pursuing death and dying." Most of the great writers, including Freud and Lewis, dealt extensively with this theme. A few comments from their writings are particularly important. How they reacted to the death of their friends and family and how each of them confronted his own death will help us understand how his respective worldview addressed this "painful riddle." Freud quotes Schopenhauer that "the problem of death stands at the outset of every philosophy." Indeed, the problem of death influenced Freud and Lewis in choosing their specific philosophy of life.

In *The Interpretation of Dreams,* Freud reveals that his awareness of death began as a young child. When he was about two years of age, his young brother Julius died. During his self-analysis, Freud claimed that he recalled his reaction to the death. Because of his jealousy of the infant, he felt guilty. "I greeted my one-year-younger brother (who died after a few months) with adverse wishes and genuine childhood jealousy; and . . . his death left the germ of [self-]reproaches in me."

Freud also recalled a discussion with his mother in which she told him that "we are all made of earth and must therefore return to earth." The young boy expressed his doubts. She then supported her statement with "proof." "My mother thereupon rubbed the palms of her hands together—just as she did when making dumplings, except that there was no dough between them—and showed me the blackish scales of epidermis produced by the friction as proof that we were made of earth. My astonishment at this ocular demonstration knew no bounds and I acquiesced on the belief which I was later to hear expressed in the words: 'Du bist der Natur einen Tod schuldig.'" (Thou owest Nature a death.)

In a letter written in 1914, Freud shared insights on war derived from his clinical work. "Psychoanalysis has concluded . . . that prim-

itive, savage, evil impulses of mankind have not vanished in any individual, but continue their existence, although in a repressed
state—in the unconscious . . ." Because these impulses "wait for op-
portunities" to be expressed and because war offers such an opportunity, wars will continue to be a recurrent part of history. As the
human race has become more educated and more knowledgeable,
wars have become not less but more frequent and more destructive.
The reason for this is "that our intellect is a feeble and dependent
thing, a play thing and tool of our impulses and emotions."

Wars demonstrate that our basic impulses have changed little
from those of our primitive ancestors, that underneath our civility
we are just as uncivilized and savage as ever. Wars show that "our
unconscious is just as inaccessible to the idea of our own death, just
as murderously inclined towards strangers, just as divided (that is,
ambivalent) towards those we love, as was primeval man."

In 1914, in a paper titled "Thoughts for the Times on War and
Death," Freud makes the interesting observation that death does
not exist in our unconscious mind. Our minds appear to be so con-
structed that we expect permanence. Freud writes: "Our unconscious then does not believe in its own death; it behaves as if it were
immortal." We cannot "imagine our own death and when we attempt to do so, we can perceive that we are in fact still spectators.
Hence . . . no one believes in his own death." Freud avoids giving
any philosophical interpretation to this provocative observation.
Perhaps Lewis would say that our minds refuse death because death
was not part of the original "plan of creation."

Freud closes his essay on war and death with the a curious suggestion: "If you want to endure life, prepare yourself for death."
Freud realized what many in psychiatry have long observed: To fully
live, one must resolve the problem of death. When left unresolved,
one spends excessive energy denying it or becoming obsessed with
it. Freud left no doubt as to how he handled the problem. He be-

came obsessed with death, extraordinarily fearful and superstitious about it. Freud dreamed about death continually. His physician described Freud's preoccupation with death as "superstitious and obsessive."

When thirty-eight years old, Freud wrote that in his opinion he would "go on suffering from various complaints for another four to five to eight years, with good and bad periods, and then between forty and fifty perish very abruptly from a rupture of the heart; if it is not close to forty, it is not so bad at all."

At fifty-three, Freud made his one and only visit to the United States. He met William James, the famous American philosopher and psychologist. James made a positive and "lasting impression" on Freud, especially the way James confronted his own death. "I shall never forget one little scene that occurred as we were on a walk together. He stopped suddenly, handed me a bag he was carrying and asked me to walk on, saying that he would catch me up as soon as he had got through an attack of angina pectoris which was just coming on. He died of that disease a year later; and I have always wished that I might be as fearless as he was in the face of approaching death."

When fifty-four years old, Freud wrote: "We have grown old since we first shared the small pleasures of student life. Now life is running out." For Freud, birthdays were not a time of joy and celebration, but of despair. "If I had known how little joy I would have on my sixtieth birthday, my first would probably not have given me pleasure either. It would be in the best of times only a melancholic celebration."

Six years later Freud continued to feel he would soon die. To a friend he wrote: "Now you too have reached your sixtieth birthday, while I, six years older, am approaching the limit of life and may soon expect to see the end of the fifth act of this rather incomprehensible and not always amusing comedy." In short, Freud was certain that he would die at forty-one; then at fifty-one; then at sixty-one and sixty-two; and when he was seventy he was certain he would die at eighty.

How did he arrive at these specific dates? The following letter to C. G. Jung illustrates the rather bizarre, superstitious process of his thinking: "Some years ago I discovered within me the conviction that I would die between the ages of 61 and 62 . . . Then I went to Greece with my brother and it was really uncanny how often the number 61 or 62 kept cropping up in all sorts of numbered objects . . . It depressed me, but I had hopes of breathing easy when we got to the hotel in Athens and were assigned rooms on the first floor. Here, I was sure, there could be no No. 61. I was right, but I was given 31 (which with fatalistic licence could be regarded as half of 61 or 62) . . ." Then Freud noticed the number 31 kept coming up even more frequently.

But when and how did he first arrive at "the conviction that [he] would die between the ages of 61 and 62"? It began to preoccupy him in 1899. "At that time two events occurred. First, I wrote *The Intrepretation of Dreams* . . . second, I received a new telephone number . . . 14362 . . . when I wrote *The Interpretation of Dreams* I was 43 years old." Like a numerologist, he concludes: "Thus, it was plausible to suppose that the other figures signified the end of my life, hence 61 or 62." Freud explains: "The superstitious notion that I would die between the ages of 61 and 62 proves to coincide with the conviction that with *The Intrepretation of Dreams* I had completed my work, that there was nothing more for me to do and that I might just as well lie down and die." Then, perhaps to reassure himself, he adds: "You will admit that after this substitution it no longer sounds so absurd."

In 1917, eight years later, he continued to believe he would die at age sixty-one. "I have been working very hard, feel worn out and am beginning to find the world repellently loathsome. The superstition that my life is due to finish in February 1918 often seems to me quite a friendly idea . . ."

Freud's "superstition" that he would die at a specific age continued even at the age of eighty and gave him no peace. At that time he was certain he would die very soon, having reached "the limit of life which my father and brother reached. I am still lacking one more year until then . . . I keep brooding on whether I shall reach the age of my father and brother, or even that of my mother, tortured as I am by the conflict between the desire for rest, the dread of renewed suffering (which a prolonged life would mean) and by the anticipation of sorrow at being separated from everything to which I am still attached."

Freud speaks openly of his fear in his letters. "As for me, I note migraine, nasal secretion, and attacks of fears of dying," Freud writes his friend Fleiss when still in his thirties. Ernest Jones writes: "As far back as we know anything of Freud's life he seems to have been prepossessed with thoughts about death, more so than any other great man I can think of . . . Even in his early years of our acquaintance, he had the disconcerting habit of parting with the words 'Goodbye; you may never see me again.'" Jones continues: "There were the repeated attacks of what he called 'Todesangst' (dread of death). He hated growing old even as early as his forties, and as he did so the thoughts of death became increasingly clamorous. He once said he thought of it every day of his life, which is certainly unusual."

In his later years he feared the pain of a terminal illness—but what was it that so tortured his younger years? And did these fears relate to his worldview?

Freud gives a hint of his fears in *The Interpretation of Dreams*. He describes this book as containing "the most valuable of all the discoveries it has been my good fortune to make." Freud observes that children often dream that a rival sibling has died and that such dreams reflect an unconscious wish that the rival go away. To those who object that children would not be so depraved as to wish for the death of another child, Freud reminds them that children do not conceptualize or fear death as do adults. He then lists what he thinks adults fear about death: "the horrors of corruption . . . freezing in the ice-cold grave . . . the terrors of eternal nothingness." He then adds that adults cannot tolerate these fears, "as is proved by all the myths of a future life." Freud believed that people accepted the religious worldview because of their fear of death and their wish for permanence. Yet "the terrors of eternal nothingness" preoccupied Freud more than most people—and he remained an unbeliever, resigned to the harsh reality of his worldview.

Lewis's case is quite the opposite. Lewis describes his state of mind before his transition as extremely pessimistic and of having no desire that life continue in any form. "Nearly all that I believed to be real I thought grim and meaningless . . . I was so far from wishful thinking that I hardly thought anything true unless it contradicted my wishes." But Lewis said there was one exception—he did acknowledge one wish.

Paradoxically, in contradiction to Freud's theory, Lewis asserts that his attraction to atheism "gratified my wishes." This wish consisted of a strong need to be free of any Authority interfering with his life, as well as a quick and easy way out when circumstances became intolerable. "The materialist's universe had the enormous attraction that . . . death ended all . . . And if ever finite disasters proved greater than one wished to bear, suicide would always be possible. The horror of the Christian universe was that it had no door marked *Exit.*"

When Freud lost a loved one through death, he felt utterly hopeless. In a letter to Jones he wrote, "I was about your age (41 years old) when my father died, and it revolutionized my soul. Can you remember a time so full of death as this?" In Freud's *Interpretation of*

Dreams, his father's death comes up frequently. He writes in the preface to the second edition that "this book has a further subjective significance for me personally . . . It was, I found, a portion of my own self-analysis, my reaction to my father's death."

In 1896, upon the event, he writes to Fliess: "Yesterday we buried the old man, who died during the night of October 23. He bore himself bravely to the end, just like the altogether unusual man he had been . . . he must have had meningeal hemorrhages . . . and spasms from which he would then awake free of fever. The last attack was followed by pulmonary edema and quite an easy death . . . I am really quite down because of it." A week later, Freud mourns: "The old man's death has affected me deeply. I valued him highly, understood him very well, and with his peculiar mixture of deep wisdom and fantastic light-heartedness he had a significant effect on my life. By the time he died, his life had long been over, but in [my] inner self the whole past has been reawakened by this event."

When sixty-four, Freud lost a young and beautiful daughter. Freud had had six children, three sons and three daughters, and he loved no one in the world more than his daughter Sophie. In 1912 she had married. Sophie and her husband had lived in Hamburg for eight years when she suddenly became ill with influenza. "Yesterday morning our dear lovely Sophie died," Freud wrote his mother on January 26, 1920. He explained that his wife Martha was too upset to "undertake the journey and, in any case, she wouldn't have found Sophie alive . . . She is the first of our children we have to outlive." And the next month, in a letter to the Swiss psychiatrist Ludwig Binswanger, Freud mentions that neither he nor his wife "has got over the monstrous fact of children dying before their parents." Perhaps Freud never fully recovered from the loss. Almost a decade later he opens a letter to Binswanger with "My daughter who died would have been thirty-six years old today." In another letter: "Since I am profoundly irreligious there is no one I can accuse, and I know there is nowhere to which any complaint could be addressed. Deep down I can trace the feeling of a deep narcissistic hurt that is not to be healed."

Within three years Freud suffered another loss in the family—Sophie's son, who had been about a year old at the time of his mother's death. The death of this child evoked the strongest reaction in Freud of any of his losses. "We brought here from Hamburg Sophie's younger son, Heinele, now aged 4.5. He was indeed an enchanting little fellow, and I myself was aware of never having loved a human being, certainly never a child, so much," writes Freud in a letter to some friends. He mentions the child lacked the proper medical care in Hamburg and came to Vienna to live with the Freuds. "The child became ill again two weeks ago, temperature between 102 and 104, headaches and . . . finally the slow but sure realization that he has a miliary tuberculosis, in fact that the child is lost. He is now lying in a coma with paresis . . . the doctors say it can last a week, perhaps longer, and recovery is not desirable . . ." Then Freud cries out in his sorrow: "I don't think I have ever experienced such grief; perhaps my own sickness contributes to the shock. I work out of sheer necessity; fundamentally everything has lost its meaning for me . . . I find no joy in life." Freud writes to the boy's father that "I have spent some of the blackest days of my life in sorrowing about the child. At last . . . I can think of him quietly and talk of him without tears." Freud admits once again he has no resources to draw on for comfort: "The only consolation for me is that at my age I would not have seen much of him." According to Jones, this is the only time recorded in Freud's life that he shed tears.

Seven years later Freud experienced still another death in the family. During the summer of 1930, Freud's mother passed away. She was ninety-five years old and Freud was seventy-four. Because of the mixed feelings Freud had toward his father and the special relationship with his mother during his childhood—recalled in his self-analysis and reflected in his Oedipus complex theory—one would expect that her loss would have been more disturbing than the loss of his father. Just the opposite appears to be the case. In a letter to Jones, Freud confessed: "I will not disguise the fact that my reaction to this event has . . . been a curious one . . . on the surface I can detect only two things: an increase in personal freedom, since it was always a terrifying thought that she might come to hear of my death; and secondly, the satisfaction that at last she has achieved the deliverance for which she had earned a right after such a long life." Did Freud experience no grief or sorrow? He acknowledged that although his younger brother experienced grief, he did not. "No pain, no grief, which is probably to be explained by . . . the great age and the end of the pity we had felt at her helplessness. With that a feeling of liberation, of release, which I think I can understand. I was not allowed to die as long as she was alive, and now I may." And then another startling admission: "I was not at the funeral." Freud was still very active, productive, and mobile. What could possibly have been the reason he missed the funeral? Was he so terrified of death he could not bring himself to attend?

Freud's intense reaction to his father's death, which so deeply disturbed him, and his experiencing "no grief or sorrow" over his mother, illustrates a frequently observed, paradoxical clinical response to death: the more negative and unresolved the feelings toward the dead family member, especially the parent, the more difficulty one has resolving the loss.

❍   ❍   ❍

Although Freud feared death and obsessed over dates he would die, he insisted he wanted to know from his physician when his time was up. "I hope that when my time comes," Freud wrote in a letter when he was forty-three years old, "I shall find someone who will treat me with greater respect and tell me when to be ready. My father was fully aware of it, did not talk about it, and retained his beautiful composure to the end."

When Freud did become seriously ill, and his physicians diagnosed cancer, his young internist, Dr. Felix Deutsch, along with the surgeon, withheld the diagnosis. Deutsch reported that Freud had asked him for help in leaving this world with decency if he were doomed to die in suffering. It was Deutsch's fear that Freud would commit suicide that made him reticent. When Freud later found out, he felt betrayed. Deutsch suggested he withdraw as Freud's physician, fearing that Freud had lost the complete trust necessary in a doctor-patient relationship. Freud agreed, and although they terminated their professional relationship, they remained friends. (Later, Felix Deutsch became an analyst and with his wife Helene, also an analyst, moved to Cambridge, Massachusetts. He was my analyst during my psychiatric training.)

When Freud moved to London to escape the Nazis, he managed to obtain visas for his whole family, his maid Paula Fichtl, and his forty-one-year-old physician, Dr. Max Schur, an internist. Schur treated Freud during the final stages of his illness. Because he was with Freud during his last months, and at the moment he died, I will lean heavily on his account of how Freud confronted and reacted to his death.

Freud and his family arrived in London on June 6, 1938, and during their trip Freud had developed what his physician referred to as "minor cardiac symptoms." He had also developed some new lesions in the roof of his mouth that his doctor feared were cancerous. A surgeon performed an operation in September of that year, and Freud healed slowly and painfully.

The Freuds moved to 20 Maresfield Gardens in Hampstead, northwest London, on September 27, 1938. Freud's death occurred in that home just one year later, on September 23, 1939.

During his last days, as Dr. Schur noted, Freud selected his books "very carefully." A few months before he died, he read *The Emperor, the Sages, and Death* by Rachel Berdach. "Your mysterious and beautiful book . . . has pleased me . . . I haven't read anything so substantial and poetically accomplished for a long time," Freud wrote to the author. "Judging by the priority you grant to death, you must be very young . . . won't you give me the pleasure of paying me a visit one day?"

Max Schur noticed how deeply the book moved Freud and read it several times himself. Berdach focuses on the reality of death, and the fear it evokes, raising many questions—e.g., is man alone cursed with the knowledge of death in the midst of life? Believers and unbelievers each share their understanding of death. One discussion, between a bishop and an Arab physician, focuses on the miraculous resurrection of Lazarus by Jesus of Nazareth and the difficulty of having to face death a second time. One of Freud's favorite poems by the writer Heine was titled "Lazarus." Did Freud's attraction to the story of Lazarus reflect his own desire for permanence? The hero of Berdach's book dies by awakening one night to an uncanny silence. Everyone in his town has gone, and only he has been left behind by the Angel of Death. He dies in a state of panic, despair, and abandonment.

On September 22, 1939, the day before Freud died by euthanasia, he selected from his library Balzac's book *The Fatal Skin* (*La Peau de Chagrin.*) Freud knew that within a few hours he would ask his doctor to end his life. Of the hundreds of books he read during his lifetime, why *The Fatal Skin*? The plot is not simple. The hero, Raphael, a "young scientific man" with a craving for riches and fame, considers himself highly gifted but unappreciated and a failure. He plans to commit suicide. "Vehement must the storms be which compel a soul to seek for peace from the trigger of a pistol," writes the author, among several comments on those who take their own lives.

Raphael meets the devil, who promises to fulfill all of the young man's cravings for fame and fortune. "I will make you richer, more powerful and of more consequence than a constitutional king," promises the devil. But as part of the pact, Raphael must take "the skin of a wild ass." With each wish the hero makes, the skin will shrink a little and shorten his life. The devil warns Raphael that "to Will consumes us: to have our Will destroys us . . . I will tell you the great secret of human life. By two instinctive processes man exhausts the springs of life within him. Two verbs cover all the forms which these two causes of death may take—to Will and to have your Will."

As the hero becomes wealthy and has more and more of his wishes granted, he finds others resent him. As he talks about himself, one can understand how Freud may have identified with him. The hero muses: "Thought is the key to all treasures . . . I have soared above this world, where my enjoyments have been intellectual joy . . . I possess the power of readily expressing my thoughts, and I could take a forward place in the great field of knowledge; and is not this the result of scientific curiosity, of excessive application, and a love of reading which possessed me from the age of seven till my entry into life? . . . My exuberant self-esteem came to my aid; I had that intense belief in my destiny, which perhaps amounts to genius . . ."

Raphael says others have "accused him of haughtiness," that he has made others aware of their "mediocrity," and they "took revenge by submitting him to a kind of ostracism." Certainly, Freud could identify with these thoughts—especially with the ostracism and rejection he experienced from the scientific and medical community.

The novel contains passages about a famous painting of Jesus Christ as well as discussions concerning the existence and nature of God. "I will not believe," Raphael says, "that the Supreme Being would take pleasure in torturing a harmless creature."

More and more of Raphael's wishes are granted. The skin continues to shrink and the hero knows his life is coming to an end. He tries to find a means of stretching the skin but fails. "It is all over with me," he cries. "It is the finger of God! I shall die!" The novel closes with the hero dying in a frantic state of despair. He falls in love with beautiful Pauline. But every time he desires her, the skin shrinks and his life shortens. So he leaves her. When she finds him, he fears he will be unable to control his desire for her and the skin will shrink one last time and kill him. "Go! go! leave me," the hero says to his lover. "If you stay, I shall die. Do you want to see me die?" He shows her the skin, which begins to shrink as his desire for her grows. Suddenly she realizes what is happening, locks herself in another room, and, to save Raphael, tries to kill herself. He realizes he is dying and shouts to her: "I want to die in your arms." He breaks down the door, rushes into the room, and takes her into his arms. Unable to control his wishes or his fear of death, he dies in a state of panic.

Many literary critics speak of Raphael as another Faust. We cannot help but remember that Goethe's *Faust* is the work that Freud quoted more frequently than any other. What drew Freud to this particular work by Balzac as the last book he read before his death? Did Freud feel he himself made a pact with the devil when he turned his back on the worldview of his parents—embracing the scientific worldview to obtain, like the hero in the novel, fame and fortune? Freud spoke of his research into the mind as being his mistress. Did Freud fear he would die in a frantic state of fear and panic as did the hero in both the book by Berdach and the one by Balzac? Freud's physician comments that Freud used the word "shrinking" to describe his father's death many years ago: "How uncanny that he should have chosen to read this book to write 'finis' to his own story."

The day after reading *The Fatal Skin,* Freud took Schur's hand and reminded him of a promise made when the physician first began treating him. "You promised me then not to forsake me when my time comes. Now it's nothing but torture and makes no sense anymore." The doctor remembered. Freud thanked him and requested that he tell his daughter Anna "about this."

After informing Anna, Dr. Schur injected Freud with two centigrams of morphine, a heavy dose that was repeated after twelve hours. At 3 A.M. on September 23, 1939, Freud died. He was cremated on the morning of September 26, 1939, at Golders Green, a small village northwest of London.

❂   ❂   ❂

C. S. Lewis also writes extensively about mortality. In *The Problem of Pain*, Lewis describes how, as an atheist, the problem of human suffering, especially "the capacity of man to foresee his own death while keenly desiring permanence," made it difficult to believe in a Creator. Before his conversion, death involved the inevitable end to a gloomy and pessimistic existence. Death equaled extinction—and though dreaded and feared, it provided a way out. When he was seventeen, Lewis wrote his friend Greeves: "My father seemed in very poor form when I got home, and fussed a lot about my cold: so everything is beastly, and I have decided—of course—to commit suicide again." Many a truth are told in jest—and we know from his autobiography that Lewis considered suicide an escape if life became unbearable.

After his conversion Lewis believed the only person to decide the time of one's death was the Person who gave one life. In *The Screwtape Letters*, Lewis's devil encourages murder and suicide. "If he is an emotional, gullible man," the devil advises his representative on earth to "feed him on minor poets and fifth-rate novelists of the old school until you have made him believe that 'Love' is both irresistible and somehow intrinsically meritorious. This belief is not much help, I grant you, in producing casual unchastity; but it is an incomparable recipe for prolonged, 'noble,' romantic, tragic adulteries, ending, if all goes well, in murders and suicides . . ."

After his changed worldview, Lewis understood death as a result of the transgression of God's laws and not part of the original plan. Death is both the result of a Fallen Universe and the the only hope for overcoming the Fall. "There are two attitudes towards Death which the human mind naturally adopts," Lewis explains in his classic work called *Miracles*. "One is the lofty view, which reached its greatest intensity among the Stoics, that Death 'doesn't matter' . . . and that we ought to regard it with indifference. The other is the 'natural' point of view, implicit in nearly all private conversations on the subject, and in much modern thought about the survival of the human species, that Death is the greatest of all evils."

But neither of these two views of death reflects the view of the New Testament, which, Lewis says, is considerably more subtle. "On the one hand Death is the triumph of Satan, the punishment of the Fall, and the last enemy." But Lewis explains that death is not only an enemy that defeats every human being; it is also the means that God uses to redeem us. "On the other hand . . . the *death* of Christ is the remedy for the Fall. Death is, in fact, what some modern people call 'ambivalent' . . . It is Satan's great weapon and also God's great weapon: it is . . . our supreme disgrace and our only hope; the thing Christ came to conquer and the means by which He conquered." Lewis reminds his readers that "Christ shed tears at the grave of Lazarus and sweated blood in Gethsemane . . ." and "detested this penal obscenity not less than we do, but more."

Lewis asserts that the central concept of the New Testament story focuses on death. The death of Jesus of Nazareth "has somehow put us right with God and given us a fresh start." This particular death "is just that point in history at which something absolutely unimaginable from outside shows through into our own world." He warns that this concept is difficult for the human mind to grasp— but that is to be expected. "Indeed, if we found that we could fully understand it, that very fact would show it wasn't what it professes to be—the inconceivable, the uncreated, the thing from beyond nature, striking down into nature like lightning."

Unlike Freud, who hated growing old and who referred to the process continually in negative, pessimistic terms, Lewis appeared to enjoy the process. Writing to a friend a month before his death, he exclaims, "Yes, autumn is the best of the seasons; and I'm not sure that old age isn't the best part of life."

Before Lewis's conversion, he noticed that many of the pagan myths he had read contained a common theme. He wrote a friend: "Can one believe that there was just nothing in that persistent motif of blood, death, and resurrection, which runs like a black and scarlet cord through all the greater myths . . . through Balder and Dionysus and Adonis . . . ? Surely the history of the human mind hangs together better if you suppose that all this was the first shadowy approach of something whose reality came with Christ—even if we can't at present fully understand that something." The great pagan myths about a dying God that so moved Lewis as a student he now saw as signposts—all pointing to that defining moment in human history, to what he called the Grand Miracle, the Resurrection.

When Lewis fought in World War I, he was wounded and thought that he was dying. He later recalled: "Two things stand out. One is the moment, just after I had been hit, when I found (or thought I found) that I was not breathing and concluded that this was death." He found himself strangely free of fear and any other feeling. "The proposition 'Here is a man dying' stood before my mind as dry, as factual, as unemotional as something in a textbook. It was not even interesting."

But except for this moment, Lewis experienced all the terror that is a part of every war. When World War II began in Europe, Lewis wrote: "My memories of the last war haunted my dreams for years. Military service . . . includes the threat of every temporal evil: pain and death which is what we fear from sickness: isolation from those we love which is what we fear from exile: toil under arbitrary masters, injustice and humiliation, which is what we fear from slavery: hunger, thirst, cold and exposure which is what we fear from poverty." He concludes that "death would be much better than to live through another war."

In a lecture given at Oxford that same year titled "Learning in Wartime," Lewis makes the point that war does not "make death more frequent." He notes that "one hundred percent of us die and the percentage cannot be increased"; that war merely "puts several deaths earlier." He observes that one of the few positive aspects of war is that it makes us "aware of our mortality." "If active service does not prepare a man for death what conceivable concatenation of circumstances would?" Lewis agrees with the Psalmist that one gains wisdom from awareness of one's mortality. "Teach us to number our days aright, that we may gain a heart of wisdom" (Psalm 90:12).

Lewis drives this point home in *The Screwtape Letters* when the devil complains that war forces people to think about and prepare for death: "How disastrous for us is the continual remembrance of death which war enforces. One of our best weapons, contented worldliness, is rendered useless. In wartime not even a human can believe that he is going to live forever." The devil considers this unfortunate. "How much better for us [devils] if *all* humans died in costly nursing homes amid doctors who lie, nurses who lie, friends who lie, as we have trained them, promising life to the dying . . . lest it should betray to the sick man his true condition!"

When twenty-three, Lewis wrote a letter to his father commenting on the death of an old teacher whom they knew well: "I have seen death fairly often and never yet been able to find it anything but extraordinary and rather incredible. The real person is so very real, so obviously living and different from what is left, that one cannot believe something has turned into nothing." This observation reflects comments by some of my medical students after first observing the corpse of a patient they knew and realizing that the person was so much more than a body.

In 1929, when Lewis was thirty years old and still an atheist, his father died. Lewis's reaction reflected the intense ambivalence he felt toward his father. In a letter to a friend he describes his feelings: "I am attending at the almost painless sickbed of one for whom I have little affection and whose society has for many years given me much discomfort and no pleasure . . . Nevertheless I find it almost unendurable . . . there is . . . though no spiritual sympathy, a deep and terrible physiological sympathy. My father and I are physical counterparts: and during these days more than ever I notice his resemblance to me." In his autobiography Lewis writes little of his father's death. "My father's death, with all the fortitude (even playfulness) which he displayed in his last illness, does not really come into the story I am telling." This is one of the few times in his autobiography that he displays little insight into himself.

In 1960, when Joy Davidman died following a long illness, Lewis wrote to a friend: "My dear Joy is dead . . . Until within ten days of the end we hoped . . . that she was going to hold her own, but it was not to be . . . At half past one I took her into hospital in an ambulance. She was conscious for the short remainder of her life, and in very little pain thanks to drugs; and died peacefully in my company about 10.15 the same night . . . You will understand that I have no heart to write more."

Lewis's published response, A Grief Observed, makes the reader feel the anger, resentment, loneliness, fear, and restlessness of the grieving process. His anger becomes palpable when he wonders if God in the final analysis is "The Cosmic Sadist, the spiteful imbecile?" He complains, "It is hard to have patience with people who say 'There is no death,' or 'Death doesn't matter.' There is death and

whatever is matters . . . you might as well say birth doesn't matter."
He struggles to force his mind to accept the loss. "I look up at the
night sky. Is there anything more certain than that in all those vast
times and spaces, if I were allowed to search them, I should
nowhere find her face, her voice, her touch? She died. She is dead.
Is the word so difficult to learn?" The reader can feel his pain when
he writes, "Cancer, and cancer, and cancer. My mother, my father,
my wife. I wonder who is next in the queue?"

Joy Davidman broke through the shell Lewis had built around
himself to avoid the risk of reexperiencing the terrible loss suffered
during his childhood. Now that his greatest fear had happened, he
cried out: "Oh God, God, why did you take such trouble to force this
creature out of its shell if it is now doomed to crawl back—to be
sucked back into it?" But Lewis, as he worked through his grief,
came to understand that "bereavement is a universal and integral
part of our experience of love. It follows marriage as normally as
marriage follows courtship or as autumn follows summer."

To understand the thoughts and feelings of Lewis once he knew
he might die, we need to read his letters and consider the books he
read at that time. Lewis never lost his sense of humor. In a letter to
a lady who wrote about how alarmed she felt when she heard Lewis
was seriously ill, he writes: "What on earth is the trouble about there
being a rumour of my death? There's nothing discreditable in dying:
I've known the most respectable people do it!"

In another letter a couple of years later, Lewis writes, "What a
state we have got into when we can't say 'I'll be happy when God
calls me' without being afraid one will be thought 'morbid.' After all,
St. Paul said just the same . . . Why should we not look forward to
the arrival . . . ?" He concludes that one can do only three things
about death: "To desire it, to fear it, or to ignore it. The third alternative, which is the one the modern world calls 'healthy,' is surely
the most uneasy and precarious of all."

A few years later Lewis tried to comfort this same correspondent after she apparently received word *she* was seriously ill. "What have you and I got to do but make our exit? When they told me I was in danger several months ago, I don't remember feeling distressed. I am talking, of course, about *dying*, not about *being killed*. If shells started falling about this house I should feel quite differently. An external, visible, and (still worse) audible threat at once wakes the instinct of self-preservation into fierce activity. I don't think natural death has any similar terrors."

And in another letter a few months later: "Can you not see death as the friend and deliverer? It means stripping off that body which is tormenting you: like taking off a hairshirt or getting out of a dungeon. What is there to be afraid of? . . . Has this world been so kind to you that you should leave it with regret?" Lewis then tries to comfort her with words that reveal his own thoughts and feelings about his death: "There are better things ahead than any we leave behind . . . Don't you think Our Lord says to you 'Peace, child, peace. Relax. Let go. Underneath are the everlasting arms . . . Do you trust me so little?' Of course this may not be the end. Then make it a good rehearsal." Lewis signed this letter: "Yours (and like you a tired traveler, near the journey's end) Jack."

In June 1961, Lewis, who suffered an enlarged prostate, developed urinary obstruction, infection of his kidneys, and eventually toxemia with cardiac symptoms. He improved during the next few months and continued to teach, write, and visit with his friends. On July 15, 1963, Lewis had a heart attack and lapsed into a coma. He again recovered, but only briefly, living the next few months quietly and happily. Records of his last days attest to a cheerfulness, a calmness, an inner peace, and even anticipation. During this time he wrote to his friend Arthur Greeves: "Tho' I am by no means unhappy I can't help feeling it was rather a pity I did revive in July. I mean, having been glided so painlessly up to the Gate it seems hard to have it shut in one's face and know that the whole process must some day be gone through again . . . Poor Lazarus!"

Though Lewis kept his sense of humor throughout his last years, he nevertheless felt keenly the separation from loved ones that death would bring. In this same letter Lewis notes that although he is "comfortable and cheerful . . . the only real snag is that it looks as if you and I shall never meet again in this life. This often saddens me very much."

To another friend he writes, "I was unexpectedly revived from a long coma, and perhaps the almost continuous prayers of my friends did it—but it wd. have been a luxuriously easy passage, and one almost regrets having the door shut in one's face . . . When you die . . . look me up . . . It *is* all rather fun—solemn fun—isn't it."

One of his biographers and a close friend notes that he spent his last days rereading his favorite books: "the *Odyssey* and *Iliad* and a little Plato in Greek; the *Aeneid* in Latin; Dante's *Divine Comedy;* Wordsworth's *Prelude;* and works by George Herbert, Patmore, Scott, Austen, Fielding, Dickens and Trollope."

In January of 1962, he wrote, "I knew I was in danger but was not depressed. I've read pretty well everything." About three weeks before his death, Lewis wrote to a friend that he was happy to have the leisure time to do what he enjoyed doing all of his life—read good literature. "Don't think I am not happy . . . I am rereading the *Iliad* and enjoying it more than I have ever done."

Two weeks before his death, Lewis had lunch with a faculty colleague, Richard W. Ladborough. They met at Lewis's invitation to discuss a book Lewis had just read. Someone had lent him a copy of *Dangerous Acquaintances* (*Les Liaisons Dangereuses*) by Pierre Choderlos de Laclos. "Wow! what a book," Lewis exclaimed. He said it was "like reading a Mozart libretto seriously: a blood curdling experience." We can understand Lewis's reading the classic works of literature that in his early years brought him great pleasure. But what attracted him to this French novel, first published in 1782?

The novel, a series of letters between members of the French aristocracy, exposes the deceit, debauchery, and corruption that prevailed in high society at that time. Both the hero, Valmont, and the heroine, Merteuil, are motivated by ambition, power, and pride; they use deceit and seduction to achieve their goals. They use social privilege to prey on the weak. Critics have described the novel as "diabolical," an "indictment of . . . privileged corruption . . . and the fate of women in a male dominated society." One critic described the main characters as "having outgrown God, they exist in a world which has no values except those which they give it."

What motivated Lewis to read it? First, a colleague loaned Lewis the book and may have recommended it as a great novel. The novel began receiving increased attention during the 1940s and 1950s and eventually critics considered it "the greatest of eighteenth-century French novels." The author's reputation placed him alongside Alexander Dumas and Victor Hugo. So Lewis may have recognized a significant work of literature—but I think the answer lies elsewhere. After all, Lewis authored *The Screwtape Letters* and other writings on the devil. He wrote often of the dangers of pride and ambition and the need of every human being for redemption. In *Dangerous Acquaintances* the schemers destroy all around them. Perhaps he found the "diabolical" aspects of the book and the depiction of the dark side of human nature fascinating and in agreement with his observations that he portrayed so compellingly in his popular *Screwtape Letters*.

During the discussion of this novel over lunch, Ladborough noted Lewis was his "usual happy and humorous self." Yet he felt Lewis was aware the end was near. "I somehow felt it was the last time we would meet and when he escorted me, with his usual courtesy, to the door, I think he felt so too. Never was a man better prepared."

How could Lewis, or anyone else, be "prepared" for death, to face this "penal obscenity" with not only cheerfulness, calmness, and inner peace, but with actual anticipation? Did his worldview provide him with the resources that made this possible? Perhaps, again, we find the answer in his own words: "If we really believe what we say we believe—if we really think that home is elsewhere and that this life is a 'wandering to find home,' why should we not look forward to the arrival?"

On November 22, 1963, Lewis's brother Warren brought Lewis his four o'clock tea. He noted Lewis was drowsy but calm and cheerful. In a letter, written two weeks after Lewis died, Warren writes: "Ever since the summer my brother had been steadily going downhill, though we all tried to shut our eyes to the fact. But not my brother." Warren wrote that Lewis knew he was going to die and was calm and peaceful in light of that awareness. "About a week before his death he said to me, 'I have done all that I was sent into the world to do, and I am ready to go.' I have never seen death looked in the face so tranquilly . . ."

Then Warren describes the last few moments of his brother's life. "On 22nd of last month I took him his tea in bed at 4 o.c., and went back to my study to do some work. At 5.30 I heard a crash in his room and ran in, to find him lying on the floor on his back, unconscious; he lived for about five minutes after that and never recovered consciousness. Would not we all wish to go the same way when our time comes?"

Epilogue

Did Freud and Lewis ever meet? The possibility is tantalizing. After Freud immigrated to England, he lived in Hampstead, in northwest London, not far from Oxford. A young Oxford professor visited Freud during this time but has not been identified. Might it have been Lewis?

We'll never know. We do know, however, of a curious connection between the families. During World War II, to escape the bombing of London, a young woman named Jill Fluett moved from her home in London to live in the suburbs with Lewis and Mrs. Moore. Before meeting Lewis, she had idolized him as an author. As she came to know him, she became infatuated with the young professor. Lewis treated her kindly and kept in touch with her for many years after she left the Lewis household. Eventually, Jill married. Her lifetime love turned out to be none other than Clement Freud, the grandson of Sigmund Freud and a member of Parliament. One day Jill Freud called the Lewis home to arrange a date for her and her family to come to dinner. She was informed that Lewis had died that very afternoon.

If Freud and Lewis did meet, if Lewis *was* the young Oxford professor who visited Freud at his home in Hampstead, the time would have been between June 1938 and September 1939, the fifteen months that Freud lived in England before his death. Freud would have been in his eighties, Lewis less than half that age.

Would they have had anything meaningful to say to one another? Certainly when Albert Einstein visited Freud many years earlier, they shared few interests and had little to discuss. In a letter to a friend, Freud wrote of Einstein's visit: "He understands as much about psychology as I do about physics, so we had a very pleasant talk."

Lewis and Freud, by contrast, would have had a great deal to discuss. They shared an interest in literature as well as in psychoanalysis. Freud, already known as the father of the new literary criticism, provided critics like Lewis with new tools for interpreting human behavior.

Perhaps they would have discussed the great authors they enjoyed. Freud listed Milton's *Paradise Lost* as one of his two "favorite books." (Curiously, his second-favorite book, *Lazarus,* by the great Jewish writer Heinrich Heine, who embraced Lewis's worldview, *also* focused on a story in the Bible.) Lewis was already an authority on Milton, though he did not publish his famous *Preface to Paradise Lost* until about three years later.

Because Freud was suffering from a fatal illness, they might also have discussed the problem of pain, which both had struggled to understand. Freud may have shared with Lewis, as he had shared with a friend a decade earlier, the pessimism and hopelessness he felt when confronted with illness and the loss of a loved one: "As an unbelieving fatalist I can only let my arms sink before the terrors of death."

Lewis, out of respect for the older Freud, would probably have avoided presenting the many arguments he wrote about in *The Problem of Pain.* He might have simply shared with Freud how he came to a personal faith that helped him through some of his most painful experiences. Because Freud admired and often quoted St. Paul, Lewis might have acknowledged that his transition, though less dramatic and more gradual than that of Paul, was no less radical and no less transforming.

Their discussion may have roamed widely and included the top-

ics of sex, love, death, happiness, and of course the most important
one—the question of God. Whatever they discussed, it would have
been an exciting experience to eavesdrop on their conversation.
Hopefully, I have provided the reader with the next-best alternative—reviewing their thoughts on these issues in their letters and
prolific publications.

✦ ✦ ✦

What accounts for the profound impact the writings of C. S. Lewis
and Sigmund Freud continue to have on our culture a half century
after their deaths? One reason for their impact may be that,
whether we realize it or not, we all embrace some form of either
the materialist worldview advocated by Freud or the spiritual
worldview advocated by Lewis. But there may be more subtle reasons. Perhaps Freud and Lewis represent conflicting parts of ourselves. One part raises its voice in defiance of authority, and says
with Freud, "I will not surrender"; another part, like Lewis, recognizes within ourselves a deep-seated yearning for a relationship
with the Creator.

Freud and Lewis agreed that the most important question concerned God's existence: Is there an Intelligence beyond the universe? Both spent a significant portion of their lives addressing this
question, realizing its profound implications for understanding our
identity, our purpose, and our destiny.

Yet Freud, and Lewis before his transition, also avoided confronting the evidence. We find this easy to do. We keep ourselves
distracted. We rationalize. We tell ourselves we will consider such
weighty (and anxiety-provoking) subjects when we are older—when
time demands will not be as great. At the moment, we have more
pressing needs. As with Lewis before his transition, we really don't
want to know—we nurture a "willful blindness" and a "deep-seated
hatred of authority." We find repugnant the notion of "a *transcen-*

dental Interferer." We feel toward our lives as both Freud and Lewis felt toward theirs: "This is my business, and mine only."

Lewis and Freud, however, also experienced deep-seated longings that haunted them persistently. Both described these feelings using the German word *Sehnsucht.* When sixty-six years old, Freud continued to speak of "strange, secret longings," now thinking these might be "perhaps . . . for a life of quite another kind." Lewis described these experiences of longing as "the central story" of his life. After his transition, he realized they were valuable "only as a pointer to something other and outer," as "signposts" pointing to the Creator. Perhaps we all experience such longings and, like Freud, remain confused by them; or, like Lewis, recognize them as signposts.

The writings of Freud and Lewis help us understand one difficulty we often have in *seeing* the signposts—namely, our tendency to distort our image of God. One of Freud's theories that has proved helpful clinically relates to the unconscious process of transference, the tendency to displace feelings from authority figures in our childhood onto those in the present, thus distorting and causing conflict with the present authority. If we possess a strong tendency to displace or transfer feelings from parental authority, especially the father, onto present-day authority figures, how much more might we distort our concept of an Ultimate Authority whom we cannot experience with our senses? If this holds true, we must be careful that our concept of God—whether the God we reject as unbelievers or that we worship as believers—is firmly based on the Creator revealed in history and not on our neurotic distortion of Him.

We must also be careful not to conceptualize or judge God by the faulty actions of his fallible creatures, whether those in the Bible, televangelists who go to jail, or priests who molest children. All fall short. Jesus of Nazareth was gentle and forgiving to the woman at the well who sought forgiveness, but severe with the religious leaders who failed to live what they professed.

Our tendency to distort and create our own God, sometimes a God not of love but of hate, may explain why, over the centuries, people have committed, and continue to commit, ungodly acts—even acts of terrorism—in the name of God. This tendency to create our own God gives us insight into why the *first* commandment is: "You shall have no other gods before me."

Freud's and Lewis's intense negative feelings toward their fathers influenced their negative attitude toward God. Lewis, after his transition, guarded carefully against this tendency in himself. He wrote: "My idea of God is not a divine idea. It has to be shattered time after time. He shatters it Himself. He is the great iconoclast. Could we not say that this shattering is one of the marks of His presence? All reality is iconoclastic."

The answer to the question of God has profound implications for our lives here on earth, both Freud and Lewis agree. So we owe it to ourselves to look at the evidence, perhaps beginning with the Old and New Testaments. Lewis also reminds us, however, that the evidence lies all around us: "We may ignore, but we can nowhere evade, the presence of God. The world is crowded with Him. He walks everywhere *incognito*. And the *incognito* is not always easy to penetrate. The real labor is to remember to attend. In fact to come awake. Still more to remain awake."

Notes

The number on the left refers to the page where you will find the cited phrase.

Prologue

2   He was recently on the cover of *Time* . . . minds of the century: *Time Magazine,* March 29, 1999.

2   ranked sixth in a book on the hundred most influential scientists: Barondes, *Mood Genes,* p. 25.

Chapter 1: The Protagonists

13   "The new Psychology was at the time . . . from Fantasy as the psychologists understand that term": Lewis, *Surprised by Joy,* p. 203.

14   "her words could be harsh . . . loved the old woman": Freud, *The Interpretation of Dreams,* in *The Standard Edition of the Complete Psychological Works,* vol. IV, p. 248.

14   "in my case . . . God Almighty and hell and who instilled in me a high opinion of my own capacities": Freud, *The Complete Letters of Sigmund Freud to Wilhelm Fliess,* p. 268.

14   As an adult, Freud would dream about her: Bonaparte et al., *The Origins of Psycho-Analysis,* pp. 219–20.

15   "for the last twenty-nine years . . . vanished, like my nurse not long before": Bonaparte et al., *The Origins of Psycho-Analysis,* pp. 222–23.

15   "universal obsessional neurosis": Freud, *Obsessive Actions and Religious Practices,* in *The Standard Edition of the Complete Psychological Works,* vol. IX, pp. 117–27.

15   "longing for Rome": Freud, *The Complete Letters of Sigmund Freud to Wilhelm Fliess,* p. 285.

15   "next Easter in Rome": Freud, *The Complete Letters of Sigmund Freud to Wilhelm Fliess,* p. 409.

15   "so much wanted to see Rome again": Freud, *The Letters of Sigmund Freud,* pp. 244–45.

15 Nevertheless, he read the Bible . . . Hebrew, and he apparently spoke Hebrew fluently: Gay, *Freud*, p. 6.

16 "My early familiarity with the Bible story . . . enduring effect upon the direction of my interest": Freud, *An Autobiographical Study*, in *The Standard Edition of the Complete Psychological Works*, vol. XX, p. 8.

16 "My dear Son . . . love from your old father": Schur, *Freud*, p. 24.

16 Unlike him, Freud never . . . Hebrew and knew only a few words of his mother's Yiddish: Freud, *The Letters of Sigmund Freud to Eduard Silberstein*, pp. xxiv–xxv.

17 Instead of going to Freud's . . . jumped to her death: Freud, *The Letters of Sigmund Freud to Eduard Silberstein*, pp. xiv–xv.

18 "I, the godless medical man . . . lest your path to salvation in the faith be cut off": Freud, *The Letters of Sigmund Freud to Eduard Silberstein*, pp. 70–71.

18 "When you and I meet . . . ideal human being": Freud, *The Letters of Sigmund Freud to Eduard Silberstein*, p. 95.

18 "I have not escaped from his influence . . . emission theory": Freud, *The Letters of Sigmund Freud to Eduard Silberstein*, p. 104.

18 "The philosopher Brentano, whom you know from my letters . . . Jesuit, which I cannot believe": Freud, *The Letters of Sigmund Freud to Eduard Silberstein*, p. 129.

19 "For the time being, I have ceased to be a materialist and am not yet a theist": Freud, *The Letters of Sigmund Freud to Eduard Silberstein*, pp. 104–105.

19 "The bad part of it . . . demand the existence of God": Freud, *The Letters of Sigmund Freud to Eduard Silberstein*, p. 111.

19 "What bound me to Jewry . . . national pride, for I have always been an unbeliever": Freud, *Address to the Society of B'nai B'rith*, in *The Standard Edition of the Complete Psychological Works*, vol. XX, p. 273.

19 "Feuerbach is one whom I revere and admire above all other philosophers": Freud, *The Letters of Sigmund Freud to Eduard Silberstein*, p. 96.

19 "We have shown that the substance . . . absolute mind is the so-called finite subjective mind": Feuerbach, *The Essence of Christianity*, p. 270.

20 "sizable pockets of anticlericalism and of secularist contempt for all religion": Gay, *A Godless Jew*, p. 7.

20 "who carried more weight with me than anyone else in my whole life": Freud, *An Autobiographical Study*, in *The Standard Edition of the Complete Psychological Works*, vol. XX, p. 9.

20 "there are no sources of knowledge of the universe other than . . . what

we call research": Freud, *New Introductory Lectures on Psychoanalysis*, in *The Standard Edition of the Complete Psychological Works*, vol. XXII, p. 139.

21 In addition, the two professors . . . anti-Semitism prevalent in Austria at that time and hinted that he might meet resistance: Gay, *Freud*, pp. 138–39.

21 "Jews were profoundly . . . illnesses": Gilman, *The Case of Sigmund Freud*.

21 "common Jewish sensitiveness . . . University, from the anti-Semitism that pervaded Vienna": Jones, *The Life and Work of Sigmund Freud*, vol. I, p. 22.

21 "I was expected . . . alien because I was a Jew": Freud, *An Autobiographical Study*, in *The Standard Edition of the Complete Psychological Works*, vol. XX, p. 9.

22 "as unheroic conduct on the part of the big, strong man": Freud, *The Interpretation of Dreams*, in *The Standard Edition of the Complete Psychological Works*, vol. IV, p. 197.

22 "not in the least frightened . . . quite prepared to kill him": Freud, *Letters of Sigmund Freud*, p. 78.

23 "Easter Sunday . . . fiftieth anniversary of taking up my medical practice": Jones, *The Life and Work of Sigmund Freud*, vol. I, p. 143.

23 Some write that opening his practice on Easter Sunday reflected the special respect Freud gave the day: Vitz, *Sigmund Freud's Christian Unconscious*, p. 91.

23 others that it reflected defiance or disrespect: Jones, *The Life and Work of Sigmund Freud*, vol. I, p. 143.

23 So the couple married in Germany . . . bride, with only a few members of the family present: Jones, *The Life and Work of Sigmund Freud*, vol. I, pp. 149–50.

24 "And in the same way a little girl . . . kill his father and take his mother to wife": Freud, *Introductory Lectures on Psychoanalysis*, in *The Standard Edition of the Complete Psychological Works*, vol. XV, pp. 207–208.

24 "I have found, in my own case too . . . presupposition of fate": Freud, *The Complete Letters of Sigmund Freud to Wilhelm Fliess*, p. 272.

25 "It is my unaltered conviction . . . Greek legend itself as an inevitable fate": Freud, *A Short Account of Psychoanalysis*, in *The Standard Edition of the Complete Psychological Works*, vol. XIX, p. 198.

25 "It became ever clearer . . . was the nucleus of every case of neurosis": Freud, *A Short Account of Psychoanalysis*, in *The Standard Edition of the Complete Psychological Works*, vol. XIX, p. 198.

27   Lewis suggested that this memory . . . taught him "longing": Lewis, *Surprised by Joy*, p. 7.

29   "the strange English accents . . . hatred for England which took many years to heal": Lewis, *Surprised by Joy*, p. 24.

30   "I feared for my soul . . . in that curtainless dormitory": Lewis, *Surprised by Joy*, pp. 33–34.

30   "No school ever had a better Matron . . . We all loved her": Lewis, *Surprised by Joy*, p. 59.

30   "Little by little . . . Occultism began to spread": Lewis, *Surprised by Joy*, pp. 59–60.

31   "Here, especially in Virgil . . . humanity tended to blunder": Lewis, *Surprised by Joy*, pp. 62–63.

31   "If the parents in each generation . . . history of education would be very different": Lewis, *Surprised by Joy*, p. 30.

31   "I have never seen a community . . . solidarity and sense of corporate honor": Lewis, *Surprised by Joy*, p. 110.

31   "system failed to cure; they were not kicked, mocked . . . flogged, and humiliated enough": Lewis, *Surprised by Joy*, p. 107.

32   "to read, write or moon about in the golden-tinted woods and valleys of this country": Lewis, *They Stand Together*, p. 53.

32   "had about it a sort of cool morning innocence . . . What it actually did to me was to convert, even to baptize . . . my imagination": Green and Hooper, *C. S. Lewis*, p. 45.

32   "The reader will remember . . . indirectly from the tone of his mind or independently from reading his books": Lewis, *Surprised by Joy*, pp. 139–40.

32   "My debt to him is very great, my reverence to this day undiminished": Lewis, *Surprised by Joy*, p. 148.

33   "great men were regarded as gods . . . educated and thinking ones have stood outside it": Lewis, *The Letters of C. S. Lewis*, p. 135.

33   "How 'I took' about sixty prisoners . . . hands up—is not worth telling, save as a joke": Lewis, *Surprised by Joy*, p. 197.

34   "She is really the mother of a friend": Lewis, *Letters, C. S. Lewis–Don Giovanni Calabria*, pp. 45–47.

34   "My ailing mother": Lewis, *Letters, C. S. Lewis–Don Giovanni Calabria*, pp. 51–53.

34   "My aged mother": Lewis, *Letters, C. S. Lewis–Don Giovanni Calabria*, p. 15.

34   "There has been a great change . . . hypocritical to pretend that it was a grief to us": Lewis, letter to Firor dated March 27, 1951 (unpublished), Marion E. Wade Center, Wheaton College, Wheaton, Ill., and Bodleian Library, Oxford University. Used by permission.

34 "Jack's relationship with Mrs. Moore . . . look after her if Paddy was killed": Sayer, *Jack*, p. 135.

Chapter 2: The Creator

36 He predicted, however, that as the masses of people . . ."the fairy tales of religion": Freud, *The Future of an Illusion*, in *The Standard Edition of the Complete Psychological Works*, vol. XXI, p. 29.

37 "Neither in my private life . . . secret of being an out-and-out unbeliever": Freud, *Letters of Sigmund Freud*, p. 453.

38 "tales of miracles . . . sober observation and betrayed too clearly the influence of the activity of the human imagination": Freud, *The Question of a Weltanschauung*, in *The Standard Edition of the Complete Psychological Works*, vol. XXII, p. 156.

38 "bear the imprint . . . ignorant times of the childhood of humanity": Freud, *The Question of a Weltanschauung*, in *The Standard Edition of the Complete Psychological Works*, vol. XXII, p. 168.

38 "distorting the picture . . . state of psychical infantilism": Freud, *Civilization and Its Discontents*, in *The Standard Edition of the Complete Psychological Works*, vol. XXI, pp. 84–85.

38 "the universal obsessional neurosis of humanity": Freud, *Civilization and Its Discontents*, in *The Standard Edition of the Complete Psychological Works*, vol. XXI, p. 43.

38 "Jesus Christ . . . is not a part of mythology": Freud, *Civilization and Its Discontents*, in *The Standard Edition of the Complete Psychological Works*, vol. XXI, p. 142.

38 "I attach no value to the 'imitation of Christ'": Freud, *Psychoanalysis and Faith*, p. 125.

39 He pursued this form . . ."without feeling much interest in it": Lewis, *Surprised by Joy*, p. 7.

41 "We shall tell ourselves . . . afterlife, but it is a very striking fact that all this is exactly as we are bound to wish it to be": Freud, *The Future of an Illusion*, in *The Standard Edition of the Complete Psychological Works*, vol. XXI, p. 33.

41 "religious ideas, which are given out . . . secret of their strength lies in the strength of these wishes": Freud, *The Future of an Illusion*, in *The Standard Edition of the Complete Psychological Works*, vol. XXI, p. 30.

42 "their names are well known . . . I am seeking to rank myself as one of them": Freud, *The Future of an Illusion*, in *The Standard Edition of the Complete Psychological Works*, vol. XXI, p. 35.

42 Many scholars have recognized . . . Voltaire, Diderot, and Darwin, in addition to Feuerbach: Gay, *A Godless Jew*, p. 42.

42 "your substitute religion . . . eighteenth-century Enlightenment in proud modern guise": Freud, *Psychoanalysis and Faith*, p. 115.

42 "all I have done . . . great psychological foundation to the criticism of my great predecessors": Freud, *The Future of an Illusion*, in *The Standard Edition of the Complete Psychological Works*, vol. XXI, p. 35.

42 "Biologically speaking . . . child's long-drawn-out helplessness and need of help": Freud, *Leonardo da Vinci and a Memory of His Childhood*, in *The Standard Edition of the Complete Psychological Works*, vol. XI, p. 122.

42 "has shown us that a personal God . . . religious beliefs as soon as their father's authority breaks down": Freud, *Leonardo da Vinci and a Memory of His Childhood*, in *The Standard Edition of the Complete Psychological Works*, vol. XI, p. 123.

43 "psychoanalysis of individual human beings . . . God is nothing other than an exalted father": Freud, *Totem and Taboo*, in *The Standard Edition of the Complete Psychological Works*, vol. XIII, p. 147.

43 "psycho-analysis infers that he really is the father, with all the magnificence in which he once appeared to the small child": Freud, *The Question of a Weltanschauung*, in *The Standard Edition of the Complete Psychological Works*, vol. XXII, p. 163.

43 "For the same person to whom the child . . . dangers lying in wait in the external world; under his father's protection he felt safe": Freud, *The Question of a Weltanschauung*, in *The Standard Edition of the Complete Psychological Works*, vol. XXII, p. 163.

44 "the effective strength of this . . . image and the persistence of his need for protection jointly sustain his belief in God": Freud, *The Question of a Weltanschauung*, in *The Standard Edition of the Complete Psychological Works*, vol. XXII, p. 163.

44 "first protection against all of the undefined dangers which threaten it in an external world—its first protection against anxiety, we may say": Freud, *The Future of an Illusion*, in *The Standard Edition of the Complete Psychological Works*, vol. XXI, p. 24.

44 "the defense against childish . . . helplessness which he has to acknowledge—a reaction which is precisely the formation of religion": Freud, *The Future of an Illusion*, in *The Standard Edition of the Complete Psychological Works*, vol. XXI, p. 24.

45 "after you have realized . . . that Power": Lewis, *Mere Christianity*, bk. I, ch. 5.

45 "as in war and everything else . . . soft soap and wishful thinking to begin with and, in the end, despair": Lewis, *Mere Christianity*, bk. V, ch. 1.

45 "rendering back one's will . . . usurpation is a kind of death": Lewis, *The Problem of Pain*, p. 9.

46 And he found himself acutely aware . . . "transcendental Interferer": Lewis, *Surprised by Joy*, p. 172.

46 "Creatures are not born with desires . . . Men feel sexual desire: well, there is such a thing as sex": Lewis, *Mere Christianity*, bk. III, ch. 10.

47 Evidence exists that the human brain is hardwired (genetically programmed) for belief: Newberg et al., *Why God Won't Go Away*.

47 "depends on the kind of philosophy we bring": Lewis, *Miracles*, p. 7.

47 "I must keep alive in myself . . . press on to that other country and to help others to do the same": Lewis, *Mere Christianity*, bk. III, ch. 10.

47 "All your life an unattainable . . . within your reach and you have lost it forever": Lewis, *The Problem of Pain*, p. 148.

47 Freud recognized a similar desire . . . German word *Sehnsucht*, the same word Lewis uses to describe the desire: Lewis, *Surprised by Joy*, p. 6.

47 "I believe now that I was never free . . . run off from my father, almost before I had learnt to walk": Freud, *Screen Memories*, in *The Standard Edition of the Complete Psychological Works*, vol. III, pp. 312–13.

48 "In the second half of childhood . . . affectionate and hostile impulses towards him persist side by side, often to the end of one's life": Freud, *Some Reflections on Schoolboy Psychology*, in *The Standard Edition of the Complete Psychological Works*, vol. XIII, pp. 243–44.

49 "With the cruelty of youth . . . elderly men, I have since regarded as lovable foibles": Lewis, *Surprised by Joy*, p. 160.

50 "those above me or who are in some other respect my superiors": Jones, *The Life and Work of Sigmund Freud*, vol. I, p. 197.

51 "My early familiarity with the Bible story . . . enduring effect upon the direction of my interest": Freud, *An Autobiographical Study*, in *The Standard Edition of the Complete Psychological Works*, vol. XX, p. 8.

52 "I was at this time living, like so many Atheists . . . why should creatures have the burden of existence forced on them without their consent": Lewis, *Surprised by Joy*, p. 115.

52 To understand what happened, we may find helpful . . . categories: *extrinsically* and *intrinsically* religious: Allport and Ross, "Personal religious orientation and prejudice."

52 Modern medical research . . . positive effect: Strawbridge W. J., R. D. Cohen, S. J. Shema, and G. A. Kaplan, "Frequent attendance at religious services and mortality over 28 years." *Am J Public Health* 87, no. 6 (June 1997): 957–61; Koenig H. G., L. K. George, and B. L. Peter-

son, "Religiosity and remission of depression in medically ill older patients." *Am J Psychiatry* 155, no. 4 (April 1998): 536–42: McCullough, M. E., and D. B. Larson, "Religion and depression: a review of the literature." *Twin Res* 2, no. 2 (June 1999): 126–36; Koenig, H. G., "Religion and medicine II: Religion, mental health, and related behaviors." *Int J Psych Med* 31, no. 1 (2001): 97–109; Koenig, H. G., D. B. Larson, and S. S. Larson, "Religion and coping with serious medical illness." *Annals Pharmacotherapy* 35, no. 3 (March 2001): 352–59; and Koenig, H. G., "Religion, spirituality, and medicine: application to clinical practice." *JAMA* 284, no. 13 (October 4, 2000): 1708.

53   In the analysis . . . "as soon as their father's authority breaks down": Freud, *Leonardo da Vinci and a Memory of His Childhood*, in *The Standard Edition of the Complete Psychological Works*, vol. XI, p. 123.

53   "when a man has once brought himself . . . we need not be greatly surprised at the weakness of his intellect": Freud, *The Future of an Illusion*, in *The Standard Edition of the Complete Psychological Works*, vol. XXI, p. 48.

53   "For the masses . . . no avail against their passions": Freud, *The Future of an Illusion*, in *The Standard Edition of the Complete Psychological Works*, vol. XXI, pp. 7–8.

53   "there has been little occasion for me to change my opinion of human nature": Freud, *Psychoanalysis and Faith*, p. 140.

54   "accepted the most varied . . . child analysis": Freud, *Psychoanalysis and Faith*, p. 10.

54   A person with OCD may experience . . . persistent, repeated impulses or images that are intrusive and cause marked anxiety: American Psychiatric Association, *Diagnostic and Statistical Manual of Mental Disorders*, pp. 417–23.

54   "the resemblance between what are called obsessive actions . . . believers give expression to their piety": Freud, *Obsessive Actions and Religious Practices*, in *The Standard Edition of the Complete Psychological Works*, vol. IX, p. 117.

55   In fact, according to a recent Gallup poll . . . God plays a direct role in their lives more than ever before: Gallup and Jones, *The Next American Spirituality*, p. 177.

55   "The religions of mankind . . . delusion ever recognizes it as such": Freud, *Civilization and Its Discontents*, in *The Standard Edition of the Complete Psychological Works*, vol. XXI, p. 32.

55   Findings from a Gallup poll published recently . . . 80 percent believe they have a personal relationship with God: Gallup and Jones, *The Next American Spirituality*, p. 177.

56 "when Freud is talking about . . . he is very ignorant": Lewis, *Mere Christianity*, bk. III, ch. 4.

56 "Our difference derives chiefly . . . pathological forms of religion and regard these as 'religion'": Freud, *Psychoanalysis and Faith*, p. 122.

Chapter 3: Conscience

58 "there are no sources of knowledge . . . in other words what we call research—and along side it no knowledge derived from revelation": Freud, *The Question of a Weltanschauung*, in *The Standard Edition of the Complete Psychological Works*, vol. XXII, p. 159.

58 "But why anything comes to be there at all, and whether there is anything behind the things science observes . . . this is not a scientific question": Lewis, *Mere Christianity*, bk. I, ch. 4.

59 "inside ourselves as an influence . . . law urging me to do right and making me feel responsible and uncomfortable when I do wrong": Lewis, *Mere Christianity*, bk. I, ch. 4.

59 "it is inside information . . . find out more about a man by listening to his conversation than by looking at a house he has built": Lewis, *Mere Christianity*, bk. I, ch. 5.

60 "the same father (or parental agency) . . . knowledge of his social duties by a system of loving rewards and punishments": Freud, *The Question of a Weltanschauung*, in *The Standard Edition of the Complete Psychological Works*, vol. XXII, pp. 163–64.

60 "are mere conventions which might have been different . . . others of them, like mathematics, are real truths": Lewis, *Mere Christianity*, bk. I, ch. 2.

61 Though some differences occur from one culture . . . "you can recognize the same law running through them all": Lewis, *Mere Christianity*, bk. I, ch. 2.

61 "All the human beings that history . . . 'I ought' or 'I ought not'": Lewis, *The Problem of Pain*, p. 21.

61 "First . . . human beings, all over the earth . . . foundation of all clear thinking about ourselves and the universe we live in": Lewis, *Mere Christianity*, bk. I, ch. 1.

61 "how very like they are to each other . . . Selfishness has never been admired": Lewis, *Mere Christianity*, bk. I, ch. 1.

61 This moral law has long . . . First Principles of Practical Reason, or Traditional Morality: Lewis, *The Abolition of Man*, p. 51.

62 "What was the sense in saying . . . unless Right is a real thing which the Nazis at bottom knew as well as we did and ought to have practiced": Lewis, *Mere Christianity*, bk. I, ch. 1.

62 "if your moral ideas can be truer . . . Real Morality—for them to be true about": Lewis, *Mere Christianity*, bk. I, ch. 2.

62 "When I came first to the University . . . baboon thinks of classical music": Lewis, *The Problem of Pain*, pp. 37–40.

63 "the stars are indeed magnificent . . . modest amount of it or scarcely enough to be worth mentioning": Freud, *New Introductory Lectures on Psychoanalysis*, in *The Standard Edition of the Complete Psychological Works*, vol. XXII, p. 61.

63 "I was grieved that you should believe . . . 'There have to be odd fellows like that, too'": Hale, *James Jackson Putnam and Psychoanalysis*, letter from Freud to Putnam dated August 8, 1910.

63 "no matter whether they publicly subscribe to this or that ethical doctrine or none at all": Freud, *Psychoanalysis and Faith*, pp. 61–62.

64 "Our best hope for the future . . . may in process of time establish a dictatorship in the mental life of man": Freud, *The Question of a Weltanschauung*, in *The Standard Edition of the Complete Psychological Works*, vol. XXII, p. 171.

64 "The ideal condition of things would of course be a community of men who had subordinated their instinctual life to the dictatorship of reason": Einstein and Freud, *Why War*, in *The Standard Edition of the Complete Psychological Works*, vol. XXII, p. 213.

64 "Perhaps I was wrong to expect it": Hale, *James Jackson Putnam and Psychoanalysis*, letter from Freud to Putnam dated November 13, 1913.

64 "A portion of the external world . . . we call this agency the super-ego and are aware of it in its judicial functions as our conscience": Freud, *An Outline of Psychoanalysis*, in *The Standard Edition of the Complete Psychological Works*, vol. XXIII, p. 205.

65 "it is in keeping with the course of human development . . . only by that means does it become a moral and social being": Freud, *The Future of an Illusion*, in *The Standard Edition of the Complete Psychological Works*, vol. XXI, p. 11.

65 "If a patient of ours is suffering . . . which it may perhaps be possible to discover": Freud, *The Question of Lay Analysis*, in *The Standard Edition of the Complete Psychological Works*, vol. XX, p. 190.

65 "We are told to 'get things out in the open' . . . 'things' are very natural and we need not be ashamed": Lewis, *The Problem of Pain*, p. 56.

65 That is, the biblical story . . . "you have broken that law and put yourself wrong with that Power": Lewis, *Mere Christianity*, bk.I, ch. 5.

66 "I consider myself . . . temptation to do so": Jones, *The Life and Work of Sigmund Freud*, vol. II, pp. 416–17.

66   He also points out that, although he stood . . . traditional in this respect:
      Jones, *The Life and Work of Sigmund Freud,* vol. II, pp. 416–18.

66   "I believe that the primary moral principles . . . we say to a man, when
      we would recall him to right conduct, 'be reasonable'": Lewis, *Mira-
      cles,* p. 35.

67   A person's need to tell others . . ."the itching, smarting, writhing aware-
      ness of an inferiority which the patient refuses to accept": Lewis, *The
      Screwtape Letters,* pp. 162–63.

67   Psychiatrists have long been aware . . . feeling of worthlessness:
      Nicholi, *The Harvard Guide to Psychiatry,* p. 282; and American Psy-
      chiatric Association, *Diagnostic and Statistical Manual of Mental Dis-
      orders,* p. 349.

68   "It is a most remarkable . . . as a periodic phenomenon": Freud, *New
      Introductory Lectures on Psychoanalysis,* in *The Standard Edition of
      the Complete Psychological Works,* vol. XXII, p. 61.

69   "the totem-feast was the commemoration . . . still survives with but lit-
      tle distortion": Freud, *An Autobiographical Study,* in *The Standard
      Edition of the Complete Psychological Works,* vol. XX, p. 68.

70   "attempts to resolve the moral experience . . . it could produce no sense
      of guilt": Lewis, *The Problem of Pain,* p. 21.

70   "when one has a sense of guilt . . . help us to discover the origin of *con-
      science* and of the sense of guilt in general": Freud, *Civilization and Its
      Discontents,* in *The Standard Edition of the Complete Psychological
      Works,* vol. XXI, p. 131.

71   "there is no doubt that this case should explain the secret of the sense
      of guilt to us and put an end to our difficulties. And I believe it does":
      Freud, *Civilization and Its Discontents,* in *The Standard Edition of the
      Complete Psychological Works,* vol. XXI, p. 132.

71   "I have reverted very much" . . . he wrote to several of his colleagues:
      Jones, *The Life and Work of Sigmund Freud,* vol. II, p. 354.

71   The book met with . . . "anthropologists united in discounting his con-
      clusions and in maintaining that he had misunderstood the evidence":
      Jones, *The Life and Work of Sigmund Freud,* vol. II, p. 360.

71   Gay also mentions that Freud . . . "publishing scientific fantasies": Gay,
      Freud, pp. 327–35.

72   "would serve to make a sharp distinction between us and all . . . reli-
      giosity": Abraham and Freud, *A Psychoanalytic Dialogue,* letter from
      Freud to Abraham dated May 13, 1913.

72   "The ethical demands . . . dangerous to link obedience to them with re-
      ligious faith": Freud, *The Question of a Weltanschauung,* in *The Stan-
      dard Edition of the Complete Psychological Works,* vol. XXII, p. 168.

72 "If the sole reason why . . . neighbor without hesitation, and you can only be prevented from doing so by mundane force": Freud, *The Future of an Illusion*, in *The Standard Edition of the Complete Psychological Works*, vol. XXI, p. 39.

73 As people became more educated . . . "they would adopt a more friendly attitude toward them": Freud, *The Future of an Illusion*, in *The Standard Edition of the Complete Psychological Works*, vol. XXI, p. 41.

73 "Christ promises forgiveness of sins . . . Moral relativity is the enemy we have to overcome before we tackle Atheism": Lewis, *Letters, C. S. Lewis–Don Giovanni Calabria*, pp. 89–91.

73 Whereas Freud spoke of the need . . . "dictatorship of Pride": Lewis, *Mere Christianity*, bk. III, ch. 8.

74 "When saints call themselves sinners . . . occasional satisfaction of them causes them to diminish, at least for the time being": Freud, *Civilization and Its Discontents*, in *The Standard Edition of the Complete Psychological Works*, vol. XXI, p. 126.

74 "Virtue—even attempted virtue—brings light; indulgence brings fog": Lewis, *Mere Christianity*, bk. III, ch. 5.

74 "Freud himself was constantly puzzled . . . He never had any doubt about the right course of conduct": Jones, *The Life and Work of Sigmund Freud*, vol. II, p. 416.

75 "But, as I said, I know nothing . . . thoroughly decent human beings is quite incomprehensible to me": Jones, *The Life and Work of Sigmund Freud*, vol. II, pp. 416–18.

75 Or, as some scientists . . . without divine assistance: Wilson, *The Moral Sense*.

Chapter 4: The Great Transition

76 "Its consolations deserve no trust. Experience teaches us that the world is no nursery": Freud, *The Question of a Weltanschauung*, in *The Standard Edition of the Complete Psychological Works*, vol. XXII, p. 168.

77 According to a recent Gallup poll, about eight out of ten adult Americans profess faith in a personal God, and about half of them report having a conversion experience: Gallup et al., *Surveying the Religious Landscape*, p. 67.

78 "If the truth of religious doctrines . . . many people who do not have this rare experience": Freud, *The Future of an Illusion*, in *The Standard Edition of the Complete Psychological Works*, vol. XXI, p. 28.

78 "I have always had a special sympathy . . . stands completely in the light of history": Freud, *Psychoanalysis and Faith*, p. 76.

79 Shortly afterward, Freud wrote an article titled "A Religious Experience": Freud, *A Religious Experience,* in *The Standard Edition of the Complete Psychological Works,* vol. XXI, p. 169.

80 The field of psychiatry . . . "a hallucinatory psychosis," etc.: Nicholi, "A New Dimension of the Youth Culture," *American Journal of Psychiatry,* 131:396-401, 1974.

80 "a marked improvement in ego functioning . . . a decrease in preoccupation with the passage of time and apprehension over death": Nicholi, "A New Dimension of the Youth Culture," *American Journal of Psychiatry,* 131:396-401, 1974.

81 "suddenly arose in me . . . but desire for what": Lewis, *Surprised by Joy,* pp. 16–21.

83 "It would almost seem that Providence . . . quite overrules our previous tastes when it decides to bring two minds together": Lewis, *Surprised by Joy,* p. 190.

83 In an interview in 1963, Lewis acknowledged . . . "Chesterton's *The Everlasting Man*": Lewis, *God in the Dock,* p. 260.

84 "I did not see to what extent this little adventure was an allegory of my whole life": Lewis, *Surprised by Joy,* p. 184.

85 "You must picture me . . . convert in all England": Lewis, *Surprised by Joy,* pp. 228–29.

85 "What I couldn't understand . . . Someone Else (whoever he was) 2000 years ago could help us here and now": Lewis, *The Letters of C. S. Lewis to Arthur Greeves,* p. 427.

86 "I was by now . . . mythical taste": Lewis, *Surprised by Joy,* p. 236.

86 "If ever myth . . . just like this": Lewis, *Surprised by Joy,* p. 236.

87 Lewis felt that as the truth . . . "imaginative beauties of the Pagan mythologies": Lewis, *Miracles,* p. 139, footnote 1.

87 "Now the story of Christ is simply a true myth . . . tremendous difference that it really happened": Lewis, *The Letters of C. S. Lewis to Arthur Greeves,* p. 31.

87 "Now as a literary historian . . . no people building up a legend would allow that to be so": Lewis, *God in the Dock,* p. 158.

87 "as real, as recognizable . . . myth must have become fact; the Word flesh; God, Man": Lewis, *Surprised by Joy,* p. 236.

87 "I am begotten of the One God . . . They were the name of God, which must not be spoken by any human being, the name which it was death to utter": Lewis, *God in the Dock,* p. 156.

88 "to beget is to become the father of . . . That is why men are not Sons of God in the sense that Christ is": Lewis, *Mere Christianity,* bk. IV, ch. 1.

88 "Now unless the speaker is God . . . forgave you for treading on other

men's toes and stealing other men's money": Lewis, *Mere Christianity,* bk. II, ch. 3.

88   "And now, just suppose I said to a patient: 'I, Professor Sigmund Freud, forgive thee thy sins.' What a fool I should make of myself": Freud, *Psychoanalysis and Faith,* p. 125.

88   "Not one of them ever made that claim . . . and the greater the man is, the less likely he is to make the very greatest claim": Chesterton, *The Everlasting Man,* p. 201.

89   "the general agreement . . . the product of a sane mind": Lewis, *God in the Dock,* p. 156.

89   "A man who was merely a man . . . He did not intend to": Lewis, *Mere Christianity,* bk. II, ch. 3.

89   "is nothing less than the loud assertion . . . nonsense of comparative religion": Chesterton, *The Everlasting Man,* p. i.

90   "it must belittle . . . new life reascends": Lewis, *Miracles,* p. 116.

91   "I have just passed on . . . Dyson and Tolkien had a good deal to do with it": Lewis, *The Letters of C. S. Lewis to Arthur Greeves,* p. 425.

91   "the intellectual side of my conversion was *not* simple": Lewis, *The Letters of C. S. Lewis to Arthur Greeves,* p. 447.

91   "Dyson and Tolkien were the immediate human causes of my conversion": Lewis, *The Letters of C. S. Lewis,* p. 197.

92   "Conversions happen in all sorts of different ways: some sharp and catastrophic (like St. Paul, St. Augustine, or Bunyan), some very gradual and intellectual (like my own)": Lewis, letter to Bodle dated December 31, 1947 (unpublished), Marion E. Wade Center, Wheaton College, Wheaton, Ill., and Bodleian Library, Oxford University. Used by permission.

93   "the ups and downs of my father's emotional life . . . embarrassing and even dangerous": Lewis, *Surprised by Joy,* p. 4.

93   "What has been holding me back . . . what the thing is": Lewis, *The Letters of C. S. Lewis to Arthur Greeves,* pp. 426–27.

94   "is always older . . . meaning to life": Erikson., *Young Man Luther,* p. 261.

Chapter 5: Happiness

99   Researchers believe that because most people . . . considerably higher: Nicholi, *The Harvard Guide to Psychiatry,* p. 290.

99   "show by their behavior . . . happy and to remain so": Freud, *Civilization and Its Discontents,* in *The Standard Edition of the Complete Psychological Works,* vol. XXI, p. 76.

100   "Happiness . . . is a problem . . . to a high degree": Freud, *Civilization*

and Its Discontents, in *The Standard Edition of the Complete Psychological Works,* vol. XXI, p. 76.

101 "has exactly . . . dictator who has seized all the means to power": Freud, *The Future of an Illusion,* in *The Standard Edition of the Complete Psychological Works,* vol. XXI, p. 15.

101 "has given us our most intense experience of an overwhelming sensation of pleasure and has thus furnished us with a pattern for our search for happiness": Freud, *Civilization and Its Discontents,* in *The Standard Edition of the Complete Psychological Works,* vol. XXI, p. 82.

101 "made himself dependent in a most dangerous way . . . unfaithfulness or death": Freud, *Civilization and Its Discontents,* in *The Standard Edition of the Complete Psychological Works,* vol. XXI, p. 101.

101 "we are never so defenseless . . . loved object or its love": Freud, *Civilization and Its Discontents,* in *The Standard Edition of the Complete Psychological Works,* vol. XXI, p. 82.

101 "of this kind, such as an artist's joy . . . convulse our physical being": Freud, *Civilization and Its Discontents,* in *The Standard Edition of the Complete Psychological Works,* vol. XXI, pp. 79–80.

102 "We are threatened with suffering . . . last source is perhaps more painful to us than any other": Freud, *Civilization and Its Discontents,* in *The Standard Edition of the Complete Psychological Works,* vol. XXI, p. 77.

102 "an attempt to procure a certainty . . . delusion ever recognizes it as such": Freud, *Civilization and Its Discontents,* in *The Standard Edition of the Complete Psychological Works,* vol. XXI, p. 81.

103 "obtained its immense power, which overwhelms 'reason and science'": Freud, *Moses and Monotheism,* in *The Standard Edition of the Complete Psychological Works,* vol. XXIII, p. 123.

103 "one feels inclined to say . . . not included in the plan of 'Creation'": Freud, *Civilization and Its Discontents,* in *The Standard Edition of the Complete Psychological Works,* vol. XXI, p. 76.

104 "the happiness which God designs for His higher creatures . . . And for that they must be free": Lewis, *Mere Christianity,* bk. II, ch. 3.

105 "God designed the human machine . . . There is no such thing": Lewis, *Mere Christianity,* bk. II, ch. 3.

105 "This sounds to me as odd as a right to good luck . . . good weather whenever you want to have a picnic": Lewis, *God in the Dock,* p. 318.

105 "refreshes us on the journey . . . mistake them for our home": Lewis, *The Problem of Pain,* p. 115.

106 "all pleasure and happiness is in its own nature good . . . less to prefer it to Him": Lewis, letter to Ms. Jacob dated July 3, 1941 (unpublished),

Marion E. Wade Center, Wheaton College, Wheaton, Ill., and Bodleian Library, Oxford University. Used by permission.

106 "When I have learned to love God . . . not suppressed but increased": Lewis, *The Letters of C. S. Lewis*, p. 248.

106 "is that it liberates you from thinking about happiness . . . unnecessary to think about money": Lewis, *The Letters of C. S. Lewis*, p. 227.

107 "when we are such as He can love without impediment, we shall in fact be happy": Lewis, *The Problem of Pain*, p. 48.

107 "The place for which He designs . . . anguish is over": Lewis, *The Problem of Pain*, p. 52.

107 "God gives what He has . . . then we must starve eternally": Lewis, *The Problem of Pain*, pp. 53–54.

107 (Research has shown . . . in life predisposes one to clinical depression): Nicholi, *The Harvard Guide to Psychiatry*, p. 623.

108 "unguarded moments am I seized by that forlorn mood": Freud, *The Letters of Sigmund Freud to Eduard Silberstein*, p. 15.

108 a long poem titled "Epithalamium": Freud, *The Letters of Sigmund Freud to Eduard Silberstein*, pp. 135–38.

109 "have lifted me out of my despondency": Freud, *Letters of Sigmund Freud*, p. 26.

109 "I have experienced during the past fourteen months . . . yet has never felt young": Freud, *Letters of Sigmund Freud*, p. 123.

109 "a big wild man . . . heights in a wonderful fashion": Jones, *The Life and Work of Sigmund Freud*, vol. I, p. 84.

109 "I take very small doses . . . most brilliant success": Jones, *The Life and Work of Sigmund Freud*, vol. I, p. 82.

109 "Today you may miss the note . . . from Paris": Freud, *Letters of Sigmund Freud*, p. 175.

109 "I mastered my depression with the help of a special diet in intellectual matters": Jones, *The Life and Work of Sigmund Freud*, vol. I, p. 303.

109 "new realization of the nature of 'happiness' . . . its threats simultaneously": Freud, *The Complete Letters of Sigmund Freud to Wilhelm Fliess*, p. 440.

109 "you think you already have it in your grasp and it is always gone again": Schur, *Freud*, p. 430.

109 "My mood is bad . . . senile depression in anyone else": Freud, *The Letters of Sigmund Freud and Arnold Zweig*, p. 101.

110 "In fact, some authorities believe . . . actually *cause* it": Nicholi, *The Harvard Guide to Psychiatry*, p. 292.

110 "Though I am supposed to be on the way to recovery . . . more sensi-

ble resignation": Jones, *The Life and Work of Sigmund Freud,* vol. III, p. 68.

110 "What good to us is a long life . . . death as a deliverer?": Freud, *Civilization and Its Discontents,* in *The Standard Edition of the Complete Psychological Works,* vol. XXI, p. 88.

110 "I am neither a self-tormentor . . . a priori assumption": Freud, *Psychoanalysis and Faith,* pp. 132–34.

111 "Strange indeed is my position . . . corresponding depression after this": Lewis, *The Letters of C. S. Lewis to Arthur Greeves,* pp. 55–56.

112 "represented adult life as one of incessant drudgery under the continual threat of financial ruin": Lewis, *Surprised by Joy,* p. 23.

112 "Working against my faith . . . a menacing and unfriendly place": Lewis, *Surprised by Joy,* pp. 63–66.

112 "the reader will remember . . . met a great dismay": Lewis, *Surprised by Joy,* pp. 62–66.

112 "a settled expectation that everything . . . what is or is not plausible": Lewis, *Surprised by Joy,* pp. 62–66.

112 "a projection of myself . . . compensate myself for my unhappiness": Lewis, *Surprised by Joy,* p. 115.

113 "I was at this time living, like so many Atheists . . . angry with Him for creating a world": Lewis, *Surprised by Joy,* pp. 114–15.

113 "began to know what life really is and what would have been lost by missing it": Lewis, *Surprised by Joy,* p. 114–17.

113 "The early loss of my mother . . . stuck in my gullet": Glover, *C. S. Lewis,* pp. 32–33.

115 "To believe and to pray . . . 'taken out of myself'": Lewis, *Surprised by Joy,* p. 233.

115 "My happiest hours . . . There's no sound I like better than . . . laughter": Lewis, *The Letters of C. S. Lewis to Arthur Greeves,* p. 26.

115 "friendship is the greatest of worldly goods . . . I know I am v. fortunate in that respect": Lewis, *The Letters of C. S. Lewis to Arthur Greeves,* p. 477.

116 "a mere mortal . . . your neighbor is the holiest object presented to your senses": Lewis, *The Weight of Glory,* p. 15.

118 "And now I advise you as a friend . . . one never knows": Freud, *Letters of Sigmund Freud,* p. 4.

118 "all my thoughts and feelings . . . might come by the old papers": Freud, *Letters of Sigmund Freud,* p. 175.

118 "Oh, they have all outstripped me in fame": Freud, *Letters of Sigmund Freud,* p. 127.

118 "We shall all of us get more gratitude . . . midst of the work": Jones, *The Life and Work of Sigmund Freud*, vol. II, p. 347.

119 "I certainly do not work because of the expectation . . . for my children later": Jones, *The Life and Work of Sigmund Freud*, vol. II, p. 400.

120 "childish of me to give free rein . . . it none the less hurt deeply": Freud, *An Autobiographical Study*, in *The Standard Edition of the Complete Psychological Works*, vol. XX, p. 49.

120 "Definitely passed over for the Nobel Prize": Gay, *Freud*, p. 571.

120 "dreams of success, fame, love . . . remarkable person I was": Lewis, *They Asked for a Paper*, p. 123.

120 "I have found out ludicrous . . . admire yourself for doing *that*": Lewis, *The Letters of C. S. Lewis to Arthur Greeves*, p. 339.

121 "The side of me which longs . . . ambitions have been given up": Lewis, *The Letters of C. S. Lewis to Arthur Greeves*, pp. 379–80.

121 "spiritual cancer: it eats up the very possibility of love, or contentment, or even common sense": Lewis, *Mere Christianity*, bk. III, ch. 8.

122 "when you pass from thinking . . . you have reached bottom": Lewis, *Mere Christianity*, bk. III, ch. 8.

122 "This Milton states in the very first line . . . subject of a fugue": Lewis, *Preface to Paradise Lost*, pp. 70–71.

122 "I am now in my fiftieth year . . . evil disease, vainglory": Lewis, *Letters, C. S. Lewis–Don Giovanni Calabria*, pp. 51–53.

123 They also found that the stronger the commitment to their spiritual convictions, the more rapid was their response to treatment: Koenig, H. G., L. K. George, and B. L. Peterson, "Religiosity and remission of depression in medically ill older patients." *Am J Psychiatry* 155, no. 4 (April 1998): 536–92.

125 "What good to us is a long life if it is difficult and barren of joys, and if it is so full of misery that we can only welcome death as a deliverer": Freud, *Civilization and Its Discontents*, in *The Standard Edition of the Complete Psychological Works*, vol. XXI, p. 88.

125 "How true it all is . . . destruction and death": Lewis, *The Letters of C. S. Lewis to Arthur Greeves*, p. 49.

Chapter 6: Sex

127 "Sexual life does not begin at puberty . . . a function which is subsequently brought into the service of . . . reproduction": Freud, *An Outline of Psychoanalysis*, in *The Standard Edition of the Complete Psychological Works*, vol. XXIII, p. 152.127

127 "In the first place sexuality . . . impulses to which usage applies the exceedingly ambiguous word 'love'": Freud, *An Autobiographical Study*, in *The Standard Edition of the Complete Psychological Works*, vol. XX, p. 38.

128 "I might have done so myself from the first and thus have spared myself much opposition": Freud, *Group Psychology and the Analysis of the Ego*, in *The Standard Edition of the Complete Psychological Works*, vol. XVIII, p. 91.

128 "We cannot avoid the resistances, so why not rather challenge them at once? In my opinion, attack is the best defense": Freud, *The Freud/Jung Letters*, p. 28.

128 "It seems to be my fate to discover only the obvious . . . wish-fulfillment as day dreams": Jones, *The Life and Work of Sigmund Freud*, vol. I, p. 350.

129 "The first organ to emerge as an erotogenic zone . . . providing satisfaction for the needs of that zone": Freud, *An Outline of Psychoanalysis*, in *The Standard Edition of the Complete Psychological Works*, vol. XXIII, pp. 153–54.

129 "Physiology should not be confused with psychology. The baby's obstinate persistence in sucking gives evidence at an early stage of a need for satisfaction which, though it originates from and is instigated by the taking of nourishment, nevertheless strives to obtain pleasure independently of nourishment and for that reason may and should be termed *sexual*": Freud, *An Outline of Psychoanalysis*, in *The Standard Edition of the Complete Psychological Works*, vol. XXIII, p. 154.

129 "the phallic one, which is, as it were, a forerunner of the final form taken by sexual life and already much resembles it": Freud, *An Outline of Psychoanalysis*, in *The Standard Edition of the Complete Psychological Works*, vol. XXIII, p. 154.

130 "we can understand . . . Oedipus in fantasy and each recoils in horror from the dream fulfillment here transplanted into reality": Freud, *The Complete Letters of Sigmund Freud to Wilhelm Fliess*, p. 272.

130 "the existence of only two basic instincts, *Eros* and *the destructive instinct.*" The psychic energy of Eros "henceforward we shall speak of as 'libido.'" Because Freud assumes that this energy called libido motivates many human interactions, he refers to these interactions as sexual: Freud, *An Outline of Psychoanalysis*, in *The Standard Edition of the Complete Psychological Works*, vol. XXIII, pp. 148–49.

131 Most professionals considered such talk, Freud said, "'a desecration of the innocence of childhood'": Freud, *The Question of Lay Analysis*, in

The Standard Edition of the Complete Psychological Works, vol. XX, p. 209.

131 "It has always seemed to me best to behave . . . inevitable resistance": Freud, *The Complete Correspondence of Sigmund Freud and Ernest Jones*, p. 32.

132 "A . . . community is perfectly justified, psychologically . . . prepared for it in childhood": Freud, *Civilization and Its Discontents*, in *The Standard Edition of the Complete Psychological Works*, vol. XXI, p. 104.

132 "the period of [religious] confirmation": Freud, *The Sexual Enlightenment of Children*, in *The Standard Edition of the Complete Psychological Works*, vol. IX, p. 137.

132 "To believe that psycho-analysis seeks a cure . . . chains of his sexuality": Freud, *Two Encyclopaedia Articles*, in *The Standard Edition of the Complete Psychological Works*, vol. XVIII, p. 252.

133 Freud persistently opposed any physical contact . . . "love became worthless and life empty": Freud, *On the Universal Tendency to Debasement in the Sphere of Love*, in *The Standard Edition of the Complete Psychological Works*, vol. XI, p. 188.

133 "Now when you decide to give a full account . . . just as I knew it before you told me": Jones, *The Life and Work of Sigmund Freud*, vol. III, pp. 163–64.

134 However, one survey of several hundred physicians . . . "obstetrician-gynecologists and general practitioners": Nicholi, *The Harvard Guide to Psychiatry*, pp. 19–22.

134 "I was modest enough . . . mysterious element that was at work behind hypnotism": Freud, *An Autobiographical Study*, in *The Standard Edition of the Complete Psychological Works*, vol. XX, p. 27.

135 "it is not a patient's crudely sensual desires . . . sake of a fine experience": Freud, *Further Recommendations on Technique*, in *The Standard Edition of the Complete Psychological Works*, vol. XII, p. 169.

135 "But psychoanalysis itself . . . every person knew something about it": Lewis, *Mere Christianity*, bk. III, ch. 4.

136 He implied that it is no accident . . . embrace this worldview: Lewis, *Mere Christianity*, bk. III, ch. 5.

136 "Repressed sexuality does not appear to the patient to be sexuality at all": Lewis, *Mere Christianity*, bk. III, ch. 5.

137 "Like all powerful lies . . . tempted at the moment is also healthy and normal": Lewis, *Mere Christianity*, bk. III, ch. 5.

137 "Virtue—even attempted virtue—brings light; indulgence brings fog": Lewis, *Mere Christianity*, bk. III, ch. 5.

137 "sex has not been hushed up . . . it had become such a mess": Lewis, *Mere Christianity*, bk. III, ch. 5.

138 "There is no getting away from it . . . 'or else total abstinence'": Lewis, *Mere Christianity*, bk. III, ch. 5.

138 "This is so difficult and so contrary to our instinct that either the rule is wrong or our sexual instinct, as it now is, has gone wrong": Lewis, *Mere Christianity*, bk. III, ch. 5.

138 He gave several illustrations . . . "excess of its function": Lewis, *Mere Christianity*, bk. III, ch. 5.

138 "You can get a large audience together . . . state of the sex instinct among us": Lewis, *Mere Christianity*, bk. III, ch. 5.

138 "By Eros, I mean of course that state which we call 'being in love'": Lewis, *The Four Loves*, p. 131.

139 "The carnal or animal sexual element . . . sexual by the simplest observations": Lewis, *The Four Loves*, p. 131–32.

139 "This act, like any other, is justified . . . by obedience or disobedience": Lewis, *The Four Loves*, pp. 133.

139 "There may be those who have first felt mere sexual appetite . . . But I doubt if this is at all common": Lewis, *The Four Loves*, p. 133.

140 "Sexual desire . . . wants *it*, the *thing in itself*; Eros [being in love] wants the Beloved": Lewis, *The Four Loves*, p. 133.

140 "For one of the first things Eros does is to obliterate the distinction between giving and receiving": Lewis, *The Four Loves*, p. 136.

140 Lewis quotes his colleague Charles Williams: "Love you? I *am* you": Lewis, *The Four Loves*, p. 136.

140 "At the height of being in love . . . prepared to behave as if it were a fact": Freud, *Civilization and Its Discontents*, in *The Standard Edition of the Complete Psychological Works*, vol. XXI, p. 66.

140 "Our advertisements, at their sexiest . . . roar of old-fashioned laughter": Lewis, *The Four Loves*, p. 139.

140 "I am sometimes tempted to wonder . . . sexual phenomena as the theory seems to demand": Lewis, *They Asked for a Paper*, pp. 129–30.

141 Venus is "a mocking, mischievous spirit . . . [who] makes games of us": Lewis, *The Four Loves*, p. 141.

141 "Banish play and laughter from the bed of love and you may let in a false goddess": Lewis, *The Four Loves*, p. 140.

142 "Being in love is a good thing . . . feelings come and go": Lewis, *Mere Christianity*, bk. III, ch. 6.

143 "I stand for an incomparably freer sexual life . . . such freedom": Jones, *The Life and Work of Sigmund Freud*, vol. II, pp. 416–18.

144 "No? Well, then you can have a good laugh . . . made me feel sentimental": Letter to Martha Bernays dated October 28, 1883, in E. Freud,
"Some Early Unpublished Letters of Freud."

144 "In Muggia, however, the women, as I said, are more attractive, mostly
blonde, oddly enough, which accords with neither Italian nor Jewish
descent": Freud, *The Letters of Sigmund Freud to Eduard Silberstein*,
p. 153.

145 "Nature has determined woman's destiny . . . in mature years a loved
wife": Jones, *The Life and Work of Sigmund Freud*, vol. I, pp.
175–77.

145 "the great question that has never been answered . . . 'What does a
woman want?'": Jones, *The Life and Work of Sigmund Freud*, vol. II,
p. 421.

146 Most of her family thought of Freud as a heathen: Jones, *The Life and
Work of Sigmund Freud*, vol. I, p. 134.

147 "The man who brings tears . . . I can be ruthless": Jones, *The Life and
Work of Sigmund Freud*, vol. I, p. 112.

147 "if there is any vanity left in your little head . . . no opinion on the matter": Jones, *The Life and Work of Sigmund Freud*, vol. I, p. 102.

147 "during their long engagement her virginity remained intact . . . hugs
and kisses": Gay, *Freud*, p. 38.

147 And Freud's official biographer, Ernest Jones . . . remained faithful
throughout his marriage: Jones, *The Life and Work of Sigmund Freud*,
vol. II, p. 241.

148 "When a man without means . . . can get everything": Jones, *The Life
and Work of Sigmund Freud*, vol. I, p. 148.

149 In 1893, thirty-seven years old . . . "we are now living in abstinence":
Freud, *The Complete Letters of Sigmund Freud to Wilhelm Fliess*,
p. 54.

149 "denied himself all enjoyment . . . sense of guilt": Freud, *Some Neurotic Mechanisms in Jealousy, Paranoia, and Homosexuality*, in *The
Standard Edition of the Complete Psychological Works*, vol. XVIII,
p. 228.

149 "On the basis of my medical experience . . . results of masturbation":
Freud, *Contributions to a Discussion on Masturbation*, in *The Standard Edition of the Complete Psychological Works*, vol. XII, p. 252.

150 "such substitutive means of sexual satisfaction are by no means harmless; they predispose to the numerous varieties of neuroses and psychoses": Freud, *"Civilized" Sexual Morality and Modern Nervous
Illness*, in *The Standard Edition of the Complete Psychological Works*,
vol. IX, p. 198.

150 "You all know the immense aetiological importance . . . faulty development of which they are indeed suffering": Freud, *New Introductory Lectures on Psychoanalysis*, in *The Standard Edition of the Complete Psychological Works*, vol. XXII, p. 127.

150 Freud thought that a clinical syndrome called *neurasthenia* . . . excessive masturbation: Nicholi, *The New Harvard Guide to Psychiatry*, p. 214.

150 "Whereas true neurasthenia arises . . . coitus interruptus": Freud, *Abstracts of the Scientific Writings of Dr. Sigm. Freud*, in *The Standard Edition of the Complete Psychological Works*, vol. III, p. 251.

150 "It has become clear to me that various obsessional movements . . . movements of masturbation": Freud, *Extracts from the Fliess Papers*, in *The Standard Edition of the Complete Psychological Works*, vol. I, p. 267.

150 "She does not claim to be treated as a woman . . . I don't think she will break the treaty": Freud, *The Complete Correspondence of Sigmund Freud and Ernest Jones*, p. 294.

151 "What I felt for the dancing mistress was sheer appetite; the prose and not the poetry of the flesh": Lewis, *Surprised by Joy*, pp. 68–69.

152 "In any case, it would be impossible . . . But perhaps you are tired of my 'affaires'": Lewis, *The Letters of C. S. Lewis to Arthur Greeves*, p. 66.

152 "I am suppressing . . . all letters that refer to my pretended assignation with the Belgian girl": Lewis, *The Letters of C. S. Lewis to Arthur Greeves*, p. 424.

152 "I hope this is not really necessary in the case of a sin so old and (I hope) so fully abandoned": Lewis, *The Letters of C. S. Lewis to Arthur Greeves*, p. 424.

152 "And I may as well say here that the feeling of guilt . . . rid of them": Lewis, *Surprised by Joy*, p. 69.

152 "I was as nearly without a moral conscience as a boy could be": Lewis, *The Problem of Pain*, pp. 37–40.

153 "on prostitutes, restaurants and tailors . . . lusts of the flesh": Lewis, *The Letters of C. S. Lewis to Arthur Greeves*, p. 214.

153 "I believe in no God, least of all in one that would punish me for the 'lusts of the flesh'": Lewis, *The Letters of C. S. Lewis to Arthur Greeves*, p. 221.

153 "some doctors said it [masturbation] could lead . . . else in his early life": Sayer, *Jack*, p. 68.

155 In an article describing her conversion, Joy wrote, ". . . the walls of arrogance . . . And God came in": Davidman, "The Longest Way Round," p. 23.

156 "from my point of view, adultery, and therefore mustn't happen": Lewis, *The Letters of C. S. Lewis to Arthur Greeves*, p. 534.

157 She wrote a friend in June 1957 that "Jack and I are managing to be surprisingly happy considering the circumstances": Green and Hooper, *C. S. Lewis*, p. 269.

157 She wrote, "You'd think we were a honeymoon couple in our early twenties," and commented openly on Lewis's sexual prowess: Green and Hooper, *C. S. Lewis*, p. 269.

158 "as persons rather than sexual objects.": Nicholi, "A New Dimension of the Youth Culture," *American Journal of Psychiatry*, 131:396-401, 1974.

159 "for any happiness . . . going to be necessary": Lewis, *Mere Christianity*, bk. III, ch. 5.

Chapter 7: Love

160 "People give the name 'love' . . . sisters of a family": Freud, *Civilization and Its Discontents*, in *The Standard Edition of the Complete Psychological Works*, vol. XXI, p. 102.

161 "Love with an inhibited aim . . . aim-inhibited love to 'friendships'": Freud, *Civilization and Its Discontents*, in *The Standard Edition of the Complete Psychological Works*, vol. XXI, p. 103.

161 "have not abandoned their directly sexual aims . . . marriage which had their origin in sexual attraction": Freud, *Two Encyclopaedia Articles*, in *The Standard Edition of the Complete Psychological Works*, vol. XVIII, p. 258.

161 "The nucleus of what we mean by love . . . humanity in general": Freud, *Group Psychology and the Analysis of the Ego*, in *The Standard Edition of the Complete Psychological Works*, vol. XVIII, p. 90.

162 "By coming to this decision, psycho-analysis . . . same 'wider' sense": Freud, *Group Psychology and the Analysis of the Ego*, in *The Standard Edition of the Complete Psychological Works*, vol. XVIII, p. 90.

162 "this only shows that men do not take their great thinkers seriously, even when they profess most to admire them": Freud, *Group Psychology and the Analysis of the Ego*, in *The Standard Edition of the Complete Psychological Works*, vol. XVIII, p. 91.

163 "almost insuperable repugnance . . . races for the colored": Freud, *Group Psychology and the Analysis of the Ego*, in *The Standard Edition of the Complete Psychological Works*, vol. XVIII, p. 101.

163 "but it is unmistakable that in this whole connection . . . ascribe an Elementary character": Freud, *Group Psychology and the Analysis of the Ego*, in *The Standard Edition of the Complete Psychological Works*, vol. XVIII, p. 101.

163 "The nature and quality of the human child's relations . . . brothers and sisters": Freud, *Some Reflections on Schoolboy Psychology*, in *The Standard Edition of the Complete Psychological Works*, vol. XIII, p. 243.

164 This process may, to varying degrees, influence our choice of a friend, roommate, spouse, or employer: Nicholi, *The Harvard Guide to Psychiatry*, p. 13.

165 "[T]he patient sees in [the doctor] the return . . . to this prototype. The fact of transference soon proves to be a factor of undreamt-of importance": Freud, *An Outline of Psychoanalysis*, in *The Standard Edition of the Complete Psychological Works*, vol. XXIII, p. 174.

165 "Essentially . . . the cure is effected by love": Freud, *The Freud Jung Letters*, pp. 12–13.

165 "The first distinction I made . . . frightened child to its mother's arms": Lewis, *The Four Loves*, p. 11.

166 "Need-love says of a woman 'I cannot live without her'; Gift-love longs to give her happiness, comfort, protection—if possible, wealth": Lewis, *The Four Loves*, p. 33.

166 "it must be the full confession . . . service of Moloch": Lewis, *The Four Loves*, p. 49.

166 "'Charity' means love . . . toil is far better and (for most of us) harder": Lewis, *The Letters of C. S. Lewis*, p. 256.

167 "And that, I have no doubt, is the original form of the thing as well as the central meaning of the word": Lewis, *The Four Loves*, pp. 53–54.

167 "Affection almost slinks . . . the sound of a sewing machine": Lewis, *The Four Loves*, pp. 56–57.

167 "affection would not be affection . . . grotesque in the sunshine": Lewis, *The Four Loves*, p. 56.

167 "Affection is modest . . . It fits the comfortable, quiet nature of the feeling": Lewis, *The Four Loves*, p. 56.

168 "almost anyone can become an object of affection . . . between dog and cat": Lewis, *The Four Loves*, pp. 54–56.

168 "the more intimate the occasion . . . subtle, sensitive, and deep than the public kind": Lewis, *The Four Loves*, p. 67.

168 "You can say 'Shut up. I want to read' . . . these are (every love has its 'art of love')": Lewis, *The Four Loves*, p. 68.

168 "Who has not been the embarrassed guest . . . ridicule of things the young take seriously": Lewis, *The Four Loves*, p. 66.

169 "there is common sense and give and take . . . in our natural lives": Lewis, *The Four Loves*, p. 80.

169 "It was of erotic love that the Roman poet . . . becomes a demon": Lewis, *The Four Loves*, pp. 82–83.

169 "Without Eros none of us . . . biologically considered, has no need of it": Lewis, *The Four Loves*, p. 88.

170 "feel uneasy when close and strong friendships . . . highest level of individuality": Lewis, *The Four Loves*, pp. 88–90.

170 "only as a disguise or elaboration . . . absorbed in some common interest": Lewis, *The Four Loves*, p. 91.

171 "so far from obliterating the distinction . . . have all a common vision": Lewis, *The Four Loves*, pp. 98–99.

171 "when the whole group is together . . . Who could have deserved it?": Lewis, *The Four Loves*, pp. 104–105.

172 "The snob wishes to attach . . . they are already attached": Lewis, *The Four Loves*, p. 118.

172 "Pride . . . is the utmost evil . . . always looking down on people": Lewis, *Mere Christianity*, bk. III, ch. 8.

172 In every group . . . "The Inner Ring": Lewis, *The Weight of Glory*, pp. 55–66.

173 "The painless death of a pious relative . . . expedite her departure": Lewis, *The Weight of Glory*, p. 60.

173 "causes perhaps half of all the happiness in the world, and no Inner Ringer can ever have it": Lewis, *The Weight of Glory*, p. 65.

174 "not all men are worthy of love": Freud, *Civilization and Its Discontents*, in *The Standard Edition of the Complete Psychological Works*, vol. XXI, p. 102.

175 "Why should we do it? . . . I put a stranger on a par with them.": Freud, *Civilization and Its Discontents*, in *The Standard Edition of the Complete Psychological Works*, vol. XXI, pp. 109–10.

175 "I must honestly confess . . . Love your neighbor as your neighbor loves you": Freud, *Civilization and Its Discontents*, in *The Standard Edition of the Complete Psychological Works*, vol. XXI, p. 110.

175 "men are not gentle creatures . . . reckoned a powerful share of aggressiveness": Freud, *Civilization and Its Discontents*, in *The Standard Edition of the Complete Psychological Works*, vol. XXI, p. 111.

176 "nothing runs so strongly counter to the original nature of man": Freud, *Civilization and Its Discontents*, in *The Standard Edition of the Complete Psychological Works*, vol. XXI, p. 112.

176 "I have not exactly got . . . my enemies do": Lewis, *Mere Christianity*, bk. III, ch. 7.

178 "personal differences—jealousy or revenge or some other kind of animosity": Wortis, J., "Fragments of a Freudian Analysis." *American Journal of Orthopsychiatry* 10 (1940): 843–49.

178 "He can go jump in the lake; I don't need him and his friendship any

more": Freud, *The Correspondence of Sigmund Freud and Sándor Ferenczi*, p. 457.

179 Freud often referred to Jung as his "son and heir": Jones, *The Life and Work of Sigmund Freud*, vol. II, p. 33.

179 "Our Aryan comrades are really completely indispensable to us, otherwise psychoanalysis would succumb to anti-Semitism": Abraham and Freud, *A Psychoanalytic Dialogue*, letter from Freud dated December 26, 1908.

179 "I must protect myself against people . . . I am not a quarrelsome person": Hale, *James Jackson Putnam and Psychoanalysis*, p. 175.

179 "As for Jung I am resolved to give up private relations with him . . . no need of his companionship myself": Freud, *The Complete Correspondence of Sigmund Freud and Ernest Jones*, p. 190.

180 "He was behaving like a drunkard . . . I think it did him good": Freud, *The Correspondence of Sigmund Freud and Sándor Ferenczi*, p. 433.

180 "lies, brutality and anti-Semitic condescension": Hale, *James Jackson Putnam and Psychoanalysis*, p. 189.

180 "So we are at last rid of them . . . friends who would not exploit and then betray me": Abraham and Freud, *A Psychoanalytic Dialogue*, letter from Freud dated July 26, 1914.

181 "Precisely because they too wanted to be Popes": Binswanger, *Sigmund Freud*, p. 9.

181 "I think I can say in my defense . . . command as few practical attractions as I had": Freud, *An Autobiographical Study*, in *The Standard Edition of the Complete Psychological Works*, vol. XX, p. 53.

181 "[B]ut why should analyzed people . . . that it should be able to realize every precious ideal": Jones, *The Life and Work of Sigmund Freud*, vol. II, p. 182.

181 "I do not break my head very much . . . ethical doctrine or none at all": Freud, *Psychoanalysis and Faith*, pp. 61–62.

181 "What personal pleasure is to be derived from analysis . . . breach must have come into existence at that time between me and other men": Freud, *Psychoanalysis and Faith*, letter from Pfister dated December 25, 1920.

182 "inclination to aggression, which we can detect . . . relations with our neighbor": Freud, *Civilization and Its Discontents*, in *The Standard Edition of the Complete Psychological Works*, vol. XXI, p. 112.

182 "to humiliate him, to cause him pain, to torture and to kill him. *Homo homini lupus* (Man is a wolf to man)": Freud, *Civilization and Its Discontents*, in *The Standard Edition of the Complete Psychological Works*, vol. XXI, p. 111.

182 "all humans pass away . . . 'Careful! this might lead to suffering'": Lewis, *The Four Loves*, p. 168.

183 "was gradually teaching me to be a prig or (in the bad sense) a Highbrow": Lewis, *Surprised by Joy*, p. 100.

183 "school life was a life almost wholly dominated . . . to arrive": Lewis, *Surprised by Joy*, p. 110.

183 "country girls, lazy, noisy and inefficient": Lewis, *All My Road Before Me*, p. 23.

183 "woman-with-the-false-eyebrows-who-tells-lies": Lewis, *All My Road Before Me*, p. 24.

183 "over-educated, affected, vain, flippant and insufferable": Lewis, *All My Road Before Me*, p. 71.

183 "the sucking, squeaking, crunching noises he makes in eating": Lewis, *All My Road Before Me*, p. 73.

183 "we were royally bored and . . . the priest . . . was about the nastiest little man I have ever seen": Lewis, *All My Road Before Me*, p. 85.

183 "the bitch": Lewis, *All My Road Before Me*, p. 91.

183 "the little ass": Lewis, *All My Road Before Me*, p. 91.

183 "repulsive dago": Lewis, *All My Road Before Me*, p. 92.

183 "childish, naive and retains many obstinate vulgarites": Lewis, *All My Road Before Me*, p. 108.

183 "a fat, amiable, ugly woman": Lewis, *All My Road Before Me*, p. 419.

184 "The female, happy or unhappy, agreeing or disagreeing, is by nature a much more *epistolary* animal than the male": Lewis, *The Letters of C. S. Lewis*, p. 242.

185 "I have sometimes had to write letters hard . . . dare not stop answering letters": Lewis, letter to Dom Bede Griffiths dated May 17, 1952 (unpublished), Marion E. Wade Center, Wheaton College, Wheaton, Ill., and Bodleian Library, Oxford University. Used by permission.

185 "He was a deeply kind and charitable man": Kenneth Tynan in *The New Yorker,* August 14, 2000, p. 65.

186 "You have never talked to a mere mortal": Lewis, *The Weight of Glory,* p. 15.

186 "a real and costly love . . . no flippancy, no superiority, no presumption": Lewis, *The Weight of Glory,* p. 15.

Chapter 8: Pain

189 "To my youthful mind, Hannibal . . . organization of the Catholic Church": Freud, *The Interpretation of Dreams*, in *The Standard Edition of the Complete Psychological Works*, vol. IV, p. 196.

190 "I put up, without much regret . . . certain degree of independence of

judgment": Freud, *An Autobiographical Study*, in *The Standard Edition of the Complete Psychological Works*, vol. XX, p. 9.

190   "there should not be such a thing . . . presentation of them may vary": Jones, *The Life and Work of Sigmund Freud*, vol. II, p. 149.

190   "We have all heard of the interesting attempt to explain psychoanalysis . . . another reproach which no one would care to put forward openly": Freud, *On the History of the Psychoanalytic Movement*, in *The Standard Edition of the Complete Psychological Works*, vol. XIV, pp. 39–40.

191   "I nurse a suspicion . . . far less resistance": Abraham and Freud, *A Psychoanalytic Dialogue*, letter from Freud dated July 23, 1908.

191   "The only serious thing about it is this . . . oil and water": Letter from Freud to L. Binswanger dated July 29, 1912.

191   "for the degree of arrogance . . . nonetheless hurt deeply": Freud, *An Autobiographical Study*, in *The Standard Edition of the Complete Psychological Works*, vol. XX, p. 49.

191   "The castration complex is the deepest . . . root for the sense of superiority over women": Freud, *A Phobia in a Five-Year-Old Boy*, in *The Standard Edition of the Complete Psychological Works*, vol. X, p. 36.

192   "the communal feeling of groups requires . . . minority encourages its suppression": Freud, *Moses and Monotheism*, in *The Standard Edition of the Complete Psychological Works*, vol. XXIII, pp. 90–92.

193   To confirm this he points to the hostile treatment by the Nazis of both Christians and Jews: Freud, *Moses and Monotheism*, in *The Standard Edition of the Complete Psychological Works*, vol. XXIII, pp. 90–92.

193   "Basically all are anti-Semites . . . masses are anti-Semitic here as everywhere": Yerushalmi, *Freud's Moses*, p. 54.

193   "I came to Vienna as a child of 4 years . . . expelled from their professions": Freud, *Shorter Writings*, in *The Standard Edition of the Complete Psychological Works*, vol. XXIII, p. 301.

194   "I am still out of work . . . etiology of this tissue—rebellion": Freud, *The Complete Correspondence of Sigmund Freud and Ernest Jones*, p. 521.

194   One of Freud's physicians would later describe it as a "grotesque nightmare": Schur, *Freud*, p. 351.

195   "We drove to the hospital together . . . imbecile dwarf": Deutsch, F., "Reflections on Freud's One Hundredth Birthday." *Psychosom Med* 18 (1956): 279–83.

196   Suddenly blood spurted from Freud's mouth, a hard crust having apparently reopened the wound: Jones, *The Life and Work of Sigmund Freud*, vol. III, p. 94.

196 "let me be impolite for once—how the devil . . . assumption that there is a moral order": Freud, *Psychoanalysis and Faith*, p. 123.

196 "obscure, unfeeling and unloving powers determine men's fate": Freud, *The Question of a Weltanschauung*, in *The Standard Edition of the Complete Psychological Works*, vol. XXII, p. 167.

197 "For us boys the real bereavement . . . something alien and menacing": Lewis, *Surprised by Joy*, pp. 18–19.

197 Lewis wrote that with his mother's death all happiness "disappeared from my life": Lewis, *Surprised by Joy*, pp. 20–21.

197 "my memories of the last war haunted my dreams for years": Lewis, *The Letters of C. S. Lewis*, p. 166.

197 "the great German attack": Lewis, *Surprised by Joy*, p. 195.

197 "Through the winter, weariness . . . concealed barbed wire": Lewis, *Surprised by Joy*, p. 195.

198 "the cold, the smell . . . grow on your feet—all this shows rarely and faintly in memory": Lewis, *Surprised by Joy*, p. 196.

198 "a little quavering signal that said, 'This is war. This is what Homer wrote about'": Lewis, *Surprised by Joy*, p. 196.

198 "suffered intensely from . . . loneliness and depression": Sayer, *Jack*, p. 132.

199 "No one ever told me that grief felt so much like fear . . . I keep on swallowing": Lewis, *A Grief Observed*, p. 1.

199 "There is a sort of invisible blanket . . . It is so uninteresting": Lewis, *A Grief Observed*, p. 1.

199 "I want the others to be about me . . . talk to one another and not to me": Lewis, *A Grief Observed*, p. 1.

199 "One is ashamed to listen . . . ant in the mouth of a furnace": Lewis, *A Grief Observed*, p. 2.

199 "I cannot talk to the children about her . . . It's the way boys are": Lewis, *A Grief Observed*, pp. 8–9.

200 "But what am I to do? . . . That's how I defend it": Lewis, *A Grief Observed*, pp. 9–10.

200 "My dear, my dear, come back for one moment": Lewis, *A Grief Observed*, p. 20.

200 "At present I am learning to get about on crutches . . . never be a biped again": Lewis, *A Grief Observed*, p. 62.

200 "Grief is like a bomber circling . . . Thought is never static; pain often is": Lewis, *A Grief Observed*, pp. 46–47.

201 "How often—will it be for always? . . . flesh is felt again and again": Lewis, *A Grief Observed*, p. 67.

201 "But go to Him when your need . . . time of trouble": Lewis, *A Grief Observed*, pp. 4–5.

202 "What do people mean when they say, 'I am not afraid of God because I know He is good?' Have they never even been to a dentist": Lewis, *A Grief Observed*, pp. 50–51.

202 "only the locked door, the iron curtain, the vacuum, absolute zero": Lewis, *A Grief Observed*, p. 7.

202 "'To him that hath shall be given' . . . temporarily destroys the capacity": Lewis, *A Grief Observed*, p. 54.

202 "Turned to God, my mind no longer . . . already been going on for some time": Lewis, *A Grief Observed*, p. 71.

203 "a rather special sort of 'No answer' . . . 'Peace, child; you don't understand'": Lewis, *A Grief Observed*, pp. 80–81.

203 "has not been trying an experiment . . . It was I who didn't": Lewis, *A Grief Observed*, p. 61.

203 "suffering is not good in itself . . . those who do the simple evil": Lewis, *The Problem of Pain*, pp. 110–11.

204 "I . . . have no dread at all of the Almighty . . . He could to me": Jones, *The Life and Work of Sigmund Freud*, vol. II, pp. 416–18.

204 "We learn from clinical experience . . . must lead to the same result": Freud, *An Outline of Psychoanalysis*, in *The Standard Edition of the Complete Psychological Works*, vol. XXIII, p. 201.

204 "There are the elements, which seem to mock . . . found, nor probably will be": Freud, *The Future of an Illusion*, in *The Standard Edition of the Complete Psychological Works*, vol. XXI, p. 16.

205 "life is hard to bear . . . a permanent state of anxious expectation": Freud, *The Future of an Illusion*, in *The Standard Edition of the Complete Psychological Works*, vol. XXI, p. 16.

205 "the pronouncements of religion promising . . . scoundrel or unbeliever": Freud, *The Question of a Weltanschauung*, in *The Standard Edition of the Complete Psychological Works*, vol. XXII, p. 167.

205 Freud argued that the notion that good is rewarded . . . square with reality: Freud, *The Question of a Weltanschauung*, in *The Standard Edition of the Complete Psychological Works*, vol. XXII, p. 167.

205 "One of the things that surprised me when I first read the New Testament . . . that is what this world is": Lewis, *Mere Christianity*, bk. II, ch. 2.

206 "The Devil would be the best way . . . wickedness which the Devil embodies": Freud, *Civilization and Its Discontents*, in *The Standard Edition of the Complete Psychological Works*, vol. XXI, p. 120.

206 "Because free will, though it makes evil possible . . . would hardly be worth creating": Lewis, *Mere Christianity*, bk. II, ch. 3.

206 "Of course God knew what would happen if they used their freedom the wrong way: apparently He thought it worth the risk": Lewis, *Mere Christianity*, bk. II, ch. 3.

206 "My argument against God . . . Consequently atheism turns out to be too simple": Lewis, *Mere Christianity*, bk. II, ch. 1.

207 "is not a system into which we have to fit the awkward . . . ultimate reality is righteous and loving": Lewis, *The Problem of Pain*, p. 24.

208 For example, Freud read Gustave Flaubert's . . . strong reaction to the book: Jones, *The Life and Work of Sigmund Freud*, vol. I, p. 175.

208 "Let us consult/What reinforcement we may gain from hope,/If not, what resolution from despair": Jones, *The Life and Work of Sigmund Freud*, vol. I, p. 173.

208 "Although it was the Devil who taught her; He cannot do it by himself": Freud (quoting Goethe's *Faust*), in *The Freud/Jung Letters*, p. 260.

209 Did Freud, at some level, feel that he, himself, had made a pact with the devil? Some scholars answer yes to that question: Vitz, *Sigmund Freud's Christian Unconscious*, p. 149; and Bakan, *Sigmund Freud and the Jewish Mystical Tradition*.

209 "In return for an immortal soul . . . the enjoyment of beautiful women": Freud, *A Seventeenth-Century Demonological Neurosis*, in *The Standard Edition of the Complete Psychological Works*, vol. XIX, p. 79.

209 "two sets of emotional impulses . . . decisive vicissitudes in it": Freud, *A Seventeenth-Century Demonological Neurosis*, in *The Standard Edition of the Complete Psychological Works*, vol. XIX, p. 81.

210 "If God were good, He would wish to make . . . either goodness, or power, or both": Lewis, *The Problem of Pain*, p. 26.

210 "Omnipotence means power . . . miracles to [God], but not nonsense": Lewis, *The Problem of Pain*, p. 28.

211 "if matter is to serve as a neutral field it must have a fixed nature of its own" and not one that changes at the whim of its inhabitants; "if matter has a fixed nature and obeys constant laws, not all states of matter will be equally agreeable to the wishes of a given soul": Lewis, *The Problem of Pain*, pp. 31–32.

211 "Try to exclude the possibility of suffering . . . excluded life itself": Lewis, *The Problem of Pain*, pp. 32–34.

211 "Love is something more stern and splendid . . . even something like contempt of it": Lewis, *The Problem of Pain*, p. 40.

211 "love, in its own nature, demands . . . opposite pole from Love": Lewis, *The Problem of Pain*, p. 46.

211 "problem of reconciling human suffering . . . trivial meaning to the word 'love'": Lewis, *The Problem of Pain*, p. 47.

212 "When souls become wicked . . . poverty and overwork": Lewis, *The Problem of Pain*, p. 89.

212 "God is good; that He made all things good . . . abuse of his free will": Lewis, *The Problem of Pain*, p. 69.

212 "I do *not* hold that God 'sends' sickness . . . suffering arises from sin": Lewis, *The Letters of C. S. Lewis to Arthur Greeves*, pp. 514–15.

213 "pain insists upon being attended to . . . megaphone to rouse a deaf world": Lewis, *The Problem of Pain*, p. 93.

213 "They will have to admit to themselves the full extent . . . endure them with resignation": Freud, *The Future of an Illusion*, in *The Standard Edition of the Complete Psychological Works*, vol. XXI, pp. 49–50.

214 "As an unbelieving fatalist, I can only sink into a state of resignation when faced with the horror of death": Freud, *The Complete Correspondence of Sigmund Freud and Ernest Jones*, p. 646.

214 "I became tired of life permanently": Freud, *The Complete Correspondence of Sigmund Freud and Ernest Jones*, p. 643.

214 Freud wondered "when my turn will come" and wished that his life would soon be over: Jones, *The Life and Work of Sigmund Freud*, vol. III, p. 19.

214 "if you ask me to believe . . . an evil spirit": Lewis, *The Problem of Pain*, p. 15.

215 "If the believer finally sees himself . . . detour he has made": Freud, *Civilization and Its Discontents*, in *The Standard Edition of the Complete Psychological Works*, vol. XXI, p. 85.

Chapter 9: Death

217 "the problem of death stands at the outset of every philosophy": Freud, *Totem and Taboo*, in *The Standard Edition of the Complete Psychological Works*, vol. XIII, p. 87.

217 "I greeted my one-year-younger brother . . . [self-]reproaches in me": Freud, *The Complete Letters of Sigmund Freud to Wilhelm Fliess*, p. 268.

217 "My mother thereupon rubbed . . . (Thou owest Nature a death)": Freud, *Interpretation of Dreams*, in *The Standard Edition of the Complete Psychological Works*, vol. IV, p. 205.

218 "that our intellect is a feeble and dependent thing, a play thing and tool

of our impulses and emotions": Jones, *The Life and Work of Sigmund Freud*, vol. II, p. 368.

218 "our unconscious is just as inaccessible . . . we love, as was primeval man": Freud, *Thoughts for the Times on War and Death*, in *The Standard Edition of the Complete Psychological Works*, vol. XIV, p. 299.

218 "Our unconscious then does not believe in its own death; it behaves as if it were immortal": Freud, *Thoughts for the Times on War and Death*, in *The Standard Edition of the Complete Psychological Works*, vol. XIV, p. 296.

218 "imagine our own death . . . no one believes in his own death": Freud, *Thoughts for the Times on War and Death*, in *The Standard Edition of the Complete Psychological Works*, vol. XIV, p. 289.

219 "go on suffering from various complaints for another four to five to eight years, with good and bad periods, and then between forty and fifty perish very abruptly from a rupture of the heart; if it is not too close to forty, it is not so bad at all": Freud, *The Complete Letters of Sigmund Freud to Wilhelm Fliess*, p. 85.

219 "I shall never forget . . . face of approaching death": Freud, *An Autobiographical Study*, in *The Standard Edition of the Complete Psychological Works*, vol. XX, p. 52.

219 "We have grown old since we first shared the small pleasures of student life. Now life is running out": Freud, *The Letters of Sigmund Freud to Eduard Silberstein*, p. 185.

219 "If I had known how little joy I would have on my sixtieth birthday, my first would probably not have given me pleasure either. It would be in the best of times only a melancholic celebration": Freud, *Lou Andreas-Salomé, Briefwechsel*, pp. 47–48 (translation F. Lee).

219 "Now you too have reached your sixtieth birthday . . . not always amusing comedy": Freud, *Letters of Sigmund Freud*, p. 339.

220 "You will admit that after this substitution it no longer sounds so absurd": Freud, *The Freud/Jung Letters*, p. 219.

220 "I have been working very hard . . . quite a friendly idea": Jones, *The Life and Work of Sigmund Freud*, vol. II, p. 194.

221 "the limit of life which my father . . . I am still attached": Freud, *Letters of Sigmund Freud*, p. 434.

221 "As for me, I note migraine . . . fears of dying": Freud, *The Complete Letters of Sigmund Freud to Wilhelm Fliess*, p. 181.

221 "There were the repeated attacks . . . certainly unusual": Jones, *The Life and Work of Sigmund Freud*, vol. III, p. 279.

222 "as is proved by all the myths of a future life": Freud, *The Interpreta-*

tion of Dreams, in *The Standard Edition of the Complete Psychological Works,* vol. IV, p. 254.

222 "Nearly all that I believed . . . contradicted my wishes": Lewis, *Surprised by Joy,* pp. 170–73.

223 "Yesterday we buried . . . quite down because of it": Freud, *The Complete Letters of Sigmund Freud to Wilhelm Fliess,* p. 201.

223 "The old man's death has affected . . . reawakened by this event": Freud, *The Complete Letters of Sigmund Freud to Wilhelm Fliess,* p. 202.

223 "Yesterday morning our dear lovely Sophie died": Freud, *Letters of Sigmund Freud,* pp. 326–27.

223 "has got over the monstrous fact of children dying before their parents": Schur, *Freud,* p. 329.

223 "My daughter who died would have been thirty-six years old today": Freud, *Letters of Sigmund Freud,* p. 386.

223 "Since I am profoundly irreligious . . . not to be healed": Jones, *The Life and Work of Sigmund Freud,* vol. III, p. 20.

224 "I don't think I have ever experienced such grief; perhaps my own sickness contributes to the shock. I work out of sheer necessity; fundamentally everything has lost its meaning for me": Freud, *Letters of Sigmund Freud,* p. 344.

224 "I find no joy in life": Schur, *Freud,* p. 360.

225 "I was not at the funeral": Jones, *The Life and Work of Sigmund Freud,* vol. III, p. 152.

225 "I shall find someone who will treat . . . beautiful composure to the end": Freud, *The Complete Letters of Sigmund Freud to Wilhelm Fliess,* p. 344.

227 "Your mysterious and beautiful book . . . for a long time": Schur, *Freud,* p. 514.

227 "Vehement must the storms . . . trigger of a pistol": Balzac, *The Wild Ass's [Fatal] Skin,* London: J. M. Dent & Sons, 1960, p. 10.

229 "How uncanny that he . . . 'finis' to his own story": Schur, *Freud,* p. 528.

230 "My father seemed . . . to commit suicide again": Lewis, *The Letters of C. S. Lewis to Arthur Greeves,* p. 128.

230 "If he is an emotional, gullible man . . . murders and suicides": Lewis, *The Screwtape Letters,* pp. 99–100.

231 "Christ shed tears . . . penal obscenity not less than we do, but more": Lewis, *Miracles,* pp. 129–30.

231 "Indeed, if we found that we could fully . . . nature like lightning": Lewis, *Mere Christianity,* bk. III, ch. 4.

232 "Yes, autumn is the best of the seasons; and I'm not sure that old age isn't the best part of life": Lewis, *The Letters of C. S. Lewis*, p. 308.

232 "Can one believe that there was just nothing ... fully understand that something": Lewis, *The Letters of C. S. Lewis to Arthur Greeves*, pp. 436–37.

232 "The proposition 'Here is a man dying' ... It was not even interesting": Lewis, *Surprised by Joy*, pp. 197–98.

233 "death would be much better than to live through another war": Lewis, *The Letters of C. S. Lewis*, p. 166.

233 "If active service does not prepare a man for death what conceivable concatenation of circumstances would": Lewis, *The Weight of Glory*, p. 31.

233 "How much better for us ... betray to the sick man his true condition": Lewis, *The Screwtape Letters*, pp. 31–32.

233 "I have seen death fairly often ... turned into nothing": Lewis, *The Letters of C. S. Lewis*, p. 59.

234 "I am attending at the almost painless sickbed ... resemblance to me": Lewis, *The Letters of C. S. Lewis*, p. 137.

234 "My father's death, with all the fortitude ... I am telling": Lewis, *Surprised by Joy*, p. 215.

234 "My dear Joy is dead ... You will understand that I have no heart to write more": Lewis, *The Letters of C. S. Lewis*, p. 293.

235 "I look up at the night sky ... word so difficult to learn": Lewis, *A Grief Observed*, p. 16.

235 "Cancer, and cancer ... who is next in the queue": Lewis, *A Grief Observed*, p. 12.

235 "bereavement is a universal and integral ... autumn follows summer": Lewis, *A Grief Observed*, pp. 58–59.

235 "What on earth is the trouble ... respectable people do it": Lewis, *Letters to an American Lady*, pp. 67–69.

235 "To desire it, to fear it ... precarious of all": Lewis, *Letters to an American Lady*, pp. 80–81.

236 "What have you and I got to do ... similar terrors": Lewis, *Letters to an American Lady*, pp. 111–12.

236 "Yours (and like you a tired traveler, near the journey's end) Jack": Lewis, *Letters to an American Lady*, p. 114.

237 "comfortable and cheerful ... saddens me very much": Lewis, *The Letters of C. S. Lewis to Arthur Greeves*, p. 566.

237 "I was unexpectedly revived ... look me up ... It *is* all rather fun—solemn fun—isn't it": Lewis, *The Letters of C. S. Lewis*, p. 307.

237 "the *Odyssey* and *Iliad* . . . Dickens and Trollope": Sayer, *Jack,* pp. 407–408.

237 "I knew I was in danger but was not depressed. I've read pretty well everything": Green and Hooper, *C. S. Lewis,* p. 295.

237 "Don't think I am . . . I have ever done": Sayer, *Jack,* p. 408.

237 "Wow! what a book": Wilson, *C. S. Lewis,* p. 292.

238 "having outgrown God . . . which they give it": David Cower in Pierre Choderlos de Laclos, *Les Liaisons Dangereuses,* Oxford: Oxford University Press, 1995, p. xxx.

238 "I somehow felt it was the last . . . man better prepared": Como, *C. S. Lewis at the Breakfast Table,* p. 104.

239 "If we really believe . . . forward to the arrival": Lewis, *Letters to an American Lady,* pp. 80–81.

239 "On 22nd of last month . . . when our time comes": Letter from Warren H. Lewis to Mrs. Frank J. Jones dated December 7, 1963 (unpublished), Marion E. Wade Center, Wheaton College, Wheaton, Ill., and Bodleian Library, Oxford University. Used by permission.

Epilogue

241 "He understands as much about psychology as I do about physics, so we had a very pleasant talk": Jones, *The Life and Work of Sigmund Freud,* vol. III, p. 131.

241 "As an unbelieving fatalist I can only let my arms sink before the terrors of death": Jones, *The Life and Work of Sigmund Freud,* vol. III, p. 140.

244 "My idea of God . . . All reality is iconoclastic": Lewis, *A Grief Observed,* pp. 76–77.

244 "We may ignore . . . Still more to remain awake": Lewis, *Letters to Malcolm,* p. 75.

Bibliography

Abraham, H. C., and E. L. Freud (eds.). *A Psychoanalytic Dialogue: The Letters of Sigmund Freud and Karl Abraham, 1907–1926.* Translated by B. Marsh and H. C. Abraham. New York: Basic Books, 1965.

Allport, G. W., and J. M. Ross. "Personal religious orientation and prejudice." *J Pers Soc Psychol* 5, no. 4 (April 1967): 432–43.

American Psychiatric Association. *Diagnostic and Statistical Manual of Mental Disorders* (DSM-IV). 4th ed. Washington, D.C., 1994.

Bakan, D. *Sigmund Freud and the Jewish Mystical Tradition.* Princeton, N.J.: Van Nostrand, 1958.

Barondes, S. H. *Mood Genes: Hunting for Origins of Mania and Depression.* New York: Oxford University Press, 1999.

Binswanger, L. *Sigmund Freud: Reminiscences of a Friendship.* New York and London: Grune and Stratton, 1957.

Bonaparte, M., A. Freud, and E. Kris, (eds.). *The Origins of Psycho-Analysis.* Translated by Eric Mossbacher and James Strachey. New York: Basic Books, 1954.

Chesterton, G. K. *The Everlasting Man.* Garden City, N.Y.: Image Books, 1955.

Como, J. T. (ed.) *C. S. Lewis at the Breakfast Table and Other Reminiscences.* San Diego, Calif.: Harcourt Brace Jovanovich, 1979.

Davidman, Joy. "The Longest Way Round," in *These Found the Way,* edited by D. W. Soper. Philadelphia: Westminster, 1951.

Erikson, Erik H. *Young Man Luther.* New York: Norton, 1958.

Feuerbach, L. *The Essence of Christianity.* Translated by George Eliot. Buffalo, N.Y.: Prometheus Books, 1989.

Freud, E. "Some Early Unpublished Letters of Freud," in *International Journal of Psychiatry* (1969): 419–27.

Freud, S. *The Complete Correspondence of Sigmund Freud and Ernest Jones, 1908–1939.* Edited by R. Andrew Paskauskas. Cambridge, Mass.: Belknap Press of the Harvard University Press, 1993.

———. *The Complete Letters of Sigmund Freud to Wilhelm Fliess, 1887–*

1904. Edited by J. M. Masson. Cambridge, Mass.: Belknap Press of the Harvard University Press, 1985.

——. *The Correspondence of Sigmund Freud and Sándor Ferenczi.* Edited by Eva Brabant, Ernst Falzeder, and Patrizia Giampieri-Deutsch. Cambridge, Mass.: Belknap Press of the Harvard University Press, 1993.

——. *The Freud/Jung Letters.* Edited by William McGuire. Princeton, N.J.: Princeton University Press, 1974.

——. *Letters of Sigmund Freud.* Edited by Ernst L. Freud. New York: Dover Publications, 1992.

——. *The Letters of Sigmund Freud and Arnold Zweig.* Edited by Ernst L. Freud. New York: Harcourt, Brace, 1970.

——. *The Letters of Sigmund Freud to Eduard Silberstein, 1871–1881.* Edited by Walter Boehlich. Cambridge, Mass.: Belknap Press of the Harvard University Press, 1990.

——. *Lou Andreas-Salomé, Briefwechsel.* Published by Ernst Pfeiffer. Frankfurt am Main: S. Fischer Verlag, 1966.

——. *Psychoanalysis and Faith: The Letters of Sigmund Freud and Oskar Pfister.* Edited by Heinrich Meng and Ernst L. Freud. New York: Basic Books, 1963.

——. *The Standard Edition of the Complete Psychological Works of Sigmund Freud.* Translated under the general editorship of James Strachey in collaboration with Anna Freud, assisted by Alix Strachey and Alan Tyson. 24 vols. London: The Hogarth Press, 1962.

Gallup, George, George Gallup, Jr., and D. Michael Lindsay. *Surveying the Religious Landscape: Trends in U.S. Beliefs.* Morehouse Publishing, 1999.

Gallup, George, and Timothy Jones. *The Next American Spirituality: Finding God in the Twenty-first Century.* Colorado Springs, Colo.: Cook Communications, 2000.

Gay, P. *Freud: A Life for Our Times.* New York: Doubleday, 1988.

——. *A Godless Jew: Freud, Atheism, and the Making of Psychoanalysis.* New Haven, Conn.: Yale University Press, 1987.

Gilman, S. L. *The Case of Sigmund Freud.* Baltimore: Johns Hopkins University Press, 1993.

Glover, D. E. *C. S. Lewis: The Art of Enchantment.* Athens, Ohio: Ohio University Press, 1981.

Green, R. L., and W. Hooper. *C. S. Lewis: A Biography.* New York: Harcourt Brace Jovanovich, 1974.

Griffin, W. *Clive Staples Lewis: A Dramatic Life.* San Francisco: Harper and Row, 1986.

Hale, Nathan G. (ed.). *James Jackson Putnam and Psychoanalysis*. Translated by J. B. Heller. Cambridge, Mass.: Harvard University Press, 1971.

Jones, E. *The Life and Work of Sigmund Freud*. Vol. I: *The Formative Years and the Great Discoveries* (1856–1900); Vol. II: *Years of Maturity* (1901–1919); and Vol. III: *The Last Phase* (1919–1939). New York: Basic Books, 1957.

Kung, H. *Freud and the Problem of God*. New Haven, Conn.: Yale University Press, 1979.

Lewis, C. S. *The Abolition of Man*. New York: Macmillan, 1947.

———. *All My Road Before Me: The Diary of C. S. Lewis, 1922–1927*. Edited by Walter Hooper. San Diego, Calif.: Harcourt Brace Jovanovich, 1991.

———. *The Four Loves*. New York: Harcourt, Brace, 1960.

———. *God in the Dock: Essays on Theology and Ethics*. Edited by Walter Hooper. Grand Rapids, Mich.: William B. Eerdmans Publishing Company, 1970.

———. *A Grief Observed*. New York: Bantam Books, 1961.

———. *Letters to an American Lady*. Edited by Clyde S. Kilby. Grand Rapids, Mich.: William B. Eerdmans Publishing Company, 1967.

———. *The Letters of C. S. Lewis*. Edited with a memoir by W. H. Lewis. New York: Harcourt, Brace, 1966. (See also the revised and expanded edition by Walter Hooper; San Diego, Calif.: Harcourt, Brace, 1993).

———. *The Letters of C. S. Lewis to Arthur Greeves (1914–1963)*. Edited by Walter Hooper. New York: Collier Books, 1979.

———. *Letters, C. S. Lewis–Don Giovanni Calabria: A Study in Friendship*. Translated and edited by Martin Moynihan. Ann Arbor, Mich.: Servant Books, 1988.

———. *Letters to Malcolm: Chiefly on Prayer*. New York: Harcourt, Brace, 1964.

———. *Mere Christianity*. Westwood, N.J.: Barbour and Company, 1952.

———. *Miracles: A Preliminary Study*. New York: Macmillan, 1947.

———. *A Preface to Paradise Lost*. London: Oxford University Press, 1970.

———. *The Problem of Pain*. New York: Collier Books, 1962.

———. *The Screwtape Letters, with Screwtape Proposes a Toast*. Revised edition. New York: Collier Books, 1982.

———. *Surprised by Joy: The Shape of My Early Life*. San Diego, Calif.: Harcourt Brace Jovanovich, 1956.

———. *They Asked for a Paper: Papers and Addresses*. London: Geoffrey Bles, 1962.

———. *They Stand Together: The Letters of C. S. Lewis to Arthur Greeves (1914–1963)*. Edited by Walter Hooper. New York: Macmillan, 1979.

————. *The Weight of Glory and Other Addresses.* Grand Rapids, Mich.: William B. Eerdmans Publishing Company, 1949.

Newberg, Andrew B., Eugene d'Aquili, and Vince Rause. *Why God Won't Go Away: Brain Science and the Biology of Belief.* New York: Ballantine Books, 2001.

Nicholi, A. M. "A New Dimension of the Youth Culture." *Am J Psych* 131 (1974): 396–401.

Nicholi, A. M. (ed.) *The Harvard Guide to Psychiatry.* Cambridge, Mass.: Belknap Press of the Harvard University Press, 1999.

————. *The New Harvard Guide to Psychiatry.* Cambridge, Mass.: Belknap Press of the Harvard University Press, 1988.

Sayer, G. *Jack: A Life of C. S. Lewis.* Wheaton, Ill.: Crossway Books, 1994.

Schur, M. *Freud: Living and Dying.* New York: International Universities Press, 1972.

Vitz, P. C. *Sigmund Freud's Christian Unconscious.* New York: Guilford Press, 1988.

Wilson, A. N. *C. S. Lewis: A Biography.* New York: Norton, 1990.

Wilson, James Q. *The Moral Sense.* New York: Free Press, 1993.

Yerushalmi, Yosef Hayim. *Freud's Moses: Judaism Terminable and Interminable.* New Haven, Conn.: Yale University Press, 1991.

Acknowledgments

My gratitude and thanks:

To Dr. Vernon Grounds, who first encouraged my interest in the field of psychiatry and, who over the years, sent me a continuous flow of articles and books to focus my attention on writing this one.

To Vester Hughes, who, more than twenty years ago, suggested I write this book and provided a grant to help me begin the research. To Howard and Barbara Dan Butt for continuing to make this research possible. And to Kenneth and Nancy McGee whose support and encouragement over many years proved crucial.

To the hundreds of students who have taken my course during the past thirty years and who have been a source of inspiration and instruction.

To Jeremy Fraiberg, Cathy Struve, Sandra Lee, and other former students who, over fifteen years, helped compile the database of the writings of Freud and Lewis. Some traveled long distances to track down unpublished material.

To Professor Peter Gomes, who encouraged me to give the Harvard Noble Lectures which form the nidus of this book.

To Marjorie Mead of the Wade Center at Wheaton College for help in finding unpublished letters.

To Victor Boutrous, Douglas Coe, Herbert Hess, Sally Frese, Paul Klassen, Jeremy Fraiberg, and Drs. Chester Pierce and Irving Weisner for their critical reading of the manuscript.

To Dean Overman and to many other friends who have encouraged me along the way, including Marcia and Robin Brown, Lessie and Brit Nicholson, Jean and Jim Petersen, and Rebecca and Andy Wasynczuk.

To Bruce Nichols, senior editor at Simon and Schuster, who suggested expanding the Noble Lectures into a book and who made many helpful emendations; and to his staff for their superb editing.

And to Frederick Lee, M.D., Ph.D., my former medical student and current teaching associate, a brilliant scientific researcher and caring physician, a friend and colleague, without whose enormous assistance this book might not have been written.

Index